Handbook of
Online
Marketing
Research

Handbook of Online Marketing Research

Joshua Grossnickle
Oliver Raskin

McGraw-Hill, Inc.
New York   San Francisco   Washington, D.C.   Auckland   Bogotá
Caracas   Lisbon   London   Madrid   Mexico City   Milan
Montreal   New Delhi   San Juan   Singapore

McGraw-Hill

A Division of The McGraw·Hill Companies

Copyright © 2001 by The McGraw-Hill Companies, Inc. All rights reserved. Printed in the United States of America. Except as permitted under the United States Copyright Act of 1976, no part of this publication may be reproduced or distributed in any form or by any means, or stored in a database or retrieval system, without the prior written permission of the publisher.

1 2 3 4 5 6 7 8 9 0 AGM / AGM 0 9 8 7 6 5 4 3 2 1 0

ISBN 0-07-136114-6

Printed and bound by Quebecor Martinsburg.

McGraw-Hill books are available at special quantity discounts to use as premiums and sales promotions, or for use in corporate training programs. For more information, please write to the Director of Special Sales, Professional Publishing, McGraw-Hill, Two Penn Plaza, New York, NY 10121-2298. Or contact your local bookstore.

 This book is printed on recycled, acid-free paper containing a minimum of 50% recycled, de-inked fiber.

To our parents. They cleared the path before us, and by example, showed us how to walk it.

Contents

16 Tracking

Preface

Marketing research is first and foremost a tool to aid in making business decisions. While we recognize the need for rigorous scientific applications of marketing research, we argue that the bottom-line measure of success is the practical ability of information to increase the quality of business decisions. We are, after all, pursuing research with the goal of increasing profits, and not for the sake of research alone.

The methods and approaches to marketing research contained in this text were selected based on their performance, accessibility, and feasibility. Just as when making a purchase decision, we traded off costs and benefits to arrive at the best approach for developing online products from a data-driven perspective. Often, conducting the highest quality research proves prohibitively expensive. Left with a choice between leveraging slightly less reliable data or making a critical business decision blind, we use the available data and keep its limitations in mind.

The Web is ever-changing. Books, by their nature, have a hard time keeping pace. Please refer to our Web site (www.sitecentric.com/handbook) for updates and more information.

Acknowledgments

The authors would like to thank:

Those we love:

- Ellen Grossnickle
- Heather Axtell Matranga
- Hope Schmeltzer
- Peter and Morgan Raskin

Our mentors:

- Rex Briggs
- Professor Cynthia Campbell
- Professor Nathan Lacey
- Professor John Probst

Our Clients:

- Clearstation/Etrade
- CNET
- E! Online
- Embark.com
- Environmental Defense Fund

- Evite.com
- iMall
- mySimon
- Snowball.com
- Sonicnet/MTVi
- Wired Digital
- ZDNet

... and all the talented staff at McGraw-Hill who worked to take this book from idea to reality.

Introduction

WHY THIS BOOK?

The commercial explosion of the Internet is, in many ways, analogous to the start of a large footrace. Initially, when the gun goes off and throngs of people charge down the pavement, it is difficult to distinguish the competitive racers from the inexperienced enthusiasts. Soon, however, the excitement wears off as fatigue sets in and the pacesetters pull away from the pack, their legs fueled by years of preparation and hard work.

The early Internet industry was flush with investor capital to fund rapidly conceived and executed ventures. Back then, the mantra was simply, "If you build and market it, they will come." Many companies spent millions scrambling in a land grab to beat competitors to market with an online product. Millions more were subsequently spent on witty advertising campaigns to build awareness in the marketplace. Now, as the dust begins to settle and we get our first good look at these newly public companies, what do we find?

In most cases, the great savings and increased efficiency promised by c-business hasn't materialized. The high cost of labor and unforeseen difficulties of conducting business online have resulted in larger than expected expenses and require higher margins to attain profitability. Gone are the days when e-commerce sites sought to dominate the marketplace virtually. Now, in addition to designing Web pages, they need to construct huge warehouses and employ hundreds of workers. Realizing this, once pie-eyed investors have become more realistic. Astronomical company valuations have headed toward the land of reality, and raising funding for new ventures has grown increasingly difficult.

The long-anticipated shakedown is upon us. Citing increased competition, poor financials, and investor flight, Forester research predicted that the majority of online e-commerce sites will fold by 2001.[1] Similar predictions that "the sky is falling" have been made in the past and proven false; but one simple fact remains: Unprofitable companies that can't raise additional capital will go bankrupt. Having spent exorbitant amounts on developing and marketing their sites, many companies are quickly running out of money and are suddenly faced with an unenviable situation.

Naysayers aside, has the time for developing new online products passed us by? Certainly not.

The Web is an incredibly dynamic and efficient medium for conducting global business. The visions of a digital future that once fueled a frenzy of investment are still possible. The proliferation of the Internet is astounding. Currently, half of all U.S. households have Net access, up from under 10 percent in 1995. Broadcast television grew at nearly the same rate, achieving near ubiquity within ten years. There is little reason to suspect that the Net will be much different. Like television and the telephone, the Internet will simply become too valuable to do without.

[1]Foresester Research. "The Imminent Demise of Most DOT COM Retailers." (April 11, 2000).

Projections for e-commerce are also astounding, rising from $63 billion in 1999 to $1.7 trillion in 2003. Undoubtedly, the opportunity to successfully develop and market well-conceived online products is alive and well. Dead (or dying) are all the half-baked, get-rich-quick schemes. The online industry is no longer a sprint to be first; it's a marathon that the most strategic and efficient companies will win.

Many factors will contribute to the success of those who survive the shakedown or launch new online products. Above all, these companies will have been able to:

1. Identify and quantify business opportunities.
2. Evaluate and satisfy the needs of customers.
3. Efficiently develop and market products.

These precursors to success are achieved through intuition, knowledge, and maybe a bit of luck. While we can't help you hone your intuition or improve your luck, we have written this book to help you increase your knowledge.

The purpose of this book is to provide the Internet business community with comprehensive information about understanding, using, acquiring, and conducting market and marketing research online. For many years, market and marketing research have been standard tools used in traditional industries to take much of the guesswork out of making critical business decisions. Without research, companies are, quite frankly, conducting their business like a game of "pin the tail on the donkey."

The advent of the Web has caused a revolution in the research community. Web technology has astronomically reduced the cost of conducting numerous types of research and simultaneously enabled the execution of more complicated and rigorous study designs. Businesses that operate entirely online, or have significant online components to their sales or marketing strategies, have a fantastic opportunity to reap the benefits of this revolution.

Unfortunately, Web companies are still stumbling around in the dark, because they lack the unique combination of research and technology skills to leverage these new opportunities. Doing so requires a thorough understanding of the types of online research currently available, and knowledge of when and how to apply each type. Additionally, not all research is created equal; users of research need to be sufficiently savvy to conduct some types of research on their own, and informed enough to select the best possible vendor to implement the remainder.

This book will remove the blindfold and provide the reader with a clear understanding of how to use online research to assist in each stage of an online venture.

CONTENTS

This text is divided into two parts. The first half of the book focuses on the types, tools, and techniques of online marketing research. We begin by outlining the research process (Chapter 1) used to evaluate when to conduct research, and to ensure that the results are actionable. Chapters 2 through 4 introduce the three fundamental types of marketing research: secondary, qualitative, and the core focus of this book, quantitative research. The remainder of the first half details the techniques of sampling, data collection, and questionnaire design that are used to conduct online marketing research.

Moving beyond the fundamentals, the second half of the book covers the process of applying online marketing research to all phases of online product conception, development, and marketing. The topics include:

- Market research—defining and understanding the market
- Segmentation—developing target markets
- Competition—assessment and positioning
- Existing online products—audience composition and performance testing

- New product concepts—development and testing
- Development—creating feature sets and interface design testing
- Testing—usability and beta testing
- Marketing—effective targeting and measuring ROI
- Tracking—developing systems for informing decisions

Handbook of
Online
Marketing
Research

P A R T

I

Fundamentals

CHAPTER 1

The Research Process

The research process is a structured approach that helps ensure all your efforts result in useful, actionable information. Far too often, companies that are anxious to gather data skip the critical early stages of the research process, and rush ahead to designing questionnaires and fielding studies. This is a dangerous practice that frequently limits the usefulness of the eventual findings.

It is tempting to ignore or pay lip service to the seemingly obvious initial planning stages of a research project. This is especially true when timing and schedules are tight—always a factor when researching online products and services. Free from many of the lengthy manufacturing and distribution processes traditional products require, online products are often conceived of, developed, and brought to market in a matter of months, not years. Such a compacted schedule is a significant challenge to the researcher who is charged with gathering actionable data.

Regardless of time constraints, it is crucial to budget sufficient time to answer some key questions before beginning any research project. The answers to these questions will directly impact the decision of whether to execute the research, and will shape the design, scope, and methodology of the ensuing study.

When we conduct research for a client, the following issues are carefully investigated and laid out in a research proposal:

- What is the budget for conducting the research?
- Can research have an impact?
- What is the objective of the research?
- Which metrics will need to be collected to attain the research objective?
- How will the data be collected?
- How will the data be analyzed?
- How will the findings be reported?
- How long will it take to complete the research?
- How much will the research cost?

Though an internal project may not require a formal research proposal, it is still advisable to create a document addressing all these questions and to review it with the key personnel involved in the project.

WHAT IS THE BUDGET FOR CONDUCTING THE RESEARCH?

It might seem premature to discuss money issues right off the bat. But having proposed and conducted research for clients of various sizes and financial situations, we can say from experience that money will be a primary driver in setting the scope of the project and determining your ability to get the project approved.

A fair amount of effort is involved in planning a research project. All your carefully crafted research objectives and ingenious study designs will be for naught if there is no money available or budgeted for research. Before jumping in with both feet, take some time to consider the research budget.

The research budget is determined by two factors:

1. the resources available in the organization, and
2. the perceived value of the research in helping to make correct or avoid poor decisions.

Obviously, large or well-funded companies can afford to invest in research, in the hope that the up-front investment will be rewarded by increased revenues in the future. Small start-ups, struggling to make payroll until their first round of financing, will probably have to minimize research expenditures as much as possible—perhaps by relying on secondary research or by conducting research in-house. Many times, this inexpensive research can be as valuable as primary research. (See Chapter 2.)

Determining the perceived value of research is more complicated than it first appears, because of the difficulty in quantifying the value of the information obtained from the research. Marketers must assign hypothetical values to the overall *cost of making a wrong decision,* and to the *chances of making the wrong decision with and without research.*

One approach, known as the Loss Method for Estimating Value of Information, can be represented mathematically:

Cost of making wrong decision = CWD
Chance of making wrong decision without research = NoR
Chance of making wrong decision with research = YesR
Maximum budget for research = MB

$$MB = (CWD \times NoR) - (CWD \times YesR)$$

Performing the necessary calculations is not difficult. The challenge is in coming up with the estimated values to plug into the equation. Companies may have a tendency to underestimate, sometimes severely, the costs and chances of making a wrong decision. Most difficult, however, is accurately assessing the degree to which research will assist in making the correct decision.

Example: With the holidays approaching, a site that sells pet food and supplies over the Internet is contemplating adding a feature to its site to allow pet owners the option of having their purchases gift-wrapped. Before implementation, the staff of the site want to conduct research to ensure that this is a desirable service that would increase customer loyalty and sales.

The costs of making the wrong decision in this instance would be the cost of building the gift-wrapping feature and having it bomb—perhaps because the majority of users were only interested in buying pet food in large quantities. The costs include the obvious development costs associated with changing the site, training the warehouse staff to wrap gifts, and purchasing wrapping supplies. Hypothetically, let's say these costs total $600,000.

There may also be costs associated with the alternate decision: not providing the service. Typically, these are less tangible issues such as effects on customer retention if you decide not to provide gift-wrapping to a customer base that desperately wants to send their sister's cat a noisy toy mouse to smack around the house. For the sake of simplicity, let's say this cost is estimated at $600,000 in lost revenue.

Now, the staffers at FurBall.com all have pets, and they give their pets presents every Christmas, Easter, and Thursday. So, it's not surprising that they think there is a 70% likelihood the idea will succeed without research. However, they concede that they don't know everything and that perhaps research could help decrease their chance of making the wrong decision from 30% to 20%.

$$MB = (\$600,000 \times .30) - (\$600,000 \times .20)$$
$$MB = (\$180,000) - (\$120,000)$$
$$MB = \$60,000$$

The maximum research budget for the gift-wrapping project is therefore $60,000. Obviously, spending the entire $60,000 on research would evaporate the potential savings that research could provide. However, a cost-effective survey of the user base, easily conducted for around $10,000 to $15,000 or far less if executed entirely in-house, is certainly warranted.

The major problem with calculating research budgets in terms of loss is that the method ignores the potential upside if the product is a success, and the role of research in affecting not only the likelihood but also the degree of success. Additional methods of calculating research budgets exist that are not covered here. Because of the difficulty involved in estimating costs and the likelihood of making a wrong decision, few companies, in our experience, even conduct this basic loss analysis before contracting expensive research.

A more common method of determining research budgets is to use a fixed percentage of development costs. This approach eliminates the headache of estimating the likelihood of making an incorrect decision with and without research. It does, however, tend to overfund projects with high degrees of certainty and underfund risky endeavors that might provide the most benefit.

CAN RESEARCH HAVE AN IMPACT?

This may seem obvious, but it is important to mention. Making sure the organization has the ability to react to research findings is critical. All too frequently, research projects are conducted during the later stages of development, after the course has been set. Findings in these studies that indicate problems typically encounter stiff resistance and often are ignored completely. Conversely, positive findings that support the wisdom of the organization's decisions result in a significant amount of back-patting, but very little action.

More difficult than determining whether the organization has time to react to research results is assessing whether it is open-minded about the findings produced by research. For a variety of reasons (negative past experience, overinflated egos, a deep belief in intuition), some executives do not believe that research can be more valid than their own assessment of the situation. Of course, research cannot make decisions on its own; it can only inform decision makers. Still, some organizations or individuals within organizations are not open-minded about research information.

It is even more common to encounter a close-minded attitude toward research findings that run contrary to a specific agenda. The executive who doggedly refuses to believe in the precepts of science might excitedly relay your results as scientific fact to colleagues, if the results supported the validity of the executive's concept. The most effective way to avoid this scenario is to work closely with key decision makers on the project to define the study objectives and the research approach. By doing so, you will be far more likely to achieve buy-in on the findings when the study is completed.

WHAT IS THE OBJECTIVE OF THE RESEARCH?

Accurately defining the research objective should be the primary focus of the preresearch phase. Once the study is under way, the research objective will maintain focus by acting as the filter for evaluating the necessity and value of each study element as the project progresses. Without a solid objective, research runs a greater risk of straying off track and resulting in muddled findings.

Research objectives should take the form of a clear, concise statement that defines the goals of the study.

> *Example 1:* Determine the value of implementing a gift-wrapping service on FurBall.com.
>
> *Example 2:* Determine the desirability of implementing a gift-wrapping service among users of FurBall.com, investigate the ideal feature set, and forecast the potential effect on brand perception and purchase probability.

Research objectives should be:

> *Attainable:* Avoid sweeping statements like the one in Example 1. It's impossible to "determine the value" because the value is an amalgamation of many variables.

Instead, shape statements that hone in on the measurable aspects that comprise the value such as *"desirability, feature set, potential effect on brand perception and sales."*

Focused: The first statement sets no limits on the scope of the research. Among whom should we attempt to understand the value? The entire nation? The Web population? Those who already use the site? Attempting to understand the perceptions of these different populations has dramatic cost implications; a good research objective focuses the research on a specific target.

Mutually agreed upon: Research objectives are best developed with the input of all the key decision makers who will be the end users of the information. The preferred method is to have decision makers themselves develop the research objectives, with input from a researcher to ensure that the statements are *attainable* and *focused.* Beyond instilling a sense of ownership in the project, this process creates consensus on the information needed to assist the decision maker(s) in determining the correct course of action.

Iterative: Everything flows from the research objective. Once an objective is agreed upon, the next steps of the preresearch process begin. What metrics will need to be collected to attain the research objective? How will the data be collected and analyzed? Every decision in these subsequent steps should be considered in relation to how it helps meet the research objective. Unfortunately, any number of issues with data collection or analysis can arise that may impact your ability to achieve the research objective. As each challenge arises, consider how it affects the research objective, and if necessary, revise the research objective to reflect the situation.

FIGURE 1.1: The Research Process

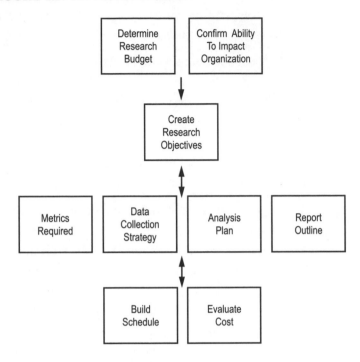

WHICH METRICS ARE REQUIRED TO MEET THE RESEARCH OBJECTIVE?

After the study objectives have been defined, the next step is to create a detailed listing of all the metrics (measures) needed to address the goals of the study.

The types of metrics available to the researcher are classification, behavioral, and attitudinal. These are covered in detail in Chapter 7. Briefly, classification metrics measure who you are, behavioral metrics measure what you do (or did), and attitudinal metrics measure what you think.

Let's return to the FurBall.com example:

Research Objective: Determine the desirability of implementing a gift-wrapping service among users of FurBall.com, investigate the ideal feature set, and forecast the potential effect on brand perception and purchase probability.

Here are some metrics we might collect to meet this objective.

Classification:

- Demographic (age, gender, etc.)
- Socioeconomic (income, occupation, etc.)
- Webographic (level of online experience, access locations, etc.)[1]

Behavioral:

- Number of visits to FurBall.com
- Number of purchases from FurBall.com
- Frequency of purchasing pet products as gifts
- Types of pet products purchased as gifts

Attitudinal:

- Overall desirability of gift-wrapping service
- Likelihood of using the feature
- Desirability of specific gift-wrapping features (ability to select paper, include personalized card, etc.)
- Ratings of different wrapping, ribbons, or cards
- Ratings of brand attributes
- Ratings of increased purchase probability

This is only one possible list of metrics that could be used to meet the sample research objective. Each situation is unique, and there are multiple methods of solving the same problem. For example, suppose that a competitive Web site had just implemented a gift-wrapping feature. Then our list would need to include metrics about the competitive product, such as awareness, usage, and satisfaction ratings. Furthermore, some of the metrics listed here may be deemed unnecessary by market intelligence previously gathered by

---

[1]*Webographics* is a term we developed to represent the group of characteristics that define a user of the Web. They could also be considered behavioral measures; but because all of our research is conducted online, we consider these to be classification metrics.

FurBall.com. If a previous study determined that the occupation of a consumer has no bearing on the purchase of pet products, for example, that metric could be removed from our list.

The list of collected metrics should be developed with the assistance of the client, who should be thoroughly briefed on the logic driving the collection of each metric. Taking the extra time up front to ensure that consumers of the research know why specific metrics are being collected will help ensure that the resulting information is used with confidence.

Unfortunately, most data is not free. There is often a wide gap between the ideal "wish list" of metrics and the practical set of data that can be acquired within the research budget. It may prove challenging (and expensive) to collect ratings of a competitive product, if doing so requires a complicated study design that directs respondents to first visit the competitor's site, then return to answer more questions. If competitive ratings are not critical to the research objective, the researcher might advise the client to forgo this information in lieu of collecting more detailed information in other areas or reducing study costs.

Evaluate each metric in terms of its cost and its benefit in achieving the research objective.

HOW WILL THE DATA BE COLLECTED?

Data collection decisions are driven by *who* and *what* the research objective is attempting to understand. Data collection is discussed in depth in Chapter 6. In simple terms:

> The *who* of data collection is called the *population,* a term that refers to the universe of people the research is attempting to understand. Populations can be large (e.g., all users of the Web) or targeted (e.g., users of a specific site). The former might require an expensive study that uses a nationally representative Web panel, while the latter could be sampled directly from a Web site for little or no cost.

The *what* of data collection is called the *study design*—how the study is structured to collect the metrics needed to answer the research objective. For example, if FurBall.com wants to determine which gift-wrapping pattern designs are most desirable, it will need to choose a data collection method that allows for the presentation of various gift-wrapping designs. Interviews conducted over the telephone or via an email survey would be ill-suited to such a research objective. A better solution would be to conduct interviews online, where sample images of each pattern design can be displayed for respondents.

The issues to consider when selecting a data collection method are quality, cost, and time. The strategy in nearly all research projects is to maximize quality while minimizing cost and time. This is more easily said than done, however, because issues of quality are often tied directly to the cost and duration of the project. The discussion in Chapter 6 of the strengths and weaknesses of each type of data collection provides assistance for making these crucial and often difficult decisions.

HOW WILL THE DATA BE ANALYZED?

Quite often, companies execute research projects with little fore-thought as to how the data will actually be utilized. It is tempting to set aside the analytic details until after data collection reveals some facts about the population. This is a dangerous habit. If it is determined after data collection that new metrics are required to perform the analysis, the study will have to be rerun or the intended analysis will have to be modified. Neither option will make anyone happy!

To avoid making costly mistakes, experienced researchers create analysis plans that detail how the collected metrics will be used to address the research objectives. Analysis plans can be as simple as reiterating how decision makers will use each metric.

Most commonly, however, an analysis plan details how two metrics (bivariate analysis) or multiple metrics (multivariate analysis) will be combined in various ways to provide insight.

> *Bivariate example:* Determine whether frequent users of FurBall.com are more likely to find a gift-wrapping service desirable, by cross-tabulating[2] "Frequency of accessing FurBall.com" with "Overall desirability of gift-wrapping service."

> *Multivariate example:* Identify a core segment of users, comprised of respondents who access FurBall.com more than once a week, purchase novelty pet products, and have purchased more than three products from FurBall.com. Cross-tabulate the core user segment with all attitudinal data to determine how these disproportionately valuable users feel about implementing a gift-wrapping service on the FurBall.com site.

As with all aspects of the research process, it is essential to distribute and review the analysis plan with the end consumers of the research. The more complicated the analysis plan, the more important it is to ensure that decision makers are comfortable with the reasons behind using specific analysis techniques and the meaning of their outputs. In our experience, clients are generally less likely to utilize complex analysis, because it may be confusing, unfamiliar, or difficult to explain to others. In other words, don't expect to conduct an ingenious cluster analysis of a site's user base and have the results unanimously accepted without providing detailed explanations and education.

HOW WILL THE FINDINGS BE REPORTED?

Research findings can be delivered in an array of formats, from simple data tables to in-depth written reports complete with charts,

---

[2]A common type of bivariate data analysis in which data tables are created that compare one variable against another.

strategic implications, and recommended action points. When planning a research project, it is important to determine how the results will be presented to the end consumer. Formal deliverables, while easier to understand and disseminate, may add unwarranted time and cost to the project.

To reach a decision about the gift-wrapping service, FurBall.com executives may only require a brief overview analysis to accompany the tabular data. If that's the case, it might make sense for the researcher to meet with key staff to review the research results, rather than delay the decision-making process by developing a formal presentation.

The degree of formality required is typically determined by the research savvy of the audience consuming the research. Decision makers who are familiar with research techniques and well-versed in the problem at hand often require little formal analysis. In fact, their familiarity with the research topic often makes these consumers more qualified to derive actionable findings than a professional researcher. Conversely, research results should be formalized to stand alone if they are to be disseminated widely throughout an organization (beyond those involved in the planning and execution of the project) or if the audience has little previous experience with research.

HOW LONG WILL IT TAKE TO COMPLETE THE RESEARCH?

Research results must be timely to be useful. Poor scheduling can cause research projects to run longer than expected and potentially miss critical decision windows. Late results can easily become worthless results, so the planning process should always include an honest, accurate assessment of the time required to deliver on the research objective.

The basic components of a research schedule are:

Questionnaire Development: The time required to develop a questionnaire goes beyond simply drafting questions. A period for review and revision of the questionnaire should be developed and agreed upon by all key individuals. In our experience, the review of questionnaires almost always takes longer than anticipated, so be certain to allocate ample time for this step.

Data Collection: Depending on the methodology, data collection can take from a few days to several months. Set-up time (such as for programming and testing an online survey) should also be factored into the time requirements for this stage.

Data Analysis: Without preplanning, unexpected delays can have a significant impact on the schedule for a research project. A thorough analysis plan will help avoid these situations and aid in accurately estimating a time frame for completing the analysis.

Reporting: Aside from data analysis, will the researcher require an additional week to create formal deliverables, such as a report or presentation?

When developing a research schedule, be realistic about the time it will take to complete each step. Make certain that key individuals commit to reviewing materials on time, and build in leeway wherever possible. Because much of research is a linear process, it is not usually possible to make up for delays by executing different parts of a project in parallel. The questionnaire must be finalized before data collection can begin; analysis cannot be done without data; and reporting requires that analysis be done first. Our advice is to be wary of conducting research on an unreasonably tight schedule. When someone takes an extra day or two reviewing the questionnaire and the data collection deadline needs to be extended, you might end up writing the report at 1:00 am on a Monday!

HOW MUCH WILL THE RESEARCH COST?

Accurately assessing the cost of the project should be a straightforward process when the data collection, analysis, and reporting requirements have been determined and scheduled. One option is to provide the research plan to outside vendors as an RFP (request for proposal) and request quotes to conduct all or part of the work. For portions of the work that will be conducted internally, assign costs to your estimates of the staff's time to complete the work and any incidental costs, such as incentives provided to study participants.

If the estimated cost of conducting the research exceeds the calculated or available budget for the research, it will be necessary to reevaluate and modify the methodology. In doing so, first attempt to determine methods of reducing costs while still addressing the research objectives. Failing this, revise the research objectives to meet the budget constraints.

CHAPTER

2

Secondary Research

M arketing research falls into two main categories: primary research and secondary research. The distinction between them is fairly simple: Primary research is original work done with your particular study objectives in mind. Secondary research is the use of previously existing resources to meet your research goals.

Though much of this book focuses on primary research, it's important to point out that a lot of time and money can be saved if you first do a bit of poking around to see what other work has already been done in your area of interest. There's little sense in reinventing the wheel, and we highly recommend that you leverage existing sources of research information before committing to more time-consuming and expensive methods.

Secondary research has many uses, and can come in many forms. In some cases, it might be the only way to cost-effectively obtain certain types of data. We find secondary research especially useful in informing our study development process by identifying issues that impact the industry and marketplace of clients for whom we are conducting primary research projects. Beyond simply

obtaining background on a subject, we've often been able to eliminate the need to conduct primary research by finding key data
points hidden in research that we acquired for little or no cost.

Any secondary research you might find began its life much as
your own primary research would. Someone, at some point, established study objectives, executed a survey or other data collection
method, and analyzed the results. Published results might take the
form of an official "syndicated" study that is available for purchase,
or a few key factoids released to the press for inclusion in a news
article. Results might be published in a scholarly journal, a govern-
ment-sponsored information database, or a host of other resources.
A vast amount of secondary research is available, and some of it
might be exactly what you need. The key is knowing where to look.

FREE (OR LOW-COST) SOURCES OF SECONDARY RESEARCH

In many cases, you can get valuable data at no cost other than your
time: making some phone calls, searching the Web, or making a trip
to the libraries in your area. Here we provide reviews of some of the
major sources of free research. In the section titled Reference
Sources later in this chapter, we list sources and their URLs. Later
in the book, we provide specific examples of how to find answers
to particular strategic questions.

Government Publications

Your tax dollars go to pay for an astounding number of things, and
market research is one of them. Government agencies like the U.S.
Department of Labor and the U.S. Census Bureau regularly commission high-quality (expensive) studies about the economy and
about the consumers and businesses that form it. International
agencies and foreign governments do the same. In recent years,
much of this information has been made accessible via the Web, so
a good first stop in your search should be the main Web pages of
the government agencies responsible for producing these reports.

General Press

Simply searching the back archives of major newspapers and magazines can yield quite a bit of useful data. Like you, reporters scour the same resources for interesting bits of data to include in their articles. If they've done the dirty work for you, why not profit from their efforts? You'll often be able to find references back to the original study that you can follow up on, view the entire study, or find even more pertinent data. In addition to data dug up in their own searches, reporters often receive copies of studies or press packets of information from studies that market research companies are promoting for sale (see Paid Sources of Secondary Research). Reporters may include just the piece of data you need in an article they are writing, and save you the expense of having to purchase the research results. Sometimes the free data isn't sufficient for your project and you'll want to purchase the study; but at the very least, searching press archives is another avenue for discovering these studies.

Industry Journals

Industry journals are magazines that are dedicated to covering even the most esoteric goings-on in their particular business. In addition to providing news such as business mergers, new product launches, CEO appointments, and the like, trade journals often quote useful statistics of one kind or another. You won't find these journals in the supermarket magazine section, so you'll have to do a bit of hunting to find the ones you want. Fortunately, the Web comes to the rescue. Sites like Looksmart (www.looksmart.com) and DirectHit (www.directhit.com) have excellent hierarchical menus and search tools that allow you to ferret out an amazing number of trade journals that either are reprinted on the Web, or provide the contact information necessary to subscribe to the print editions or to search back issues. The National Directory of Magazines (www.media finder.com/mag_home.cfm) maintains links to a vast array of periodicals, including industry and trade publications. If you aren't able to find trade journals directly, chances are that an industry or trade association can point you in the right direction.

Trade Associations

If a trade journal doesn't exist for the industry you are attempting to study, chances are that there is still an organization that exists to promote the common interests of people in that line of business. These groups are treasure chests of useful information and people. Larger associations often publish major industry journals and sponsor industry-wide research. If not, they will likely have available a list of useful publications and fact sheets about their constituency. Even better, the staff at these organizations can usually point you in the right direction more quickly than your own detective skills would.

Public Company SEC Filings

Publicly-traded companies regularly file reports with the Securities and Exchange Commission (SEC). These reports may contain explicitly useful marketplace data, such as estimates of market size or growth prospects, though this is more the exception than the norm. What they all have, however, is information about financial performance that can be creatively used to deduce all kinds of important data points. We give specific examples of "creative deduction" in Part II, where we address the strategic application of market research tools. Public company filings can usually be found on the companies' Web sites, but an even more convenient way to locate them is through EDGAR Online (www.edgar-online.com). Edgar allows you to search for public company filings by company name, ticker symbol, industry classification, or key word; you can quickly zero in on the companies you want to look at. Currently free user registration is required to access EDGAR; select "Visitor Membership."

Investment Brokerages and Information Services

Perhaps no one puts as many brains and dollars behind understanding the marketplace as do the firms that sell investment services. Analysts constantly monitor and assess various industries' potential, and often write opinions on the future of various industry sectors and of companies within those sectors. These opinions and analyses can be fantastic sources of information that can help satisfy your research needs. Fortunately, much of the information is available, free of charge, via the Web sites of investment and brokerage houses.

Library Reference Desk

In this day of electronic information, it might seem outmoded to suggest a visit to a person in the musty old library. Beware preconceived notions! Reference librarians spend most of their education and their entire careers refining the art of finding information (however esoteric it might be). Though much information is available online, many resources have not yet been computerized. Even those that have been can be difficult to ferret out. Reference librarians know where to go, online or off, so pay them a visit before you spend time spinning your own wheels. Librarians love to help researchers and they'll often go out of their way to make your life easier.

Newsgroups and UseNet

USENET is one of the oldest online institutions and consists of thousands of publicly available discussion groups. These discussion groups are commonly known as Newsgroups, even though you'll be more likely to find discussions than news articles there. People in USENET groups may be discussing topics of broad or esoteric appeal. Chances are good that there will be a group discussing something related to your research project, and that they've been discussing it for a while. A number of USENET search and archive tools are available on the Web to help you zero in on particular groups and discussion "threads" and to read what has been said on the topic. If you don't find the exact answer to your question, simply post the question to the members of the group. Participants of the discussion might be able to point you in the right direction.

Discussion Lists

In recent years a vast number of Email-based and Web-based discussion lists have been developed to provide Internet users even more ways of exchanging ideas. Originally, these lists were highly scattered and grew only by word of mouth. As the idea of commercial enterprise built on community and affinity groups has come into favor, a number of companies have capitalized on the opportunity to aggregate lists in one place and have provided tools to make the lists easier to use and read. Several notable services are EGroups (www.egroups.com), OneList (www.onelist.com), Topica (www.topica.com), and Liszt (www.liszt.com). All of these services publish lists broken down into major categories and subcategories of interest that are very easy to search and use. Subscribing and unsubscribing to the lists is simple, as is reading the archives. Use discussion lists much as you would USENET to find your secondary research information.

Search Engines

More than likely, if you're anything like us, the first thing you'll do when hunting down data is turn to your favorite search engine(s). Theoretically, if it's out there someplace on the Web, one or all of the search services will find it for you. Sometimes this holds true, sometimes not. Ironically, the growth of the Web and its potential to allow access to limitless amounts of information have hampered the ability to actually *find* this information.

Search engines, contrary to many of their marketing claims, only search and index a small fraction of what's actually out there. Much of the indexing priority is based on how recently the data was submitted to the engine, so older (not necessarily much older!) content that has not been updated recently is likely to have dropped off the map. In our experience, this includes old market research reports. That said, search engines provide a great on-ramp into your exploratory search of the Web by bringing you to pages that may link to much more useful (and chock-full-o'-data) pages.

When using search engines, remember that all are not created equal. Try your searches on different engines, being creative and flexible with your search techniques to see which ones are most effective. A great way to query multiple search engines at once is to use one of several freely available search assistant programs, such as GO Network's Express Search (http://express.infoseek.com/) or the search tool embedded in Microsoft Internet Explorer 5.x. These tools hit a number of specified search engines with your query, remove duplicates, and bring you one set of results—a definite time-saver for serious searchers.

Directory Services

Sometimes, simply throwing your search query out to the four winds and slogging through all the returned results isn't effective. Old pages may not be indexed, even though they're out there; or they might be hiding under result #10,050 and never see the light of day. Another approach is to use any number of hierarchical directory-style search services, like Yahoo! or Looksmart, to hone in on the sites that are likely to contain your desired information or to give you another list of relevant links to chase down.

Assisted Searching Services

One of our favorite new search products, introduced recently in an effort to win over fickle users, is the assisted search service. On an assisted search service, you can type a question, no matter how vague, in plain-old English; send it to the search service; and receive a personalized, well-thought-out response listing suggested places to look for an answer. This is truly the lazy person's approach to searching, and we've found some very useful resources in this way. We have no idea how these services manage to make a profit, or even hope to support such a labor-intensive service; so we make no guarantees that such services will remain free (or even exist!) at the time of this book's publication. Check Looksmart Live (www.looksmart.com/live/) or Answers.com (www.answers.com). Other companies, such as Allexperts.com (www.allexperts.com) and KnowPost (www.knowpost.com), are building services in which communities of "experts" volunteer to help out with answering your questions. They're excellent places to throw out your queries; you never know what they might come up with.

Market Research Firms' Web Sites

You may already have stumbled upon some market research firms during your Web searches on search engines, but it definitely pays to hunt down market research sites directly and spend some time browsing their content. As we mentioned earlier, a lot of useful content is not indexed by the search engines. The best way to uncover what market research sites have to offer is to do some digging yourself.

Market research firms often publish very useful documents, called white papers. White papers typically distill some learning gained from prior research into short reports (usually fewer than 20 pages) that are often freely available on these sites. Companies provide them for a couple of reasons. First, it helps advance the level of learning in the field. Second, it's a very respectable way to enhance the firm's reputation for having an innovative, knowledgeable staff of researchers. Regardless of the motives for publishing white papers, they might contain information very useful to your cause.

While perusing research firms' sites, you might also find sneak previews for syndicated research products they have for sale. If you are looking for generally broad data, these previews might suffice. You probably won't find much detailed data, because they hope to entice you to purchase the entire study; but it never hurts to look. Finally, you may find useful factoids on the site that were gleaned from primary research the firm conducted for its clients. It's not typical for the results of an entire privately commissioned study to be published; but if it served the client's and research firm's purposes, bits and pieces might be available.

Competitors' Sites

In addition to the information available from publicly-traded company's filings, you may find useful data points on the Web sites of other companies in the line of business you are researching. Knowing what the competition is up to is an important part of any strategy, so you will probably already be looking at these sites. Particularly check out the "About Us" sections, where companies typically talk about their business models and missions, and sometimes mention data to support their claims. You may also wish to check out the press release sections of the sites, where companies may make mention of the results of a study they commissioned, or one that brought to light relevant data for their (and your) business strategy. If you're not sure where to find your competitors' sites already, a good hierarchical directory site like Yahoo! Companies (biz.yahoo.com/industry) or one of numerous company search engines, such as COMFIND Business Search (www.comfind.com) or Dun and Bradstreet's Companies Online (www.companiesonline.com), provide the Web addresses of many privately-held companies.

Public Relations Newswire Sites

Quite a lot of the "news" you read in trade publications actually gets its start in a press release issued by a commercial enterprise.

These releases are typically placed on one of a number of newswire services that are read by journalists looking for new story ideas or content. You can get the same information by visiting a few PR sites, such as PRNewswire (www.prnewswire.com) or Business Wire (www.businesswire.com). Both sites offer search and archive capabilities.

Research Destination Sites

With countless Internet and high-tech news sites, rumor sites, and opinion sites just a mouse-click away, sometimes it seems as if half the Web consists of sites documenting their own existence. Not wanting to leave market research out of the act, several useful sites have been developed that generate content based on snippets of data gleaned from a large variety of syndicated research studies on Web and high-tech topics. The data tends to be presented as mini-analyses about an industry trend, and can provide background insight on the overarching issues facing your marketplace, as well as specific data points, at no charge. NUA's Internet surveys site (www.nua.ie) is a searchable and well-categorized site, as is Internet.com's CyberAtlas (www.cyberatlas.com). Both sites are updated frequently and have email newsletters to keep you abreast of the latest study findings. A relative newcomer to the scene is DeepCanyon (www.deepcanyon.com). This is a destination we can't recommend highly enough. In addition to providing useful free access to Dun & Bradstreet's company database (which provides quick estimates of market size, competition, and sales figures), it provides links to and comprehensive reviews of countless research and marketing resources on the Web. You could easily spend days exploring all the information provided.

PAID SOURCES OF SECONDARY RESEARCH

The resources mentioned in the previous section may go a long way toward satisfying your early research requirements, such as obtaining general background data on the industry. But as you begin to narrow and refine your research needs, you will probably have some holes to fill. Before you start thinking about doing your own primary research studies, consider exploring the research data that is available for purchase.

One nice thing about actually purchasing secondary research is that the profit motive that drives information services tends to result in an easier searching experience. The companies that have data to sell want to make it as quick and painless as possible for you to find what you need and make the purchase. You'll find a host of information and news retrieval services, data warehouses, and research vendors that have developed robust search tools to get the job done quickly.

Before we delve into the different types of paid research data, a word of caution is in order. Just because you have to pay for something, that doesn't necessarily mean it's any good! Data is only as reliable as the study upon which it was based. We recommend that you spend some time learning about the background of the study and the company that generated the data before making a purchase. We discuss issues related to study methodology in Chapters 5 and 6. Review those chapters and bone up on the do's and don'ts of executing marketing research; then determine whether the data you are considering measures up to quality research practices.

Subscriber Information Services

A good example of a subscriber information service is a news and research service such as LEXIS-NEXIS. Those who remember systems like LEXIS-NEXIS from college days will be pleased to learn that you no longer have to conduct your research at a university terminal or other proprietary workstation. Now, most information services leverage the power of the Internet and the Web to allow you to search their catalogs from any connected computer. Much of what you find on an information service is taken from other sources, and much of it is freely available, if you had the time to dig around for it. Pay-for-use information services add value by making the search process more relevant and more comprehensive than you might otherwise achieve on your own. LEXIS-NEXIS, for example, claims to pull data from over 22,000 individual sources. Clearly, you would not be able to cover that much ground on your own. More and more companies are appearing on the Web offering their search services for nothing more in return than a free membership registration and a few ad banners.

Syndicated Research

Syndicated research gets its name from the fact that a company conducts one research project and sells the results to multiple clients. Some syndicated studies are highly branded, widely distributed, and actively marketed with a catchy brand name like the Yankelovich Monitor (www.yankelovich.com). Others are more targeted, have specific areas of focus, and are difficult to find without some assistance.

Syndicated research might not seem quite as attractive as free research, but it may end up being more cost-effective in the long run. The adage "You get what you pay for" applies. If you are basing a $500,000 decision on your research, paying a few hundred dollars for a key piece of data is a small and worthy investment. It will almost certainly be less expensive in terms of personnel cost than doing the research work yourself. If you've grown weary of your quest for free data, you'll be pleased to learn that finding information available for purchase is more straightforward. Data has a limited shelf life, and firms that produce and sell syndicated research have a vested interest in making it as easy as possible for prospective clients to learn about and buy studies.

Syndicated research comes in three different forms: published one-offs, tracking studies, and research newsletters.

Published one-offs are studies that were executed in the past and, unlike tracking studies, are unlikely to be conducted again in the future. Good quality syndicated research is expensive to produce; if the demand for a particular study wasn't high enough to warrant multiple editions, a one-off is the result. Unless you are interested in a broad topic that's likely to have wide appeal to induce companies to engage in a regular program of research, one-off studies will comprise the majority of what you'll find in your syndicated research hunt.

There are literally tens of thousands of one-off reports available, so obviously tracking them all down could be problematic. Fortunately, a number of saintly companies have done the dirty work for you. You can quickly determine what's available by using one of the noteworthy services mentioned at the end of the chapter.

Tracking studies are conducted multiple times during their life spans (typically as long as people keep demanding and paying for the study). The main objective of a tracking study is to provide the most up-to-date information on the population or issues being studied. Tracking studies have an additional objective: to measure changes or trends that occur over time. Companies recognize that they must meet the market as it turns the next corner, so they attempt to identify future trends by analyzing past behavior. A distinguishing characteristic of a tracking study is that it is executed over and over, in largely the same form each time (questioning, order of questions, sampling methodology, etc.). This is done so data from each wave of interviewing can be compared to previous waves. Tracking studies often include a report from the research firm that analyzes the shifts in the population over time. Many tracking studies are done in the online sector, because the Internet is changing so rapidly and businesses place a high value on the ability to take the pulse of the marketplace on a regular basis. Tracking studies are often named with the word "Track" or "Trak" or "Monitor" somewhere in the title.

A third source of syndicated data is *research newsletters*. Publishers of these newsletters tend to focus on a particular area of the market, and often subscribe to (or receive free copies of) syndicated research reports. They read the reports and distill the data into what they see as the most pertinent bits for their particular focus. Research newsletters don't usually contain data that couldn't be found elsewhere, but they do a nice job of scanning what's out there and keeping the busy executive informed on the latest situations. Again, there are thousands of newsletters available (only some of which focus on research) so you'll need to isolate the ones that have meaning for you. Pay a visit to MediaFinder (www.mediafinder.com), which indexes over 24,000 newsletters and scores of other periodicals.

Continuous Tracking Services

Regular tracking studies are conducted on a periodic basis—quarterly, for example. That is typically sufficient to measure shifts in the overall state of a population, but it falls short in the ability to link these shifts with other factors that may be influencing the market, or to catch significant events that may have occurred between studies. This is akin to the idea that a snapshot of your child, taken at the same time each year, might give you some idea of how the child's life is progressing; but a movie that documented the entire year would prove far more telling. Continuous tracking is marketing research's attempt to "film" the marketplace. Continuous tracking typically falls into three categories: brand tracking, purchase behavior tracking, and media measurement.

Brand Tracking

Millward Brown first popularized continuous tracking in the early 1980s as a tool to measure the impact of marketing efforts (primarily advertising) on people's awareness and perceptions of brands. Rather than executing a few big studies each year with large sample sizes, continuous brand tracking is based on a continuous program of interviewing small samples (approximately 50 to 100 respondents per week). The line of questioning is typically very focused on the main objective of the study (determining consumers' awareness of and preference for a brand, for example) and the resulting data are plotted over time. Overlaying other variables of interest (e.g., ad spending in a particular geographic region) allows the analyst to measure the impact of one on the other.

Online Brand Tracking

Understanding the relationship between advertising and brand attitudes continues to be a primary application of continuous tracking in traditional markets, and more recently, online as well. Millward Brown Interactive's Voyager program for online advertisers utilizes a large panel of online consumers coupled with innovative tracking software to register the impact of advertisements viewed by panelists. Clients can pull a sample of panelists who have viewed their ad campaigns and survey them on their brand attitudes and preferences much as they would with traditional (phone-based) tracking studies.

Purchase Behavior Tracking

Beyond simply measuring consumers' stated opinions, attitudes, and preferences for brands, some companies have instituted tracking programs that measure actual purchase behavior. By using huge databases of point-of-purchase data (usually obtained via scanning of product bar codes) coupled with shopper affinity cards (e.g., the Safeway Club Card or Shopper's Hotline card), subscribers to services like Information Resources' InfoScan can link their marketing efforts directly to their bottom-line sales figures. Purchase tracking systems are obviously very appealing to marketers, but there are limitations. Foremost among them is the fact that the purchase decision process and purchase cycle for many products is longer than can be effectively measured using this approach. Someone who is considering a new automobile may spend several years gathering information, saving money, and being deluged with advertising before actually making the purchase. The impact of an advertising campaign in 1996 may indeed have influenced the purchase of a car in 2000, but the correlation would be difficult to measure, if not impossible. Because of this limitation, purchase behavior tracking is typically only employed for packaged goods products such as toothpaste, food items, and beverages. Until recently, purchase behavior could only be linked to offline media activities like radio, print, and television. Information Resources recently announced a partnership with MediaMetrix, a media measurement firm, to provide a linkage between online media consumption and offline purchase behavior. The service is new and the sample is small, but we expect to see further development of this type of research in the coming years.

Media Measurement

If you are familiar with the Nielsen Ratings, you are familiar with media measurement. This type of research is the primary tool of media planners, who use the information to decide on the placement of their advertising campaigns. Media measurement provides the subscriber with estimates of the number of people who consume various types of media (radio, TV, print, online, outdoor, etc.) and the characteristics of those people. Using this data, planners can learn which types of people will be reached by placing advertising in these locations.

The data obtained from these services can be very detailed. For example, you might learn that the 2.3 million viewers who watch the typical *Baywatch* episode average 23 years of age, are 90% likely to be male, own 6.5 video game titles, and are 60% likely to drive an American sedan. If a media planner's advertising strategy called for reaching 2 million male consumers in their early twenties, it might choose *Baywatch* as its media location.

Media measurement is typically done via a panel of consumers, selected to be nationally representative, who agree to let the research firm monitor their media consumption habits. This monitoring may be done passively or actively. In passive monitoring, a special device tracks the programs (for television). For online tracking of Web site usage, a software application installed on the panelist's computer does the job. In active monitoring, the research firm depends upon the panelist to keep a diary of media consumption. The diary system (sometimes supplemented with telephone interviews) is typically used for radio, since radio media consumption happens in many locations throughout the typical day (car, home, office). Print-based tracking is typically done via a readership survey of each publication and an audited measurement of the publication's circulation.

Media measurement has been around for a long time. It is the bread-and-butter line of business for a number of major research companies. As the online advertising market heats up, dozens of firms are scrambling to cement a leadership position in the measurement of online media consumption. MediaMetrix (formerly PC Meter) and Nielsen's NetRatings are the leading contenders.

TRENDS IN FUTURE DEVELOPMENT
OF SYNDICATED PRODUCTS

It used to be that secondary research, whether paid or free was available in "one-size-fits-all" form. Information was typically delivered in a fixed format, often in the form of mountainous piles of printed data tables. Primary research would get you exactly what you needed, but would eat up your entire research budget in the process. Secondary research was a compromise you'd make in order to cut costs.

With the sweeping changes brought about by the Internet and computerization, the line between primary and secondary research is blurring. Syndicated research is now available in far more customized form. Companies like USADATA (www.usadata.com) take the data from massive syndicated studies and place it online in innovative systems that allow you to slice and dice the information to get exactly what you need. Instead of being locked into purchasing a large, expensive study, you pay only for the data you can use (learning the market penetration of tennis enthusiasts in Austin, Texas, for example).

Media planners note similar trends in the measurement tools they use. NetRatings and Media Metrix both allow subscribers to drill down into reports to quickly isolate the required information, without having to custom-order a data processing run.

REFERENCE SOURCES

The Web provides a vast storehouse of information for marketing researchers. Intrepid surfers don't have to stray from their desks to find more resources than they can possibly handle. We've listed some suggested starting points; but you'll discover far more than what is contained in these few pages. A resource we can't recommend highly enough is DeepCanyon (www.deepcanyon.com). It is a source for syndicated research products available for sale; a comprehensive guide to marketing research companies; a directory of numerous free sources of data; and marketing-related news. If you anticipate focusing a good deal of your research efforts on using secondary sources, we recommend picking up Kalorama's *Finding Market Research on the Web* (www.marketresearch.com/Web_book.html). It's a bit pricey ($235), but will more than pay for itself by giving you the fastest route to the secondary information you seek.

Government Resources

U.S. Census Bureau (www.census.gov)

The primary government portal to a vast array of demographic, economic, and business statistics on the U.S. population. The site is searchable and has menus, but be prepared to be spun around several times during your visit. Nonetheless, it's a worthwhile visit. The site contains volumes of free data and links to much more. Some major areas of interest are:

American FactFinder
(factfinder.census.gov/)
A nice set of tools that enable customized queries and reports on massive census databases.

Annual Capital Expenditures Survey
(www.census.gov/csd/ace/index.html)

Information on capital investment in new and used structures and equipment by nonfarm businesses. The survey is based on a sample of approximately 34,000 companies with one or more employees and approximately 12,000 nonemployers.

Annual Survey of Manufactures
(tier2.census.gov/asm/asm.htm)

Contains estimates of the value of product shipments for approximately 1,750 classes of manufactured products, based on reports from a representative sample of about 55,000 manufacturing establishments.

International Statistical Agencies
(www.census.gov/main/www/stat_int.html)

Firms wanting to tackle international markets will appreciate this convenient list of links to foreign agencies comparable to the census bureau.

The Statistical Abstract of the United States
(www.census.gov/statab/www/)

A great resource for frequently requested data points gathered by federal agencies and private organizations.

U.S. Consumer Expenditure Surveys (stats.bls.gov/ csxhome.htm)

The U.S. Bureau of Labor Statistics conducts ongoing research into the buying habits of American consumers, as well as the characteristics of those consumers. This data is leveraged by many for-profit data agencies (like Claritas) into detailed buying profiles of various product and service categories; but you can obtain much of the same information at little or no cost directly through the government site.

STAT-USA (www.stat-usa.gov)

A subscription-based service of the U.S. Department of Commerce that aggregates data and publications from dozens of governmental trade and economics agencies. Purchase of reports is handled on a pay-as-you-go basis.

General Press

Looksmart (www.looksmart.com) maintains a convenient and comprehensive listing of major (and esoteric) news sources available on the Web. Some that we've turned to on a frequent basis are:

Associated Press (wire.ap.org)

Barron's(www.barrons.com)

Boston Globe (www.boston.com/globe/)

Business 2.0 (www.business2.com)

Business Week (www.businessweek.com)

CNET News.com (www.news.com)

CNN (www.cnn.com)

The Economist (www.economist.com)

Fast Company (www.fastcompany.com)

Financial Times (www.ft.com)

Forbes (www.forbes.com)

Fortune (www.fortune.com)

inc.com (www.inc.com)

Industry Standard (www.thestandard.com)

Kiplinger Online (www.kiplinger.com)

Los Angeles Times (www.latimes.com)

Money (www.money.com)

MSNBC (www.msnbc.com)

Nando Times (www.nandotimes.com)

New York Times (www.nyt.com)

Newsweek (www.newsweek.com)

Red Herring (www.redherring.com)

Time Magazine (www.time.com)

US News and World Report (www.usnews.com)

Wall Street Journal Interactive (interactive.wsj.com)

WashingtonPost.com (www.washingtonpost.com)

ZDNet News (www.zdnet.com/zdnn/)

Industry Journals

There are online and print publications documenting the latest developments in even the most obscure specialties (Prehistoric Antiquities & Archaeological News Quarterly springs to mind). There are literally thousands out there, so including them all would be a book in itself. Fortunately, tracking them down has become easier than ever. Your first stop should be the National Directory of Magazines (www.mediafinder.com/mag_home.cfm). If you don't get more leads than you can handle directly from this site, hierarchical Web directories like Looksmart (www.looksmart.com) and Yahoo! (www.yahoo.com) also provide useful backup.

Trade Associations

There are more than 100,000 trade associations in the United States alone. Many of them exist specifically to promote the interests of certain business sectors, providing a wealth of information on the competitive environment, statistics, and, frequently, helpful staff who can point you in the direction of resources you might not have considered. The hunt for your desired organization isn't as difficult as you might expect. Most well-equipped public or university libraries have *The Encyclopedia of Associations—National Organizations of the United States,* published by Gale Research. If you want a $500 copy of your own, check out their Web site at (www.gale.com). Much of the same information can be obtained for free (and without leaving your desk) at Association Central (www.associationcentral.com) or the American Society of Association Executives (www.asaenet.org/Gateway/OnlineAssocSlist.html)

Public Company SEC Filings

SEC filings are available on publicly-traded companies' Web sites (typically within the Investor Relations' section. A quicker and more convenient place for one-stop shopping is EDGAR Online (www.edgar-online.com), which aggregates all information submitted to the Securities and Exchange Commission. EDGAR Online requires a free user registration (select "Visitor Membership") but offers useful features like customized email alerts and extensive searching capabilities.

Investment Brokerages and Information Services

Analysts constantly monitor and assess various industries' potential, and often write opinions on the future of various industry sectors and of companies within those sectors. These opinions and analyses can be fantastic sources of information that can help satisfy your research needs. Fortunately, much of this information is available, free of charge, via the Web sites of investment firms and brokerage houses.

Brokerages

Ameritrade (www.ameritrade.com)

Charles Schwab (www.schwab.com)

Datek (www.datek.com)

DLJdirect (www.dljdirect.com)

E-Trade (www.etrade.com)

Fidelity Investments (www.fidelity.com)

Hambrecht & Quist (www.hamquist.com)

Morgan Stanley/Dean Witter Online(www.online.msdw.com)

Wit Capital (www.witcapital.com)

Investment Information Services

ClearStation (www.clearstation.com)

CNN Financial News Network (www.cnnfn.com)

Companies Online (www.companiesonline.com)

Corporate Information.com
   (www.corporateinformation.com)

Dun & Bradstreet (www.dnb.com)

Hoover's Online (www.hoovers.com)

Individual Investor (www.individualinvestor.com)

Investext (www.investext.com)

Market Guide (www.marketguide.com)

Money Magazine (www.money.com)

Motley Fool (www.fool.com)

Silicon Investor (www.siliconinvestor.com)

Smart Money (www.smartmoney.com)

The Street (www.thestreet.com)

Zacks Investment Research (www.zacks.com)

Newsgroups and USENET

USENET is a network of thousands of message boards, also known as newsgroups. People on USENET groups may be discussing topics of broad or esoteric appeal. Chances are, there will be a group discussing something related to your research project.

Rather than browsing the groups directly, we recommend using a search and archiving service to comb through the archives of available material. Most major search services provide USENET searching capabilities, though you may need to dig into the advanced search options to access the tools. They typically obtain their functionality from two main providers, who you may wish to access directly for enhanced features.

Remarq (www.remarq.com) is our favorite tool for the job. Remarq has numerous features designed to make searching and keeping tabs on USENET much easier than it ever was. One particularly useful feature is its email alert, which will send you notification when any of your watched newsgroups post content related to your objective.

Deja.com (www.deja.com) also provides USENET searching features, though they've shifted the focus of their destination site toward consumer product reviews rather than strictly USENET functionality. Because of all the clutter caused by their shift of business focus, you'll be more likely to get real value out of Deja by accessing it via one of the major search services, rather than going directly to the main site.

Discussion Lists

Beyond USENET, a large number of private and public accessible discussion forums have been developed. Originally, they were scattered across the Internet in fragmented email lists and Web-based bulletin boards. Now, most of these groups have been aggregated and made accessible via one of the community services listed here. If you don't find a list discussing your topic on one, check the others.

EGroups (www.egroups.com)

ForumOne (www.forumone.com)

Liszt (www.liszt.com)

TileNet (www.tile.net)

Topica (www.topica.com)

Search Engines

Almost every search for secondary resources will involve using at least a few major search services. Among the tried-and-true services are:

Altavista (www.altavista.com)

Excite (www.excite.com)

Go (www.go.com)

HotBot (www.hotbot.com)

Lycos (www.lycos.com)

WebCrawler (www.webcrawler.com)

These services have been around for quite a while and generally offer good performance. We especially like Altavista and HotBot for conducting highly-focused searches. However, new searching technologies and approaches have been developed in recent years that are definitely worth a try. In fact, we tend to get better results on average using three newer services:

Ask Jeeves (www.ask.com)

DirectHit (www.directhit.com)

Google (www.google.com)

Directory Services

Sometimes you don't know exactly what you're looking for, or it simply gets lost in the clutter of the returns from a "pure" search service. In such cases, turn to a hierarchical directory and drill your way down to publications that meet your general criteria. You'll have to do further searching once you visit the sites a directory suggests; but the search functionality on the destination site is often far more accurate than what you'd get through a search engine, and can turn up useful resources that you wouldn't have picked up otherwise. Most of the major search services (Altavista, HotBot, Lycos, etc.) have integrated some degree of hierarchical directory functionality to keep up with the originator, Yahoo! You might also check out a few of the services that primarily focus on building comprehensive directories rather than maintaining their own archiving and searching databases.

About.com (www.about.com)

Looksmart (www.looksmart.com)

NetGuide (www.netguide.com)

Search Engine Guide (www.searchengineguide.com)

Yahoo! (www.yahoo.com)

Assisted Searching Services

Allexperts.com (www.allexperts.com)

Answers.com (www.answers.com)

KnowPost (www.knowpost.com)

Looksmart Live (www.looksmart.com/live)

Market Research Firms' Web Sites

ActivMedia Research (www.activmediaresearch.com)
Consulting firm specializing in e-commerce and Internet market research.

Audits & Surveys Worldwide (www.surveys.com)
Conducts the National Retail Census and numerous other syndicated studies.

CyberDialogue (www.cyberdialogue.com)
Online researcher offering syndicated and customized research solutions. Publishes the American Internet User Survey and CyberCitizen studies.

Forrester (www.forrester.com)
Respected provider of research and strategic consulting services on the impact of major shifts in technology on high-level business strategy. Reporting tends to take a broad perspective.

Frost & Sullivan (www.frost.com)
Major provider of syndicated research on high-tech industries, including telecommunications, information technology, and semiconductors.

Gallup Organization (www.gallup.com)
Most famous for its public opinion polls, but also maintains
full lines of business in marketing research consulting for
high-tech and service companies.

Gartner Group (www.gartner.com)
World's largest information technology consulting firm.
Owns Datapro and Dataquest, both specialty firms that
study computing and communications industries.

Giga Information Group (www.giga.com)
Discount provider of syndicated research and analysis in the
information technology and telecommunications fields.

IDC (www.idc.com)
Another major player in the crowded information technology
research arena.

Instat (www.instat.com)
Digital communications research specialist.

Intelliquest (www.intelliquest.com)
Specializes in high-tech branding, positioning, and other mar-
keting-centered topics. Maintains a large panel comprised
of technology users and purchase influencers.

Jupiter Communications (www.jup.com)
One of Forrester's main competitors, but targets its efforts
more squarely on Internet-related technologies and consumers. Frequently quoted in both mainstream and specialty press.

Millward Brown Interactive (www.mbinteractive.com)
Online research consultant specializing in understanding marketing communications on the Web. Maintains a panel that
is primarily utilized for advertising effectiveness research.

NFO Interactive (www.nfoi.com)

Online presence of NFO Worldwide (www.nfow.com), a major international consumer research firm. NFO Interactive conducts custom research and offers a variety of syndicated products on online consumer behavior. It also maintains a large Web consumer panel.

NPD Group (www.npd.com)

International research firm that focuses on consumer products and issues, rather than high-tech and business-to-business topics. Parent company of Media Metrix.

PC Data (www.pcdata.com)

Tracks software, hardware, and video game sales in the U.S. and U.K.

Roper Starch (www.roper.com)

Firm specializing in consumer attitudes, behavior, and advertising effectiveness.

Yankee Group (www.yankeegroup.com)

Another major provider of market research and strategy services for the IT and related fields.

Yankelovich Partners (www.yankelovich.com)

Authority on consumer attitude research. Specializes in branding, positioning, and other social consumer research. Conducts the Yankelovich Monitor, a long-running study of consumer values, attitudes, and beliefs.

Zona Research (www.zonaresearch.com)

Subsidiary of Intelliquest. Specializes in business-to-business topics related to Internet and intranet development.

Competitors' Sites

Searching the sites of the competition can yield a surprisingly rich assortment of data. The trick is to track down these sites. We recommend starting your search with one of these resources:

> *COMFIND Business Search (www.comfind.com)*
>
> *Companies Online (www.companiesonline.com)*
>
> *Corptech (www.corptech.com)*
>
> *Dun & Bradstreet (www.dnb.com)*
>
> *Hoover's Online (www.hoovers.com)*
>
> *Wright Investors Service Company Profiles (profiles.wisi.com)*
>
> *Yahoo! Companies (biz.yahoo.com/industry)*

Public Relations Newswire Sites

> *Businesswire (www.businesswire.com)*
>
> *PR Newswire (www.prnewswire.com)*

Research Destination Sites

> *CommerceNet (www.commercenet.com)*
>
> *CyberAtlas (www.cyberatlas.com)*
>
> *DeepCanyon (www.deepcanyon.com)*
>
> *Digitrends (www.digitrends.com)*
>
> *EMarketer (www.emarketer.com)*
>
> *Iconocast (www.iconocast.com)*
>
> *Internet Surveys (www.nua.ie)*
>
> *StatMarket (www.statmarket.com)*

Subscriber Information Services

> *Dialog (www.dialog.com)*
>
> *Dow Jones (www.djinteractive.com*

> *Dun & Bradstreet (www.dnb.com)*
> *LEXIS-NEXIS (www.lexis-nexis.com)*
> *Proquest (proquest.umi.com)*

Syndicated Research

Syndicated research is offered by hundreds of firms in tens of thousands of studies. To find studies that were conducted at one point in time (one-offs), you'll have the best luck searching the catalogs of the research resellers or aggregators listed here. A bit like travel agencies, these firms offer listings and descriptions of the studies they have available for sale. Some, like USADATA, allow you to purchase only the key metrics you need, rather than buying an entire study.

Aggregators and Resellers

Bitpipe (www.bitpipe.com)
CommerceNet (www.commercenet.com)
DeepCanyon (www.deepcanyon.com)
ExportHotline (www.exporthotline.com)
IMR Mall (www.imrmall.com)
Kalorama (www.marketresearch.com)
Multex Research on Demand (www.multex.com)
Profound (www.profound.com)
ResearchPortal (www.researchportal.com)
USADATA (www.usadata.com)

Newsletters

MediaFinder (www.mediafinder.com)

Continuous Tracking Studies

Brand Tracking:
  Intelliquest (www.intelliquest.com)
  Mediamark (www.mediamark.com)

Millward Brown (www.millwardbrown.com)

NFO Worldwide (www.nfow.com)

Online Brand Tracking:

CyberDialogue (www.cyberdialogue.com)

Harris Interactive (www.ecommercepulse.com)

Millward Brown Interactive (www.mbinteractive.com)

Purchase Behavior Tracking:

Information Resources (www.infores.com)

PC Data (www.pcdata.com)

Scarborough (www.scarborough.com)

Media Measurement:

@Plan (www.webplan.net)

Aribitron (www.arbitron.com)

Audits & Surveys Worldwide (www.surveys.com)

MediaMetrix (www.mediametrix.com)

NetRatings (www.netratings.com)

Nielsen Media Research (www.nielsenmedia.com)

Simmons (www.smrb.com)

CHAPTER 3

Qualitative Research

While a large number of secondary research products and resources are available to you, they all share a common characteristic: They weren't designed with your problem in mind. At some point, you will have a question that simply can't be answered by a search of previously conducted (and published) material, you will need to do the research yourself. When you decide to conduct original research, the first major decision you'll face is whether to use a qualitative or quantitative approach.

QUALITATIVE VERSUS QUANTITATIVE: WHAT'S THE DIFFERENCE?

It's surprising that market researchers, with their knowledge of branding and the importance of a clear marketing message, didn't choose more distinct-sounding names for these two very different types of research. It is important to understand the distinction (at least to avoid embarrassing yourself at the conference table), so let's review the major differences. A detailed discussion of quantitative research is presented in Chapter 4.

Qualitative research is soft and fuzzy. Quantitative research uses charts and graphs. Qualitative research resides at the touchy-feely end of the research spectrum. Traditionally, it involves face-to-face contact with the consumer and uses in-depth interviews to explore issues that arise. It is free-form and open-ended, and as such, provides an excellent way of taking a first look at the factors surrounding your particular question. Qualitative research is concerned with getting a subjective "feel" for the topic and usually involves small numbers of participants. The *focus group* is one example of a qualitative research technique.

Quantitative research, on the other hand, is structured and is characterized by surveys, pie charts, and statistical reliability. When you need to know hard facts or take reliable measurements, you'll need to turn to quantitative research.

Qualitative research can probe into hard-to-define areas, like the underlying reasons for attitudes and opinions. Quantitative research is strongest when measuring hard facts. Qualitative research has high value as an investigative tool that allows researchers to quickly understand the mind-set and perspective of the customer. In the hands of a skilled practitioner, it can be highly effective at identifying the complicated thought processes that consumers go through when making decisions to purchase or use products. Its flexibility and format allow it to easily adapt to scenarios that were not anticipated when the study was designed.

Conversely, quantitative research must be highly planned out in order to be effective, and is less suited to investigating the nuances surrounding a research problem. The tradeoff in flexibility is made up for by a significant increase in data reliability; in practice, the two techniques are often used as complementary stages of an overall project.

Quantitative research can provide a representative picture of the population being studied. Qualitative research cannot. While qualitative research provides a rich, contextual perspective on the issue, the interviewing techniques and small number of interviews conducted leave open the possibility that the results are an anomaly; that is, the degree to which the identified situation exists in the actual population may be significantly less or more than indicated in the qualitative sessions. Other issues may be missed altogether.

STRENGTHS OF QUALITATIVE RESEARCH

Ideal Exploratory Tool

The beauty of qualitative research is that its free-form design allows anything to happen. It can be used as an extension of the brainstorming sessions that often precede the tackling of product development or marketing problems. Bouncing ideas off your customers is a valuable way to get a fresh perspective from the people who matter most to your business. The team that is directly involved with the project is often too close and too heavily invested in the idea to have an objective view of the situation. Introducing the customer into the mix can have a profound impact.

Suppose you are designing a new way to pay for online purchases. To create an appealing product, you might sit down with a group of potential customers (online shoppers) and talk to them about their online buying experiences, especially what they liked and didn't like about the payment process. Based on their feedback, you might come up with a list of features for your new online payment method and turn them into good selling points for your product. This information could then drive a more extensive quantitative study, conducted with a representative cross-section of your marketplace, that could measure the extent to which those issues features appeal to your customers.

Increase the Value of Subsequent Quantitative Research

Qualitative research can serve as an excellent planning tool for any quantitative research you are considering further down the road.

Before you embark on more sophisticated and expensive adventures, a bit of time spent in qualitative sessions can be a big help if you're not sure you understand all the issues well.

In order for quantitative research to be effective, you need to know what questions to ask. Ask the wrong questions and you get back data that is of limited or no value (the "garbage in, garbage out" principle in action). In established businesses, you might already know the major issues; but in uncharted territory (and online business is largely uncharted), qualitative research will help you take a first rough cut and avoid a costly mistake later on.

Suppose you were attempting to identify the top reasons that consumers prefer to make clothing purchases in physical stores. You design and execute a quantitative survey in which you provide a list of reasons why consumers might prefer to purchase in physical stores and ask them to choose which (if any) are most relevant to them. The data comes back and you find that the top two issues are "Afraid to use my credit card online" and "Enjoy the experience of shopping in stores." But what if the real issue is that customers need to try clothing on before they purchase? If you didn't ask the question, you'd never know. By conducting some qualitative research beforehand, you would likely have identified that issue and included it in the survey.

Obtain Visceral Feedback Instead of Just Number Crunching Data

When conducted using a face-to-face format (whereby both researcher and customer are physically present), qualitative provides the subtle, visceral feedback that might not come through in a structured quantitative approach. Because the researcher can observe what participants do as well as what they say, a skilled practitioner can come away with much richer insight than data-centric methods might provide, and also can have a context for interpreting the findings.

Group Dynamics Enhance Results

Often, qualitative research is conducted in a group setting, in which participants have the opportunity to interact with one another. This technique, which was borrowed from psychotherapists, has a tendency to draw out ideas and opinions that may not have come up in one-on-one situations. Focus groups elicit feedback on both an individual and a group level. To encourage interaction, the moderator must encourage quiet participants to talk and tone down the most vocal members to keep them from dominating the group.

Customers Are People, Not Pie Charts

Perhaps the best thing about qualitative research is that it provides the human perspective. Consumers of research—those who will act on the findings—can forget that behind all the charts, graphs, averages, and medians are real customers who are people, not data points. Qualitative research results are accessible and understandable; people feel comfortable using the information. And because it is familiar, it is an excellent first approach to introduce your organization to the research process.

LIMITATIONS OF QUALITATIVE RESEARCH

Small Number of Participants

The nature of qualitative research makes it prohibitively costly to involve large numbers of participants. Because the number of consumers interviewed using qualitative techniques rarely exceeds 30, you cannot be confident that the results are representative. When you use small sample sizes, the possibility exists that you interviewed a group that was significantly different from the rest of the marketplace. When the costs of making a wrong decision are high (expensive development of an inappropriate feature, for example), the findings from qualitative research should be confirmed with more rigorous quantitative research before proceeding.

Moderator's Skill Level Has High Impact

Qualitative research is typically conducted in real-time, with a moderator guiding a discussion and helping to draw out feedback from the group in an unbiased manner. During these sessions, something might be mentioned that seems insignificant at first; but with skillful probing, something important might be uncovered. A good moderator possesses detailed knowledge of the subject being studied; the keen, analytical mind of a psychologist; and a friendly personality. We've seen qualitative sessions conducted by both excellent and poor moderators. We can attest to the fact that a lot of weight rests on this person's shoulders. This doesn't mean that you can't do qualitative research on your own; it does mean that, when you are thinking about basing a critical decision on the findings, it makes sense to have groups led and analyzed by experienced, qualified researchers.

Dependent on Personal Interpretation

While all marketing research may become the victim of the personal biases of the analyst, this is particularly so in the case of qualitative research. So much of the findings are dependent upon the researcher's ability to interpret what took place and distill it into something meaningful that there is a lot of room for "artistic license." This may be especially problematic when the person(s) conducting and interpreting the research is a member of the project team or may otherwise be influenced by organizational factors. In other words, the designer who has spent the past 400 waking hours designing an interface mockup is not the most objective person for the job! For this reason, it's a good idea for several key decision makers to observe the proceedings directly (or indirectly by reviewing transcripts or recordings of the sessions); take notes; and draw their own conclusions, to be compared with those of the lead researcher on the project.

Difficult to Capture a Geographically Representative Sample

Because qualitative research is usually conducted in person, it is expensive to conduct sessions in all of the geographic areas where you will potentially have markets for the product. When companies pull out all the stops, they may conduct groups in several major cities (New York, Chicago, and Los Angeles, for example) and maybe a few smaller towns. More often, when the research is to be done on a shoestring budget, sessions are held in the local area of the company or the researcher. Both approaches share the risk that a significantly different and perhaps strategically critical group of consumers will be overlooked simply because they don't live in the right city. Online applications of qualitative research are helping to overcome this problem (see Online Focus Groups), but they currently don't provide the same level of information that in-person approaches provide.

APPLICATIONS OF QUALITATIVE RESEARCH

Because qualitative research means essentially taking the opportunity to sit down with your customer and have a structured dialog, there are limitless ways in which you can conduct qualitative research. Here are a few examples:

Ideation Session

"Ideation" is another word for brainstorming. When a project team is just getting started on an idea, they'll often hold formal or informal internal creative sessions to warm up to the project. Including target consumers in the sessions will provide excellent insight, especially if the brainstorming is designed to identify the issues that are to be addressed by a new product or service.

Brand Identity "Taste Test"

Companies that are developing a brand identity (naming, logos, taglines, etc.) or reworking an existing one often have several versions to choose from. Personal biases of the internal team may make it difficult to arrive at a mutually agreeable conclusion. Have a group of consumers in the target market provide feedback on their overall opinions of each identity treatment and the brand associations each one elicits, to arrive at the best choice for your brand.

Brand Personality Assessment

An established company might use qualitative research to take stock of its brand "personality"—that is, the associations users make with the brand name and products. For example, an automobile manufacturer that wants to reposition itself in new markets needs to understand current perceptions in order to determine the effort required to drive brand perceptions in a new direction.

Concept Testing

Though we believe that quantitative online research can provide excellent, projectable feedback on new concepts, qualitative research is often utilized to get early customer input before further research or development takes place.

Advertising Creative Pretesting

Before spending large sums on advertising campaigns, qualitative research can be used to confirm that consumers are taking away the right message from an advertising concept. We discuss numerous methodologies for measuring advertising response in Chapter 15.

QUALITATIVE RESEARCH FORMATS

While there are nearly limitless applications for qualitative research, there are a few major formats for gathering the information. We present the four approaches that are most relevant to the development and marketing of online products and services:

In-Person Formats

Focus groups: In-person group discussions whereby a moderator leads the session to touch on areas of interest and to encourage feedback.

Usability testing: Observation and interviewing of consumers as they have a hands-on experience.

Online Formats

Email feedback: Most people are surprised to learn that they are involved in research when they access "Contact the Webmaster" links. This form of feedback can be very valuable in several areas, and should be leveraged whenever possible.

Online focus groups: The newest approach to conducting focus groups, whereby participants spend time in your chat room instead of your boardroom.

FOCUS GROUPS

Focus groups are what most people think of when they think about qualitative research, and they are the most popular qualitative format. Essentially, they consist of a group of participants who are selected to reflect your target market; a moderator or two; a private room; and a conference table. The conference table isn't critical, but you want to create an environment where all the participants can comfortably interact with the moderator and with each other.

Focus groups are well-suited to initial research studies, because the group discussion brings out more ideas and issues than any individual could have thought of. We've been involved in groups in which our initial thinking on an issue was blown out of the water by the time a group of eight consumers had bounced their opinions off each other. If those eight people had been interviewed one at a time, chances are that many of the issues would never have come up.

In addition to using focus groups to do preliminary research on any topic, you can use them successfully to explore new product concepts, product redesigns, advertising concepts, branding ideas, or even interface mockups. The one thing focus groups are not good for is obtaining specific feedback on the usability of your product. Because the average Web user doesn't have seven friends coaching him or her through the exploration of a site, use a one-on-one approach to obtain usability information (see *Usability Testing*).

Planning a Focus Group

Obtain a Facility

There is an entire industry that does nothing more than provide qualitative researchers and their clients with a high-tech place to conduct their research. The typical focus group facility has a large conference room equipped with the latest in ergonomically correct furniture, a variety of audiovisual equipment (for showing commercials, demonstrating Web sites, and pilot testing new situation comedies), cleverly disguised video and audio recording equipment, and an adjacent room where the commissioners of the research can sit and watch the proceedings behind a one-way mirror. The facility provides a number of services that address the logistics of conducting groups, such as:

- receptionist and waiting room to register and manage participants when they arrive;
- food and beverage service for both participants and the sponsors in the back room; (one of our favorite perks of doing full-scale qualitative)
- high-speed Internet access;
- photocopying and AV duplication services (so you can walk out with a permanent record of the proceedings).

Of course, these services don't come cheap. Renting a facility with all the bells and whistles can easily cost you in excess of a few thousand dollars per evening. For some companies, it is money well spent.

If you are on a tight budget, you can easily cut costs by conducting focus groups in a facility you provide yourself. If you have an office with a conference room (or at least a conference table), that's perfect. If not, you'll need to be more creative. If your office, filled with overworked engineers, designers, and a few hundred empty coffee cups, is the last place you'd want to invite potential customers to discuss their perceptions of your brand image, you'll need to go outside the office. Hotels will rent you small meeting rooms for a fraction of the cost of a specialty facility. Likewise, restaurants often have private rooms you can reserve for a few hours for a reasonable cost. Both options have the advantage of food service on-site, which will ease your logistical burdens. But remember that, aside from the table and chairs, you'll probably have to bring most of the additional materials yourself. Here is a checklist of some of the most commonly used items:

- pens
- paper
- note cards
- computer equipment and monitor
- computer projection device
- Internet access
- video camera and microphone(s)
- drawing easel and paper
- whiteboard or blackboard
- powerstrips and extension cords

Create a Discussion Guide

One way to approach the focus group is to go in unprepared and trust that your intimate knowledge of the issues at hand and your uncanny ability to keep everything organized in the midst of a rapid-fire discussion will do the job.

This, of course, is the wrong approach.

A bit of planning will go a long way toward ensuring a positive experience for yourself and your participants (and your boss, if he or she is watching). Planning the topics to be addressed in a focus group is done in a document called a discussion guide. As with all research planning, it is best created with the input of all the parties who will be using the research. This provides two principal benefits: First, obtaining input from multiple parties helps ensure that important issues aren't overlooked. Second, involving interested parties makes them far more likely to be invested in the outcome of the group, as opposed to dismissing the results if they don't meet their assumptions. Research only has value if the organization is willing to consider the information with an open mind, so creating organizational involvement is something that *we cannot stress the value of enough* (in any type of research).

The discussion guide need not be a highly polished, formal document. It can be rough or refined, so long as it provides a structured approach to guide the session's activities and discussion. We usually create discussion guides with lots of space on the paper to write notes that will assist us in summarizing the outcomes of the session.

Obtain Participants

The best-planned focus group, run by the best-trained moderator, and executed in the highest-quality facility, will be of minor value if the participants do not represent your target market. It may be easier for you to coerce immediate friends and family into a room to discuss their opinions of your idea for a baby toy Web site; but if none of them have babies (or plan to), how much weight do you really want to place on their feedback?

Instead, whenever possible, we recommend putting a bit more effort toward recruiting participants who closely resemble the market you have envisioned for your product. Depending on the situation and your budget, here are some of the tools at your disposal:

Professional Recruiters: Just as there are full-service facilities available for your sessions, there are full-service recruiters who will find you warm bodies to fill those ergonomic seats. Recruiters may be part of a large company or independent operators. Sometimes recruiters pull from their personal databases of pre-screened candidates; at other times they recruit new candidates. This is an important distinction: We've observed scenarios in which recruiters have filled up rooms with "professional participants" who have clearly been involved in many past projects, and are attending out of an innate need to share their opinions again and again, eat a nice meal, and pocket an extra $50.

A good recruiter can be a valuable asset. The recruiter can take over much of the drudgery of finding and scheduling qualified consumers, while you concentrate on the objectives of the study. Recruiters can be pricey, however. Expect to pay around $80 per qualified respondent in larger metropolitan areas. By employing the power of the Web and a little creativity, you can often save costs and achieve better results if you do your own recruiting.

Posters or In-Person Solicitation: If you find the online approach to soliciting people for a focus group a bit too high-tech for your taste, you can employ tried-and-true methods. Get out in your neighborhood and at area colleges and post flyers; or stop people on the street and try to solicit them. We use this approach from time to time when the deadline for conducting the group is close and we know where to find concentrated populations of target users. When you take this approach, you'll naturally need a way to follow up on your leads (Web pages with information, phone numbers, email addresses, etc.). For this reason, we're big fans of using the Web.

Online Recruitment: Assuming you want to speak to Web-enabled consumers, there is little reason why you shouldn't use the Web and the Internet as much as possible in your recruitment process.

1. *Represent your current customer base.* If you have a customer base or an established Web presence, leverage the relation-

ships you have already developed. In many cases, your current customer base represents the "lowest-hanging fruit," and strategic developments should always be approached with them in mind. In addition, you may have significant information available about your customers or users that will facilitate the recruitment process. Many of these approaches are discussed in depth in Chapter 4, as they are also options for obtaining participants in quantitative research.

Proprietary Email Lists: If you have an established Web presence, or at least have an email address database of customers or sales leads, you can leverage this resource to contact a wide sample of potential candidates. This approach is especially effective if you are researching topics that will affect your current customer base, such as a product redesign. If you are planning to conduct focus groups locally or in specific regions, mention the regional requirements in the email message, or use the ZIP code data you may have associated with these addresses to select only suitable contacts.

Hyperlinks on Your Site: If you don't have a list of email addresses to contact your users, you can still recruit by placing a link on the front page or other appropriate page of your site. The link can direct interested users to an information page or Web-based screening interview. Be aware of the bias you may introduce depending upon where you place the link. For example, if you place a link on the front page of the site, you'll probably recruit a decent representation of the total traffic that crosses through the site (assuming that most people enter through the front page before moving elsewhere on the site). If you place the link on a page that specifically caters to one type of user, you'll probably recruit users who fit that profile.

2. *Represent the outside marketplace.* If you are introducing a new product from scratch, and don't have an established population to call upon, you can still use the Web to launch a targeted recruitment approach. Even when you do have an established customer base, chances are that your planning is designed to both maximize your success with your current customers and reach new ones.

Newsgroups: The Internet offers a number of publicly available means of reaching targeted groups of consumers. Newsgroups (also known as USENET) are international discussion groups that may be highly segmented into areas of interest. People in USENET groups discuss topics of broad or limited appeal, such as the nuances of maintaining saltwater fish tanks, building ham radios, or stock picking techniques.

The best way to learn about USENET newsgroups is to poke around in them a bit. Major search services like AltaVista (www.altavista.com), Excite (www.excite.com), and InfoSeek (www.infoseek.com) are excellent tools to aid your exploration, as are specialty services like Remarq (www.remarq.com) and Deja.com (www.deja.com). Each offers USENET searching options and allows you to search for specific terms of interest (e.g., kites, pets) and pull up the USENET discussion lists that contain posts meeting your criteria. When you find some groups that seem to be populated by the types of customers you want to reach, you can word a targeted, professional solicitation for your focus group and post it to the newsgroup.

Ideally, the solicitation should ask users to take a short Web-based survey (see *Screen Candidates*) whereby you can determine the users' appropriateness for the group. Alternatively, you may have them contact you by phone or email to accomplish the same goal.

A word of caution: USENET is one of the oldest institutions on the Internet, and was originally a very noncommercial environment where users could freely exchange ideas and information. In recent years, commercial interests found it an effective way to market products and services. There is a mixed response to this type of usage, and you must use discretion in leveraging this resource. Many news groups have "charters" that dictate the types of information that can and can't be posted on the group. It is poor etiquette to operate contrary to these charters, so we urge you to review them before using this technique for solicitation. Typically, the charter can be found in the group's FAQ section (short for Frequently Asked Questions). FAQs for each group can be found at: (www.lib.ox.ac.uk/internet/news/faq/by_group.index.html)

Other discussion lists: Outside of USENET, a vast number of email-based and Web-based discussion lists have been developed to provide Internet users even more ways of exchanging ideas. Originally, these lists were scattered and grew only by word of mouth. Today, a number of companies have capitalized on the opportunity to aggregate these lists in one place and provide tools to make the lists easier to use and read. Two notable services are EGroups (www.egroups.com) and Topica (www.topica.com). Both services publish lists broken down into major categories and sub-categories of interest, and are very easy to use. Use of these types of discussion lists is subject to the same caveats as USENET.

Rental lists: The biggest drawback to using either USENET or other discussion lists for recruiting is that the subscribers are there principally to share ideas in a noncommercial format. They may not be receptive to the idea of providing feedback on products or other commercial endeavors. Fortunately, there are many other lists that are also highly segmented and composed of users who specifically stated that they were interested in being contacted to hear about such things. This is known as opt-in email marketing and is very different from unsolicited email marketing (aka *spam*). These lists are obviously very interesting to direct marketers and, as such, usually don't come free. They are typically handled by list brokers who have inventories of lists, their major topic classifications, and the list size. You generally pay to contact these users on a cost-per-user basis. A very convenient way of accessing online lists is via PostMasterDirect (www.postmasterdirect.com), which offers an easy-to-use interface and hundreds of targeted lists to contact. We've used them with great success in both qualitative and quantitative research recruitment.

External Web links: If you can get a banner or hyperlink on an external site for little or minimal cost, you might consider this recruitment method as well. Be wary of paying a lot for banners or links, though, because the level of response you'll likely get will be too low to make this type of recruitment cost-effective.

Provide Incentives

You'll almost certainly need to compensate your participants for their time if you hope to get them to spend the 1½ hours necessary to conduct a good focus group. A good rule of thumb is that the busier and more affluent the target customer is, the more you'll have to dish out in the way of incentives. Typically, the cash incentive paid to a respondent is anywhere from $20 to $200, though even higher amounts have been paid to gain the feedback of top-level decision makers in large companies. Think about paying around $50 to each participant as a start, and see how the first round of recruiting goes. Depending on the response, you can raise or lower the amount as you see fit. Incentives are usually paid in cash at the end of the group, to make sure that your participants have a good reason (aside from altruism) to stick around and pay attention till the bitter end.

Screen Candidates

After you've figured out a way to identify interested candidates, you'll need to determine whether they are the kind of people whose feedback you want to consider. This process is called *screening*. Screening can take place via phone, in person (at the time of solicitation), or on the Web. We are, of course, big fans of using the Web to do our dirty work whenever possible. One of the biggest advantages of using the Web is that your Web page can be on duty 24 hours a day and take sign-ups whenever the participants have a few spare moments to go online.

Whatever method you choose, screening has three objectives:

A. Determine whether the candidate is appropriate for your objectives.
B. Determine what type of consumer the candidate represents.
C. Determine the candidate's availability and schedule the candidate to meet your study's requirements.

A. Is the candidate appropriate? Your screening process should be driven by the target market you wish to study during the focus group. The definition may be very narrow (e.g., female golfers who play in competitive leagues) or broad (sports enthusiasts). To determine whether your candidate fits the definition, come up with a short set of questions that can be asked and answered quickly over the Web, on the phone, or in person. For example, to create a focus group of female golfers who play in competitive leagues, you might ask three simple questions:

1. What is your gender? (If male, thank and terminate interview.)
2. Do you play golf? (If no, thank and terminate interview.)
3. Do you ever play golf in competitive leagues or clubs? (If no, thank and terminate interview.)

B. What type of consumer does the candidate represent? In practice, you'll probably have a broader target market definition and a broader range of candidates you'll want to include in your groups. As such, your screening questions will probably have a wider range of possible answer choices; the choices will allow you to segment candidates into distinct types of consumers you'll try to understand. We provide more detail on the segmentation process in Chapter 9; for now, this simple approach will give you the general idea.

We once conducted focus groups for an online investment Web site. Our objective was to understand the reactions of different types of investors to the brand identity, feature sets, and subscription model. To do this, we broke the total market into segments that had meaning for our client:

- experienced versus beginning investors;
- heavy traders versus light traders; and
- fundamental versus technical stock pickers.

Segments were based on a composite of all three attributes; for example, inexperienced, light-trading consumers who base stock picks on fundamental factors. When we screened candidates, we asked a number of questions that allowed us to assign the candidate to a segment and fill the focus groups with participants who represented each type of consumer. When we conducted the groups, we noted what comments came from which type of consumer so that we could interpret feedback in the appropriate context.

C. Determine candidates' availability and schedule the groups. In-person focus groups are usually scheduled to start in the early evening (6 to 6:30) so participants don't have to take time out of the workday. Often several sessions take place, with one starting around 6 and another starting around 8:30 to provide an option for those who work later hours. There is no golden rule for the scheduling of groups; but the schedule should cater to the needs of the type of consumer you are studying. When scheduling, try to get participants to agree to a few possible time slots so you have some flexibility in creating the right mix of consumers for your groups. Once you see who is available and when they can come in, you can do a bit of juggling to create groups that are to your liking, then contact participants with the final schedule. Like the airlines, you may want to overbook your sessions by a few participants to account for no-shows, as long as you can accommodate everyone if they do all show up (or at least provide the same incentives to the ones you don't end up interviewing).

Assuming you have several sub-types of consumers to interview (e.g., heavy users, light users), we suggest that you schedule similar consumers together in the same session. In other words, hold one session for the heavy users and another session for the light users. Unless you find value in observing the interplay between opposing viewpoints, keeping some degree of homogeneity in the group is helpful because it allows you to focus on one group's needs and opinions at a time.

Deciding how many people to include in your groups and how many sessions to hold depends on the number of consumer types you seek to interview, the material you want to cover, the level of input you want to obtain from any given participant, and your budget and time constraints. In general, focus groups seem to have a good flow when between 6 and 10 participants are involved in any given session. Try to have at least two or three sessions with similar participant makeup to make sure that the results from one group were not a complete anomaly.

Running a Focus Group

A focus group is an organic entity, and not something that lends itself to step-by-step instructions. You'll find that practice makes perfect, and after conducting a few groups you'll have a much better idea of what works best in different situations. In the interest of getting you started out on the right foot, here are some useful guidelines that will go a long way toward making your first focus groups positive, valuable experiences:

Remain Objective

If you are intimately involved with the project being studied, you will invariably have a number of preconceived notions, biases, and opinions on the subject. Leave those at the door. It is far too easy to shape the conversation and resulting conclusions into a mirror image of your personal opinions on the subject. If you're going to the trouble of asking your customers what they think, why not listen to what they have to say?

Follow the Discussion Guide, but Be Flexible

Your job as the moderator is to keep things on track without making the session feel stiff and regimented. If something comes up during the discussion that was never considered previously, investigate the new issue further. Sometimes you'll arrive at a dead end; at other times you'll find the breakthrough idea that puts your product on the top of the heap.

Don't Dominate the Session

The idea of having a captive audience is appealing to the ego-maniac in all of us, but focus groups are far more valuable if you let the participants do most of the talking. Play the role of the psychotherapist, encouraging the group to express their feelings on the subject and coaching them into exploring particular areas of interest. As a general rule, the moderator should speak no more than 20 percent of the time.

Give Everyone an Opportunity for Input

Frequently, one or two assertive participants dominate the conversation and intimidate the more passive group members. Keep these people in check, and elicit feedback from the quieter participants, who have equally valid opinions but can't manage to get a word in edgewise.

Record the Session

Because it's next to impossible to take good written notes while you are attempting to interact with the focus group, making audio- or videotapes is essential. You'll find these recordings extremely useful when you do your post session analysis, and they will make it easy to share the proceedings with skeptical colleagues who couldn't attend the session. We prefer videotapes, because you can see who is making a comment and cross-reference it against the person's consumer characteristics (see *What type of consumer does the candidate represent?*).

Have Relevant Observers Present, but Not Actively Participating

Videotapes of the sessions provide one way to share results with the commissioners of the research, but it's even better if a small contingent of them can actually observe the proceedings. If an idea piques their interest, they can ask you to probe deeper into that issue. The act of attending the sessions makes decision makers more vested in the process and more likely to value the findings. To avoid intimidating the participants or biasing the results, the observers should ideally watch the sessions from another room, via closed-circuit TV or a one-way mirror.

Interviewing Techniques and Activities

There are many texts dedicated to the art of focus group research, and urge you to study a few of them if you think you'll be making extensive use of focus group techniques. In the meantime, here are some tips we've found helpful in doing this type of work.

Use Appropriate Visual Aids

People tend to react better when they've got something to look at other than the person on the other side of the table. Simply writing ideas on a whiteboard can keep people focused and thinking about the topic at hand. Obviously, the more information you can give participants, the more they'll have to consider and respond to. When testing out new concepts such as products, logos, and advertising ideas, show the group as much about what you've got in mind as possible.

Apply Indirect Questioning to Get at Touchy Areas

Some questions (such as income, spending levels, or other personal issues) that you need to pose to the group might be particularly sensitive and may cause participants to give erroneous information or become offended (and clam up for the rest of the session). To overcome this obstacle, use indirect questioning to provide some distance between the subject and the respondent and to make the topic more comfortable to address. If you circle around and warm up to the subject a bit, the respondent may end up telling you exactly what you want to know without feeling put on the spot. If you must gather personal information that is explicitly stated, consider having participants fill out brief exit surveys when they pick up their incentive money.

Use Word Association and Personification Techniques to Draw Out Abstract Concepts

When you are trying to get a read on customers' emotional responses to a topic, realize that it might be difficult for them to articulate their feelings. This is especially true when you're trying to figure out abstract ideas, like whether the blue or the red background design makes men feel like ordering perfume for their wives.

Having participants call out words that they might associate with the issue at hand is a great way to get the discussion rolling. For example, we might place several brand identity concepts on a projection screen and ask respondents to call out the words they'd associate with each concept. A review of all the words they offer will often lead you into a valuable discussion with the group on the underlying issues.

A related technique, personification, asks respondents to convert the product or brand into a "person" who has a personality (psychographics), along with demographic and behavioral characteristics.

Use Sorting Exercises

In a focus group that centers on determining the best alternative among several options (a logo, design interface, product packaging, feature mix, etc.), participants will have an easier time with the task if they are given some props to work with. Cards, labeled or illustrated with the alternatives, can be sorted in order of the respondents' preference and then reviewed to discuss the motives behind their choices.

USABILITY TESTING

While focus groups are typically used to obtain feedback on abstract issues or for exploratory research, usability testing centers on evaluating the ability of a Web site to meet user requirements in functionality (accomplishing tasks), navigability (getting around), and aesthetics (appearance). Usability testing, also known as UI (User Interface) testing, is generally done late in the game, when you've already made most of your strategic decisions and are putting the final polish on your latest creation. It is not the time to investigate strategic issues, branding issues, feature development, or other issues that require earlier research attention. As the name implies, you'll probably have a usable version of your product ready for evaluation when you decide to do the testing; mockups and demos can be employed if the actual product isn't available.

Planning a Usability Testing Session

If you've read through the guidelines for planning a focus group session, you have a good idea of what's involved in putting together a usability testing project. Because so much is the same, we'll highlight the major differences here.

Facility

If you're going to have users interacting with your site, you'll need computers suited for the job. Assuming the site is online somewhere, you'll need machines with Internet access and an appropriate browser. Try not to use equipment that is significantly different from your typical Web user's equipment; you don't want to introduce an artificial factor that impacts the usability of the site. Consider the equipment's processing speed, the size of the monitors, and so on.

There are two schools of thought on the appropriate Internet connection speed to use in testing. The speed at which a site downloads can have a big impact on a users' satisfaction, so some UI researchers recommend that you mirror the connection speeds of your intended market (i.e., modem speeds for products targeted to home users, and high-speed connections for corporate users). We take the position that your interface designers should already be doing everything possible to keep load times to a minimum, and that your testing time can be better spent on issues other than "Your &^%#$ site is so slow!" There are already a number of interesting automated products, such as Keynote Systems (www.keynote.com) WebCriteria (www.webcriteria.com), for gathering objective performance metrics like load times. If you want to obtain usability feedback with consideration given to the connection speed of your users' equipment, conduct some sessions at modem speeds and others using high-speed connectivity.

A final facility and equipment consideration is a recording device capable of capturing the users' interactions with the site. Some elaborate facilities dedicated to UI research have testing stations that combine the video output of the computer with the feed of a video camera to create a tape that records the users' expressions, eye tracking, and verbal feedback with a picture-in-picture display of the computer screens they were viewing. You can assemble something similar to this yourself using a simple video mixer (consumer models are available for less than $500). A cheaper approach is to use a software product such as HyperCam (www.hyperionics.com/www/hypercam.htm), which can capture and play back a session (mouse movement, clicks, and screen display), along with audio commentary recorded from the computer's microphone, in an AVI video format.

Discussion Guide

A usability test is not so much a discussion as it is an observational exercise. As such, you probably won't need a discussion guide per se, but you will want to work with your designers and development team to make a list of interface elements and site areas that are of particular concern to them. In addition, compile a list of typical tasks a user might perform when using the product. Then be sure to prompt your subjects to check out areas that might not otherwise be explored, to ensure that key functionality is up to par. The discussion guide will also provide a convenient and structured place to write down observational notes during the session.

Participants

Gather UI test subjects in much the same manner as you would focus group participants. When recruiting and screening, consider the level of Web experience of your testers in addition to all the other customer characteristics you'd be considering in focus group recruitment. Beginning and advanced users may have different needs from the product and interface; gauge your product's ability to meet both groups, unless your product is specifically targeting one type of user.

Unlike focus groups, where the group dynamic adds value, usability testing is generally done one-on-one, with the researcher observing the subject's usage. Web surfing is not usually done with the aid of a support group, and it makes sense to keep the subject in a realistic environment. In a group session, it would be difficult to capture nuances that might mean the difference between a work of UI genius and disaster. If you have the luxury of multiple researchers working on the project with you, it can be advantageous to schedule several one-on-one sessions in parallel, so that you can conduct a group debriefing afterward to capture users' overall impressions of the site design and usability.

Scheduling for usability testing is a bit more tricky than scheduling for a focus group, because of the one-on-one format. We don't recommend overbooking for these sessions, because you'll have your hands full if you end up with multiple users for a single observer. Give yourself some leeway between scheduled sessions, so you can spend some extra time with especially interesting subjects, collect your thoughts, and make any necessary adjustments to equipment. If you factor in an extra evening or two for the UI testing, you'll get the required number of participants without having to worry about overbooking a particular session or being too pressed for time.

Running a UI Test

In its simplest form, a UI test consists of having a user move around the tested site while the researcher observes what seems to be happening. If you had an unlimited amount of time with the subject, and the subject was naturally inclined to experience all the areas of the site that were to be tested, this would work fine. In reality, you have only a limited amount of time (perhaps 30 to 45 minutes), and many things to cover, so a bit of guidance will be necessary.

In moderating the UI test, you'll need to strike a balance between allowing users a completely natural experience and moving them through the site to be sure that critical areas are reviewed.

The Catch-22 in providing guidance to your subject is that the site should be able to speak for itself. After all, you won't be there later to help your befuddled visitor slog his or her way through a confusing interface.

To balance the need for a complete review of the site with the goal of evaluating the interface's ability to speak for itself, we recommend that you employ this five-step approach:

1. Gauge the initial reaction to the front page. Before providing any input, pull up the front page of the tested site and ask a few questions about the respondents' first impression of the site. What do they expect the site will do for them? Is it reliable? Is it trustworthy? The front page of a site is a critical evaluation point for a new visitor, and the "Back" button is all too handy. Your testing should confirm that the first screen quickly and accurately conveys the site's overall value proposition.

2. Allow the user to surf around naturally for 10 minutes or so. Assuming that you've recruited subjects who have some level of interest in the category your site serves, you shouldn't have to drag your subjects through the site like overtired children in a clothing store. They'll probably be eager to dive in and see what it is you've brought them in to test. As they surf, pay close attention to the navigational elements they do and don't use. Ask follow-up questions as they move along, to determine whether expectations were met about various links and features. During the first few sessions, you'll probably notice a few areas that stand out as presenting particular problems.

3. Ask the user to perform some typical site usage tasks. Presumably, your site is designed to serve some need or other (finding a new car, reading your horoscope, etc.). After some natural exploration has occurred, focus the user on some typical ways to use the site, to see how your UI theory compares with reality. As they perform the tasks, ask probing (not leading) questions to uncover any problems they might be having. If your competitors serve a similar need on the Web, ask the participants to use a current preferred site to accomplish the same task. As they do so, probe into what they like (and dislike) about the competitor's approach. It's not usually necessary to reinvent the wheel when designing an interface. In fact, following popular or familiar approaches eliminates one hurdle a consumer will have to overcome in order to adopt your product.

4. Move subsequent testers past identified problem areas. If your first few testers have major problems with certain design elements, chances are others will too. There's little point in wasting valuable time on the same few issues; make note of them and move on to other, unexplored areas. After the problem elements have been fixed, you can retest. A word of caution, however: If one person has an issue with an element, that doesn't necessarily mean that all users will. Before steering all test subjects around the pothole, it is a good idea to have the same issue tested by several subjects with differing characteristics (e.g., Web experience level, involvement in the site subject matter, etc.). You may find that your site (or certain elements of it) appeals to some groups but not to others. That's a significant finding; we'll address it again in Chapter 14.

5. Have participants engage in a group discussion after the hands-on session. If you are conducting multiple testing sessions simultaneously, a useful exercise is to have the subjects discuss their experiences in a group setting. You'll have the opportunity to compare the reactions of different types of users, and to obtain suggestions on improving the problem areas. (Obtaining suggested improvement feedback is best done outside the actual testing session, to avoid disrupting the session's flow.) When conducting the group debriefing, it is advisable to have a computer and projection device (or large monitor) handy so you can pull up the site and display the element being discussed.

Learning More about the World of UI Design and Testing

In the past few years, there has been an explosion of interest in Web site usability. Entire departments of companies have been created to focus solely on the UI (user interface) of sites. The study of computer–human interaction is not new, and many experts in the software field have crossed over to the Web in an effort to bring their knowledge to the online world.

Countless books are written about good Web design, but usability encompasses more than aesthetics. One oft-quoted leader in the usability field is Jakob Nielsen. His Web site, Useit.com (www.useit.com), is an excellent resource for understanding the nuances of human–computer interaction and the performance evaluation process. We also recommend his book on the subject: *Designing Web Usability: The Practice of Simplicity.*

EMAIL FEEDBACK

Many sites conduct qualitative research without realizing it. In fact, the "Email us your comments or suggestions" link on most sites is probably the most widely used form of qualitative research today. Because it is free, you should make the most of it. Generating email feedback can be as simple as including a "mailto:" hypertext link on a page; or it can involve a feedback Web page, powered by a CGI back-end that formats comments, along with other pertinent information, and mails them to a support person.

Structured versus Unstructured Feedback

Email feedback can be structured or unstructured. Unstructured feedback is the most common type, and it can be up and running in seconds. But as many highly trafficked sites soon find out, information overload can swamp the team dedicated to dealing with this feedback, and lots of useful information can be lost in the confusion. Instead of adding a legion of support personnel, you can obtain the same useful information for a fraction of the cost by adding structure to the feedback process.

Adding some standardized form elements to a Web page, along with a place to enter free-form commentary, can go a long way toward managing your support problem. The form elements (text boxes, selection boxes, pulldown menus, etc.) can structure user comments and ease interpretation of the feedback. For example, you can have users check menu options that will identify the type of issue they are writing about (e.g., bug report, poor content, or security question) and have the CGI direct the comment to the employee assigned to deal with that area.

Use a Mini-Survey to Learn More about the User

If you really want to get the most out of email feedback, ask users a few questions that will help you identify the type of users they are. Then, when you see a comment about the site being too hard to use, you can also see that it is coming from a visitor who is new to the Web. Interpreting feedback within the context was given in is a powerful capability that can be yours with just a bit more preplanning.

If you're running an investing site, ask users how often they trade; how long they've been trading; how many times they've been to your site; and what features they use when they come to the site. You might also ask what other investing sites they visit regularly. At the bottom of the feedback page, be sure to provide an open-ended space for them to voice their opinions freely. The open-ended feedback will make a lot more sense when you examine it within the context of the respondents' relationships with the category and your site.

Avoid Overinterpreting Email Feedback

Because email feedback is so widespread and familiar, we've known site owners to misappropriate the data and use it as a tool to under-

FIGURE 3.1: Structured feedback form

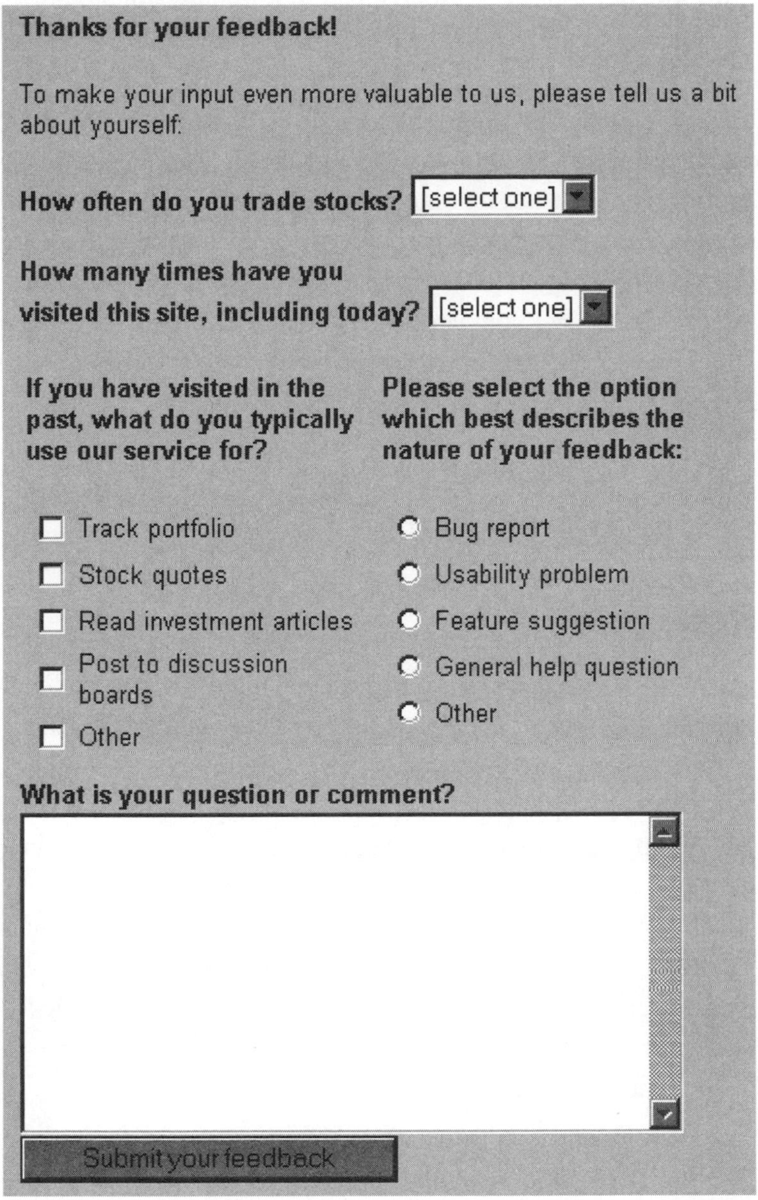

Thanks for your feedback!

To make your input even more valuable to us, please tell us a bit about yourself:

How often do you trade stocks? [select one] ▼

**How many times have you
visited this site, including today?** [select one] ▼

If you have visited in the past, what do you typically use our service for?	**Please select the option which best describes the nature of your feedback:**
☐ Track portfolio	○ Bug report
☐ Stock quotes	○ Usability problem
☐ Read investment articles	○ Feature suggestion
☐ Post to discussion boards	○ General help question
☐ Other	○ Other

What is your question or comment?

[   ]

Submit your feedback

stand their user base (bad) or make critical strategic decisions (even worse). Email feedback is an excellent tool for debugging your site and obtaining usability-related information. It lets your users know that they have a way of interacting with the site's creators, and allows them to identify issues that your own staff would never have otherwise noticed. But because email feedback is unsolicited (users must actively seek out this means of expressing themselves), you cannot take the information received as representative of the entire audience. Your email inboxes may be flooded with the missives of only a few seasoned complainers, who have little or nothing to do with the rest of your audience. On the other hand, their observations may be valid and their opinions may be similar to those of people in your target market, but you can't count on it. Consider yourself warned: Use email feedback as a warning flag, but undertake more rigorous approaches before you commit to a plan of action.

ONLINE CHAT SESSIONS

Online focus groups consist of a group of subjects and a moderator all getting together in the virtual space of an online chat room to discuss the issues via text-based "chat." Before the concepts of intercept sampling and online panels were developed, the online focus group was actually one of the first research applications on the Internet. The ability of a chat room to bring together people from all over the world was a very appealing concept, and the market research industry was quick to see its potential. Over the years, experience has shown that online focus groups are not the quick-fix they were hoped to be; they have their strengths and weaknesses, like any other research tool.

Strengths

Facilitate the attendance of low-incidence or hard-to-reach consumers. Because traditional focus groups require participants to take a big chunk of time out of their day, it can be very difficult and expensive to get high-quality people. Executive-level decision makers may be exactly the type of consumer you are trying to reach, but they may not be willing or able to rearrange their schedules to come to an in-person meeting. If they are willing, chances are that they'll demand a high price for their time. The ability to log on to an online focus group from anywhere in the world makes it easier to get these types of people involved.

Provide geographic representation at a fraction of the cost. Many full-budget focus groups are executed in multiple cities to account for regional differences in attitudes or habits. But "full-budget" might be far beyond your budget. Perhaps the costs associated with traveling and operating in multiple locations are too high, even though you believe that having only local representation will give you a distorted picture. Including consumers from rural areas may be an issue as well, because traveling the back roads of America may take too long or cost too much to be effective. The online chat room can solve these problems by allowing people to interact in the same space, no matter where on the planet they might be sitting.

Eliminate facilities costs and reduce the need for respondent incentives. Because you are conducting the groups in virtual space, you have no need to rent facilities, provide audiovisual equipment, or pay respondents large premiums to come to an in-person session. Beyond eliminating logistical headaches, these cost savings can easily add up to several thousand dollars.

A transcript of the session is created automatically. Everything in a chat session can be logged automatically, so you end up with written documentation of exactly what transpired. There can be no question about what was said, and user quotes can easily be included in later analysis.

Limitations

Traditional focus groups have largely gained their strength from the in-person format, so it is not surprising that the limitations of online focus groups all stem from the anonymous, text-based nature of the chat session. As improved videoconferencing technologies and higher bandwidth Internet connections become more widespread, we may see less and less reason to use in-person focus groups; for now, four limitations apply.

The typewritten format may inhibit the free exchange of ideas. The need to type out the exchange that occurs in an online focus group may put some artificial constraints on the discussion. Some participants feel less comfortable discussing ideas in written form, and some are simply poor typists. The flip side, of course, is that the additional step may result in a more considered response to a question. Depending upon the objectives of the study, receiving a more considered response can be a benefit, so take this factor into account when selecting a methodology.

Controlling information is difficult. Focus groups are often used to address strategic issues that your organization may wish to keep confidential. In an in-person group, you can do a good job of controlling the information by collecting all handouts, having participants sign confidentiality forms, and so on. Online, there is a greater chance that something might end up in the hands of the competition or the press.

The online format affords no in-person contact or observation of participants. A skilled qualitative researcher looks at what the subjects do, as well as listening to what they say. Key emotional cues can be lost or distorted when translated to written form, and the researcher will have no other means of determining what is real from what is an intentional projection of the participant's.

Moderating a chat session is challenging. Having run several online focus groups, we can attest to the fact that keeping all the respondents talking (typing, actually), driving the discussion in the right direction, and actually reacting to what is going on in the session is a very challenging proposition. In fact, we suggest that several individuals share the task of moderating the group. If you've never run an online focus group in the past, shadow someone with prior experience in conducting research in this format before you attempt it yourself.

CAN I DO IT MYSELF?

In a word: Absolutely. But *should* you? It all depends on the situation. Obviously, many readers have purchased this book because they wish to roll up their sleeves and get some firsthand experience in doing marketing research. Because there is virtually no technical component to most qualitative research, it is an excellent place to get your feet wet.

The first advantage of doing qualitative research in-house is that you and your team probably know the product or topic at hand better than any hired researcher. Second, if you do the research, you will experience firsthand the interaction with the customer and will be able to judge for yourself the validity of the feedback you get. Finally, quality focus groups, conducted in professional facilities with professional moderators, can easily exceed $15,000 per study, not counting travel costs. If you are working on a shoestring budget in the earliest stages of your product's development, the do-it-yourself approach is sometimes the only option. And although an experienced professional moderator can provide a high level of value, you can definitely do a decent job on your own.

IS THERE EVER A REASON TO OUTSOURCE?

Qualitative research is so tangible that it is tempting to assume that you can always do the job yourself and apply the money saved toward other projects. That is not always the case.

Availability of Internal Resources versus Budget Availability

This may seem obvious, but it is often the deciding factor in the make or buy decision. If you have sufficient human resources to do the work, and the human resources have an interest in conducting the sessions and performing the accompanying analysis, this might be a good option. However, if you have plenty of money and not enough staff, you'll probably have to outsource research efforts, like half the projects that you are current undertaking at this stage of the game.

Expenditure Level and Strategic Importance of the Decisions Driven by the Research

If you are planning to make a decision that involves hundreds of thousands of dollars of spending (ad campaigns, new product developments), it probably makes sense to allocate a bit of money and have a professional do some (if not all) of the research for you. The make or buy decision can be calculated according to the guidelines illustrated in Chapter 1, which can be paraphrased as follows: The greater the cost and likelihood of making a mistake, the more you can justify spending on the research.

Organizational Culture

We've had clients whose company cultures automatically place more merit on the work and input of external consultants and "experts" than on the work of internal teams that are closest to the issues. We won't debate the validity of such attitudes; but consider your company's culture before deciding whether to do the work internally or to outsource. If your organization automatically considers internal projects inferior, all your hard work and valuable analysis may be for naught. Fortunately, this attitude is most prevalent in companies with large consulting budgets, so hopefully you won't be caught between a rock and a hard place.

Outsourcing Qualitative Research on a Tight Budget

If money is very tight (for either real or political reasons), you can cut some costs and hire professional assistance where it will have the most impact. The easiest cost-cutting measure is to use your own facilities instead of renting official focus group rooms (for a saving of several thousand dollars). We've conducted very effective qualitative research with a few hundred dollars to pay for participant incentives, a dozen pizzas, and the rental of a video camera to record the proceedings.

Another major cost of large-scale qualitative work is travel and lodging. When focus groups are conducted nationwide, the qualitative team must travel to the location, typically stay overnight, and rent facilities in each city. Because travel expenses can easily exceed several thousand dollars per employee, carefully consider whether there is a strong need to gather opinions from outside your local area. If you are using qualitative research as an exploratory tool to drive more representative quantitative research later on, you can save a considerable amount of money by holding sessions only in your local area. If you must include geographic variety in your research, but can't afford to travel, an online focus group may be a good compromise.

Finally, if you are planning to conduct both qualitative and quantitative research, you may be able to reduce the costs of each component by having the same vendor manage both parts. Volume discounts apply in research too; be aware of the ability to negotiate costs when shopping around or publishing your request for proposal.

4

Quantitative Research

Q uantitative marketing research is the measurement of consumer characteristics, behaviors, and attitudes. It forms the core of marketing research, because these measurements can be scientific, rigorous, and representative. As such, they can be used confidently to make critical business decisions. As a general rule, research data is quantitative when you can chart it, graph it, or tabulate it.

STRENGTHS OF QUANTITATIVE RESEARCH

Reliable: The underlying principle of quantitative research is that, when it is done correctly, the results are an accurate representation of the population being studied. For example, a quantitative study could determine with a measurable degree of certainty what share of a particular Web site's users were women, parents, or single mothers. A focus group or other qualitative technique could never provide this type of information. Hence, when research is being used to drive an extremely critical decision, the data should nearly always come from a quantitative methodology.

Large-Scale: To provide increased confidence that the results are not an anomaly, quantitative studies interview considerably more consumers than qualitative research methods do. For consistency, quantitative studies also necessitate the standardization of questionnaires and interview techniques. Hence, quantitative research can easily cross geographic boundaries and include respondents from the entire target population. This is especially relevant online, where automated interview techniques allow large sample sizes, and the global nature of the Internet invites the inclusion of respondents from all over the world. It's quite common for a basic profiling study of a Web site's audience to have a sample size of more than 4,000 randomly selected respondents, 15% of whom are typically from outside the United States.

In-Depth Analysis: An array of statistical techniques can be applied to quantitative data. Reviewing simple averages or frequency distributions is often enough to provide valuable insight into the nature of a population. However, the possibilities extend far beyond these simple statistics, to complicated multivariate procedures like cluster analysis (to establish target segments), conjoint analysis (to determine the ideal feature set of a new product), or factor analysis (to identify driving forces behind brand preference or spending behavior).

Replicable and Trackable: Another basic principle of correctly executed quantitative research is that, if identical studies were conducted in tandem among the same population, the results would be nearly identical. Therefore, changes in a population can be tracked over time (longitudinally) by executing the same study at regular intervals. Tracking studies are exceptionally valuable for monitoring changes in customer characteristics, behaviors, and attitudes. A common example of tracking research is an advertising effectiveness study that evaluates the effect of advertising on brand awareness, brand perception, and sales. Longitudinal tracking of established success metrics is an excellent method of evaluating business decisions on an ongoing basis, and can provide critical early feedback on the impact of a marketing or product development decision before it impacts the bottom line. The online environment lends itself well to developing and executing these studies affordably. Previously, tracking studies were available only to large brands at high cost from established research companies.

Automated: An economic benefit of quantitative research over qualitative techniques is the ability to refine the process over time to dramatically decrease the cost of conducting subsequent research studies. Once systems are in place for collecting, analyzing, and reporting on data, research studies can be executed quickly to answer pressing business questions as they arise. This is especially true online, where the interviewing and data collection process can be built once and used repeatedly. The economics are somewhat less favorable when research is conducted offline or contracted to an outside vendor. Despite the advantages (both economic and performance), many companies execute copious amounts of qualitative research in situations that would be better addressed with quantitative techniques, because they lack the requisite research knowledge or tools to conduct quantitative studies.

LIMITATIONS OF QUANTITATIVE RESEARCH

Some of the factors that make quantitative research reliable and easily replicated can also be drawbacks.

Limited for Exploration: The standardization of questionnaires and interviewing techniques tends to limit testing to predetermined hypotheses. Questionnaires have respondents react to specific question and answer lists created by the researcher. Therefore, some potentially interesting spontaneous or tangential responses may be missed or excluded. For this reason, quantitative research is not always the best choice for exploratory research. To get the best of both worlds, researchers often use a two-pronged approach: They use qualitative methods to help determine the issues surrounding a research topic, and then establish the degree to which these issues exist using quantitative research.

Response to Innovative Concepts: Quantitative research is strongest when utilized to understand established brands or markets. This is largely because it is challenging to convey innovative concepts to interviewees. Imagine if someone had conducted a survey 20 years ago about the desirability of interacting with friends, family, and coworkers via messages typed into a computer and sent over phone lines. Email, which has since proved to be an invaluable communication tool, may not have initially rated very highly among consumers. Who knew then that computers would become ubiquitous or that email would provide the ability to communicate with increasingly busy friends and family? Because personal experience and hearsay shape opinions, respondents have difficulty reacting to surveys regarding subjects that are entirely foreign.

This issue is somewhat less relevant online, where studies can utilize powerfully descriptive multimedia tools to help convey concepts to interviewees. Graphics, sounds, movies, and product demos can all be employed online to help familiarize respondents with concepts. These aids often provide the personal experience necessary to fuel the formulation of opinions.

Accessibility: Quantitative data is an abstraction, and as such can be difficult for some decision makers to relate to. Hearing a few consumers describe their opinions about a product though examples of personal experience is far easier for many people to understand than tables and charts full of feature-set ratings, behavioral habits, and personal characteristics. Lack of ability to interpret quantitative research drives many companies to conduct qualitative research when more rigorous quantitative methods would be cheaper and more appropriate.

Potentially Misleading: Perhaps the greatest limitation of quantitative research is the fact that the results from poorly conducted studies are often perceived as irrefutable truth by individuals with limited experience. Charts, graphs, and tables have empirical implications, and it is only natural to accept them as fact. But in some cases, information confidently offered up as "truth" is completely unreliable. Any number of factors can affect the legitimacy of quantitative research: Questionnaires can contain leading questions; data collection methods can introduce bias; margins of error due to small sample sizes may render findings insignificant; or an analyst may present only those findings that support an unseen agenda. Just as with qualitative research, the skill of the researcher in interpreting data in an unbiased but meaningful way has a major impact on the project's value.

APPLICATIONS OF QUANTITATIVE RESEARCH

Nearly every aspect of the marketing process can be investigated using quantitative research techniques. Generally, however, survey research is best suited to measuring concrete and easily categorized attributes such as market factors or consumer characteristics and behavior. Quantitative research is routinely used to measure customer attitudes and preferences. However, collecting accurate measures of these complex factors poses an interesting set of challenges for the researcher. We investigate these issues further when we discuss questionnaire design, in Chapter 7.

The most common applications of quantitative research are determining market factors, identifying customer characteristics and behaviors, and measuring the attitudes and opinions of consumers.

Market Factors

Market Size: Measures the overall number of individuals who may potentially use a product or service. For example, the total number of people who use search engines online.

Consumption Levels and Frequency: Measures how often a product is used or consumed combined with the market size and economic value of consumption, to provide the overall value of the market. Suppose it is determined that 50 million Web users access search engines an average of twice a week and conduct an average of five searches on each visit. From this we can calculate that the total usage level of the search market is 26 billion searches per year. If search engines earn $.02 per search (via advertising revenue), then the total value of the search industry might be $520,000,000. Of course, many other factors go into a market's value, but this is a principal component.

Segmentation: This involves identifying and measuring the size of distinct groups of consumers based on specific characteristics and behaviors that have a bearing on their relationship to the category. The age-old 20–80 rule is a prime example of segmentation. Assume that 20% of Web search engine users complete an average of 40 Web searches per week. These users account for 80% of the total searches, and hence, advertising revenue. When 20% of your customers account for 80% of your revenue, it is critical to develop a set of metrics to identify these core customers, understand their needs, and tailor your business practices to suit them. This does not mean the other 80% of users should be ignored. The point is simply that by developing segmentation variables, the divergent needs of each group can be understood and addressed.

Consumption Patterns: These metrics provide a more robust understanding of the category being studied. They are category-specific measures. In the Web search industry, such metrics might include:

- types of information most commonly searched for;
- percentage of searches conducted for business versus leisure purposes; and
- the relative share of directory service versus text string searches.

There is obvious value in obtaining a thorough understanding of how customers relate to the category. This value can be increased by combining usage patterns with the segmentation definitions described. Understanding that the heaviest 20% of users tend to search for technology information from work by using advanced text string searches will provide strategic insight toward developing products to satisfy the needs of this disproportionately valuable customer base.

Distribution Channels: Many markets have several channels that compete to satisfy the consumer need for the same products or services. A Web site selling software, for instance, competes against both online competitors and off-line distribution channels such as catalogs, warehouse clubs, computer stores, and general merchandisers. While the gross number of software purchasers may be the total *potential* market size for an online software retailer, the *actual* market size might be much smaller if the majority of consumers prefer to purchase software from warehouse clubs. The difference between potential and actual market sizes can have significant business ramifications, because the additional marketing cost of convincing off-line consumers to purchase online may prove to be greater than the potential return.

Market Share: Awareness and usage levels of competitive products define the landscape of your marketplace. Establishing a hierarchy of competitors based on total size or similarity to your product offering creates a competitive set against which to position your product. In our search engine example, such an investigation might reveal that a few leading search engines, like Yahoo!, Lycos, and AltaVista, dominate the search engine market and account for 75% of all Web searches. Further analysis might indicate that, while Yahoo! and Lycos have enormous numbers of users, nearly all of them are light searchers (fewer than 5 searches per week). On the other hand, AltaVista might prove to attract fewer but heavier searchers (more than 40 searches per week). Thus, AltaVista might be considered your closest competitor if you've decided to target your search service by catering to heavier users.

Customer Characteristics and Behaviors

Demographics, Webographics, and Socioeconomics: One of the most basic and common applications of quantitative research is the profiling of customers by their fundamental personal characteristics. This is especially relevant online, where the anonymous nature of the relationship gives businesses little, if any, direct contact with the customers they serve. Customer profiles are easier to come by in the brick-and-mortar world, where retailers observe and interact with customers consistently. Online quantitative research studies are leveraged to determine whether customers are more likely to be males or females, students or business owners, and experienced users who are comfortable with the Web or newbies who require a good deal of hand-holding.

Psychographics: Consumers are more than the sum of their demographics. They have hobbies, political affiliations, personality types, and any number of other characteristics that define them and can be major drivers in consumer behavior. These characteristics can be measured, analyzed, and then leveraged to develop appealing products and effective marketing programs.

Consumption and Purchase Habits: Advertising-supported Web sites are in the business of matching advertisements for their client's products and services to the qualified eyeballs of their user base. Therefore, a standard application of online marketing research is determining how many (and which) types of computers, automobiles, books, vacation packages, cell phones, pens, and personal hygiene products you purchase regularly. This information, aggregated along with general demographic data, is then used to demonstrate the value of advertising on a particular site.

Attitudes and Opinions of Consumers

Product Requirements and Feature Preferences: By measuring the desirability of attributes that could be included in a product or service, this process identifies a set of attributes that are core to the success of a product, others that are important but non-critical, and still others that contribute little to the customer's purchase decision. Returning to our search service example, a survey of user attitudes might reveal that search speed, relevance of results, advanced searching capabilities, and ease of use are the four attributes that rate as the most important to search engine users. The same study might also show that appealing design, directory listings, and largest database also rate highly, but not as high as the former four features. Other features, such as stock quotes, links to shopping, weather reports, and personalized home pages might be identified as not critical to the purchase decision.

Brand Perceptions: Before consumers try a product or service, various forms of marketing messages and word of mouth opinions shape their preconceptions of the brand (and may even influence their attitudes toward the brand after trial). Because one of the primary challenges for any company is to encourage trial of its products, many quantitative methods have been designed to evaluate how consumers perceive brands. An understanding of how the marketplace views brands helps uncover marketing opportunities to enhance the positive and combat the negative perceptions. Suppose a quantitative study revealed that our search engine enjoyed an awareness level of 40% among search engine users, but only 25% of those users had ever tried the service. Investigating the brand perceptions of the 75% who had not tried the service might reveal that they felt our search engine was designed for less-experienced users of the Web, because it was perceived as lacking advanced searching capabilities. This finding might spark new product development or the aggressive marketing of existing capabilities.

Product Performance: While positive brand perceptions encourage initial trial, meeting expectations with excellent product performance creates loyal customers. Conversely, the inability to meet expectations creates dissatisfied customers who not only are nearly impossible to recapture, but will likely cost you further customers by voicing negative reviews. It is critical to ensure that your product's performance is up to par and supports the claims made in marketing messages. Before our search engine begins heavily marketing its new or existing tools for advanced searching, it would be well-advised to ensure a positive experience for new users by testing the performance of those features.

TYPES OF QUANTITATIVE RESEARCH

Quantitative research can be grouped into three major categories. The first obtains information through observation of consumer behavior. The second utilizes interviews to understand customers. The third combines observational and survey techniques to obtain a comprehensive understanding of customers and their behaviors.

Behavioral Data

Observational or behavioral research monitors customer's purchases, media consumption, advertising exposure, and online usage to keep marketers abreast of *what* is going on in the marketplace. Typically, behavioral data is collected continuously to track changes as they occur. Researchers analyzing this data are often able to infer the forces driving changes by mapping the data against current business activities.

Two types of behavioral data are purchase data and Web server log data.

Purchase Data: A record of products that customers purchase is perhaps the simplest example of behavioral data. It represents a bottom-line measure of the success of all the marketing components (product development, promotions, distribution). A comparison to sales of competitive products provides information on market size, market share, and product preference.

Major product development and promotional activities often cause significant changes in purchase levels. Many factors affect sales, though, so it is impossible to track the effects of small changes in business strategy by evaluating purchase data alone. A downward trend could be the result of competitive marketing activities, seasonal demand, distribution problems, or a number of other factors.

Web Server Log Data: One of the truly exciting aspects of conducting research online is that every action of a user on a Web site can be collected in something called a Web server log. These logs have the ability to provide an array of useful information, such as where on the Web users initially came from, how many pages they viewed, which pages they visited, and how long they spent on each page.

Sites aggregate log information to determine the number of daily visitors to the site and the total number of pages viewed. For many content and marketing sites, these numbers are fundamental indicators of success, much as purchase data are to a product-oriented company. Log data, however, shares the same limitations as all behavioral data: While effective at tracking changes in site usage, it is difficult to isolate which of many possible factors is responsible for the changes.

The value of server log data goes far beyond simply understanding how many users visit your site in total. The information can be sliced and diced any number of ways, to provide insight into how users interact with your Web site. In many cases, server logs are the only connection site developers have with the customers they serve. Most sites, for instance, track the number of page views to predefined areas of the site to determine which are most popular. E-commerce sites commonly compare the number of users who access product pages to the number who make purchases to evaluate the conversion rate of browsers to buyers. Evaluating the number of pages each user views provides a measure of involvement with a site. The logs even have the capability to track the path that individual users take though your site.

These are just a few examples of what can be learned through an analysis of the Web server logs. In Chapter 16, we discuss some methods of using server logs to track the performance of your site on an ongoing basis.

In our experience, the responsibility for intelligently collecting and reporting on server log data typically falls to the same person in the organization charged with conducting primary research. If this means you, it's important that you understand how log servers collect data. Every time a user requests a file from a Web server (a hit), the server writes a record of the request in the server log. The log is a text file with one entry per line. Because the server log tracks hits, an HTML page with four pictures on it shows up in the server log as five hits (one request for the page and four requests for the images). It's quite easy to imagine how server logs can quickly grow to an unmanageable length. Even a medium-size site that attracts 20,000 users a day can produce daily logs with 500,000 entries if users view an average of five pages, each containing four images.

When dealing with files of this size, it is important to take a structured approach to culling through the data and producing reports. A number of intelligent companies have developed products that process and convert raw server log data into tools that allow for convenient analysis. We discuss these companies, such as Web Trends (*www.webtrends.com*) and Accrue (*www.accrue.com*), in more detail in Chapter 16.

Interview Data

As we mentioned earlier, observational methods track changes, but do little to explain *why* these changes take place. To understand the driving force behind observed market events, the researcher turns to the second type of quantitative research—interviews. Interviews provide an in-depth understanding of a customer's personal characteristics, relationship to the category, product requirements, and any number of other measures that help explain and predict the customer's behavior.

This type of quantitative data that is typically collected via surveys is the cornerstone of marketing research and a primary focus of this book. There are fundamental differences between survey data and observational data. The latter is a recording of actual events, while survey data is provided by imperfect human beings. Behavioral data from polling centers might show that 33% of registered voters participated in the last national election. A nationwide survey might find that 55% of registered voters reported voting in the same election. A number of factors could be responsible for the 22% inaccuracy of the survey data; they are discussed in detail in the chapters on sampling, data collection, and questionnaire design. For now, it is sufficient to say that accurate collection and interpretation of survey data requires specialized marketing research skills.

Survey data may be less precise than behavioral observation; but when collected and analyzed carefully, it is the most reliable method of researching the characteristics and attitudes of those who report voting, and more important, those who did not vote. Without survey data, your analysis would begin and end with one accurate measure. With survey data, you obtain an in-depth understanding of the factors driving Americans' decision to participate in the electoral process.

Here are some examples of interview-based research studies:

Ad hoc research studies are custom designed to explore a specific business issue. These studies, which are the most common type of survey research, can cover a broad range of topics. The simplest ad hoc studies collect basic classification data, such as age and gender, to develop consumer profiles. More advanced applications may, for example, explore opportunities to steal customers away from competitors by identifying shortcomings in competitive products, or evaluate the ability of a marketing-based Web site to affect users' perceptions of the featured brand.

Often, little is previously known about the population being studied in an ad hoc research project. The study may be the first conducted by a company about its users, or it may be an exploration into an entirely new base of potential customers. In our experience, these studies tend to be characterized by long questionnaires that collect a vast amount of data. Afraid to miss any metrics that may prove relevant to the analysis, researchers tend to throw the kitchen sink in along with measures that are core to proving their hypotheses.

In addition to their length, ad hoc studies require more planning time and extensive analysis. They are, therefore, often costly to conduct—especially if outsourced to a research vendor.

Research Products: After conducting ad hoc research projects, many research vendors have "productized" approaches to address common business questions. Some companies have specialized techniques to measure the effectiveness of advertising; others focus on evaluating brand perceptions; and still others have methodologies to help ensure products are being developed in line with customer expectations.

Chances are good that you're not the first person to consider conducting research on the issue facing your business. In many cases, there may be a research company with a standardized study that would exceed the quality of a custom-designed ad hoc study. This is the case because researchers conducting these studies have invested much time and many resources into perfecting the questionnaire, study design, and analysis. These studies also tend to be cheaper than ad hoc research, because they benefit from increased efficiency and economies of scale. So before developing an extensive and expensive ad hoc study, it often pays to take the time to research the products of a few research companies. This can usually be accomplished simply by checking their Web sites, calling sales representatives, or emailing contacts within the company.

Tracking Studies: While ad hoc studies can delve deeply into an issue, they only capture a single snapshot of the environment. Marketers turn to tracking studies to understand how the marketplace changes over time. By interviewing respondents at regular intervals, or preferably on a continuous basis, these studies provide longitudinal (over time) data. These continuous results can be analyzed to identify trends or can be plotted against the execution of business activities (marketing campaigns, new product pricing) to determine their impact.

Tracking studies are often the result of extensive ad hoc research. The preliminary studies identify the metrics that have the greatest influence on a company's success. These might be metrics that segment customers into distinct target markets, measures of brand perceptions the company is actively attempting to influence, or any other mission-critical information.

Tracking studies are powerful strategic tools, coveted by decision makers. Until recently, however, the benefits of these studies were only available to large companies, because the cost of developing, executing, and maintaining a tracking study proved prohibitively expensive for smaller companies. This was due to that fact that, traditionally, interviews were conducted via phone, requiring a dedicated staff of interviewers to conduct surveys and a dedicated staff of analysts to manage the project.

This is not the case with Web sites. One of the most significant differences between conducting surveys online and conducting them off-line is that there are almost no incremental costs associated with online research. The costs of online research occur either before the project is executed, with questionnaire development and programming, or after the study is completed, with analysis and reporting. Once a Web survey is up and running, it automatically interviews respondents and stores their responses. Thus, from an interview and data processing perspective, there is virtually no difference in cost whether you survey 10, 1,000, or 10,000 respondents.[1]

---

[1]Incentives are often used in online research to boost response rates. Larger sample sizes require increased expenditures on incentives, but the incremental costs range in the hundreds of dollars, not thousands.

While off-line surveys also incur the development costs, they suffer from incremental data collection and processing costs. Phone surveys require that every respondent be individually located, called, and interviewed by a paid person on the other end of the phone. It's easy to see, therefore, that interviewing 200 people via traditional phone methods can be expensive, and that doing so every week would be astronomically expensive. Other traditional data collection methods are as, if not more, expensive than phone surveying.

Tracking studies executed online are essentially ad hoc studies that are never turned off. As long as the researcher continues soliciting respondents through various sampling methods (discussed in Chapter 5), the automated survey process continues to collect and store interviews. The analyst can collect current or past data from the server at any time, and provide answers within minutes to pressing business questions. We talk more about online tracking studies in Chapter 6.

Combined Behavioral and Interview Data

Observational data excels at describing *what* customers are doing, while survey data helps explain *why* customers act the way they do. The obvious next step is to combine these two types of data to obtain a complete understanding. Unfortunately, doing so is not always as easy as dipping chocolate into peanut butter.

The sources used for observing customer behavior are seldom the same sources used for interviewing customers. Purchase data, for instance, is collected at cash registers around the nation via scan logs. Customer data, on the other hand, is largely collected via phone or mail-in surveys. To effectively combine the data types, a log of each respondent's purchase habits would have to be combined with a survey of their characteristics and attitudes. Until recently, the logistics required and the lack of high-powered computing made the tracking of an individual's purchases nearly impossible. Recently, increases in processor speed and the proliferation of relational databases have created an entire new type of quantitative research.

Here are two examples of combined data types:

Frequent shopper cards provide perhaps the best example of combined observational and interview data. Retailers both large and small now commonly provide customers with cards that identify them as individuals, and incentives to use them on every purchase occasion. Often, when the cards are issued, they are accompanied by a short survey that collects basic classification metrics (gender, age, etc.).

Through an analysis of this information, marketers, brand managers, and store owners can determine the types of products different people purchase. More significant, this information can be tracked over time to determine consumption patterns. By linking the purchase data to marketing, pricing, or other factors with the potential to influence consumer behavior, powerful insight can be gained into the impact of the marketing mix on a product's success. Shopper cards are most commonly employed in packaged goods industries (food, household consumables, etc.) whose purchase cycle is short enough to allow researchers to observe changes in behavior in a relatively short time frame.

Integration of logs and survey data. We've briefly discussed both the value of tracking users actions via server logs, and the immense potential of conducting tracking studies online. Similar to frequent shopper cards, Web sites can also combine these two types of information to create powerful tools for the ongoing analysis of business activities.

Web sites can assign each new user a *cookie,* which is a unique identifier somewhat like an online version of the frequent shopper card. This information can then be stored as a field in the Web server's log or other database, along with information about where the user went on the site and when. Like a frequent shopper card, the cookie enables longitudinal (over time) analysis about a user's relationship to the site. With it, sites can derive many valuable metrics, such as what share of their traffic is driven by new, occasional, or frequent users. Furthermore, the usage patterns of these groups can be compared to determine what types of content or services are valued most by each segment. E-commerce sites utilize cookies to evaluate the purchase cycles of users, by tracking how many times they visit a site before making a purchase, and what areas of the site they access on each visit.

To take this information a step further, a site might continually sample a subset of users accessing the site and interview them about mission-critical issues—a tracking study. The salient metrics collected through the survey could then be encoded into the cookie along with the unique identifier. Now, instead of knowing only how first-time users are using the site, a Web site developer can determine how users in the primary target market used the site—a segment defined by any number of variables that are available only though surveying. Web hosts can also evaluate their marketing efforts by tracking which mechanism of driving awareness delivered the greatest number of coveted users. The ability to obtain this level of insight into a customer's relationship with a product marks a truly revolutionary development in marketing research, which we delve into more deeply in Chapter 16.

CHAPTER 5

Sampling

O ne of the first decisions you'll make when conducting primary survey research is who you will interview to collect your results. In an ideal world, you would interview every member of the population you were attempting to understand. In a few cases, this population is manageably small and easily accessible. In most cases, the population you'll be dealing with will be very large, and in many cases, it will be extremely large—so large that conducting interviews with every member of the population would take years and cost hundreds of millions of dollars. The U.S. Census Bureau is charged with just such a task: contacting all adults in the United States. The process is so expensive and time-consuming that it only occurs only every 10 years.

Because conducting a census of the population is impractical, researchers rely on various methods to select a subset of the population to interview. High-quality research practice dictates that the selection process be random. Why? Because a basic precept of statistical theory holds that a random sample of significant size will mirror, within measurable limits, the population from which it was taken.

This is not a statistics textbook, so we won't bore you with the details. That said, you should understand a few fundamental concepts of sampling so you can develop studies that provide reliable data (and identify studies whose methodologies are suspect).

THE CENTRAL LIMIT THEOREM

The reason we are able to talk to a small subset of a population— and then project their answers out to the other people whom we didn't talk to—hinges on the central limit theorem. The central limit theorem states that if you were to calculate the mean (average) of a measurement (e.g., age, weight, number of apples consumed in the past month) among a number of independent random subsets of the population, the means of each sample would fall around the true mean of the population in the shape of a normal (bell-shaped) curve.

An illustrated example might make things clearer: If we were to randomly select 50 independent samples of 500 users from a Web site and chart the average age of each sample, the resulting chart would be in the shape of a normal distribution. (See Figure 5.1.)

FIGURE 5.1: Normalized Distribution

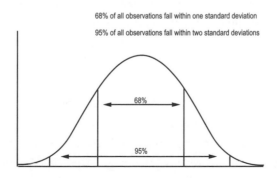

68% of all observations fall within one standard deviation

95% of all observations fall within two standard deviations

68%

95%

Statistical theory also tells us that 68% of all the sample means will fall within a set distance from the actual population mean. This distance is called the *standard deviation.* The theory also holds that 95% of all observations will fall within two standard deviations of the mean.

Why is this important? Because when we do a survey, we can reverse-engineer this theory to state that any statistics we obtain from the sample will have a 95% likelihood of being within a defined range from the actual population value. In marketing research, we call this range the *confidence interval,* and we call the likelihood that the statistic is within this range the *confidence level.* When CNN reports on the results of its opinion polls, for example, it states that the poll is accurate to plus or minus 5% at the 95% confidence level.

We can combine the confidence interval and the confidence level to make a new term, the *sampling error.*

SAMPLING ERROR

Three factors determine sampling error:

1. *Sample size:* The larger your sample, the more likely it is to represent the actual population. Assume that our research objective was to profile the age, gender, and income of users of a major Web site like Yahoo!. If we were to randomly sample only 10 of Yahoo!'s visitors, we would have a difficult time determining even the basic ratio of men to women, much less the more varied ranges in age and income. With a sample of only 10, it's very possible that we might select 3 women and 7 men, leading us to believe that Yahoo!'s audience was significantly male. If we were to increase our sample size to 100 or even 500, however, we significantly reduce the role of chance in our results. We might find that Yahoo!'s users are more evenly split in terms of gender.

TABLE 5.1: Sampling error

	Sampling Error at the 95% Confidence Level			
	Sample Size			
% reported	100	500	1000	3000
50%	*10.5%*	*4.9%*	*3.2%*	*2.5%*
80% or 20%	8.4%	3.9%	2.6%	2.0%
95% or 5%	4.6%	2.1%	1.6%	1.1%

2. *Variability in the population:* If the population you're sampling is relatively homogeneous on a specific variable (say, the ages of college students), then the sample size needed to obtain an accurate representation is far smaller than if the population is highly diverse (say, the ages of U.S. adults). Therefore, sample proportions that are either very high (95% of college students are 18 to 25 years of age) or very low (3% of college students are over 25) result in smaller sampling error than middle-of-the-road statistics (50% of college students are male).

3. *Sampling method:* All the statistics we've discussed assume that each of the samples was drawn from the population at random. Non-random sampling methods, while often implemented due to cost or logistical constraints, can introduce an immeasurable amount of bias into the results. The nature of the bias cannot be known with certainty, nor can it be corrected for, so the sampling error associated with nonrandom samples is potentially much higher than that for random samples. A higher sampling error translates to less reliable data, so random samples are always preferable to nonrandom samples. In practice, however, collecting samples that are purely random is not always feasible. In these cases, utilizing non-random samples can be a viable option. Much of this chapter is devoted to a review of the merits and methods of random and non-random approaches to sampling.

NONRESPONSE BIAS

Another factor that can affect the reliability of survey results is non-response bias. This is the bias introduced into the data when a person selected for a survey either cannot be contacted or refuses to participate. Unlike sampling error (which can be calculated), non-response bias typically has an unknown effect on data reliability. This is because it is not known whether the reason behind the non-response is random or systematic in nature. In many cases, the factors driving nonresponse are systematic. Nonresponders may be wealthier, more educated, younger, or have any other number of characteristics that directly affect how they would have responded to the survey questions.

The amount of potential nonresponse bias in a survey is indicated by the *response rate:* the percentage of people the researcher attempted to contact who actually completed the survey. If a survey has a response rate of 50%, one in every two attempts resulted in a competed survey. One in ten responders equals a response rate of 10%; and a dismal 1 in 100 response rate results in worthless data.

Nonresponse bias is a growing problem in marketing research—especially off-line. These days, people are busy and often not at home. When they are home, they are constantly fielding calls from people pitching newspapers, time-shares, and phone surveys. Response rates, which were once quite high, have slowly dropped to 30% or lower as people become more unwilling to participate in telephone and mail surveys. The nonresponse bias associated with the inability to contact respondents is alleviated in online sampling; potential respondents are typically selected as they visit a Web site and must actively opt to participate or not. Online research also has the advantage of being novel. Consumers who would never take the time to complete a telephone interview may be willing to spend the same amount of time taking an online survey.

The fact that not everyone answers a survey does not necessarily mean that the data is riddled with nonresponse bias. While nonresponse bias cannot be measured precisely, there are ways of assessing its severity. One common method is to compare the data collected in the survey to known values in the population. In a study that intends to provide a nationally representative picture, for example, you might turn to the U.S. Census to obtain the known values. There is definitely cause for alarm, for instance, if 80% of your survey respondents are women, when they comprise only 51% of the population. Another method is simply to ask those who do not wish to participate in the study to answer a small subset of questions. In all likelihood, you'll obtain a much higher response rate to this succinct questionnaire, and hence have a smaller degree of nonresponse bias associated with the mini-survey. This data, which is more likely to be representative than the main survey that obtained a lower response rate, can then be compared to the main survey to identify significant differences between responders and nonresponders.

Once the source of nonresponse bias is identified, a process known as data weighting can be employed to help bring the sample data into line with expected population values. A full discussion of data weighting is beyond the scope of this book; for a brief description of the process, see Chapter 11.

SAMPLING FRAME

There is a key distinction in sampling between the population the research is attempting to study and the population that is available for sampling—that is, people who are able to be contacted and solicited to participate. This available subset of the population is called the *sampling frame*. The goal is for the sampling frame to include every member of the actual population. The greater the difference between the sampling frame and the population, the greater the sampling error and the less confidence we have in the data.

Unfortunately, exactly mirroring the population in the sampling frame is more easily said than done; in practice, it is nearly impossible. For instance, a study may have the stated objective of interviewing the population of a company's customers, U.S. adults, or a Web site's user base. The sampling frames for these studies may end up being a list of customers who have filled out product registration forms, all the phone listings in the United States, or all users who access a Web site over a defined span of time. Note the differences between the populations being studied and the sampling frames: The list of customers may not be complete; many U.S. adults may not have phones or may have unlisted numbers; and the Web site sample includes only those who access the site during the time span of the study.

RANDOM SAMPLES (PROBABILITY SAMPLES)

A random sample is defined as a sample in which each member of the sampling frame has an equal probability of being sampled. When correctly executed, random samples have a known sampling error, and therefore enable the researcher to make definitive statements about the sampling frame from which the sample was drawn. Aside from conducting a census of the population, random sampling is the only method of collecting information that can be reliably projected to the population from which it was drawn.

Keep in mind that samples are selected from sampling frames, not from the entire population. Typically, the term *random sample* is reserved for samples that closely a mirror the population by making every reasonable effort to include each member of the population in the sampling frame. However, it is possible to take a random sample from a sampling frame that is biased. When reviewing research from a random sample, understand how the sampling frame was constructed.

Because of the cost and difficulty involved in defining an accurate sampling frame and developing a method to sample respondents from it at random, collecting true random samples may not always be an option.

Off-Line Techniques of Random Sampling

List Sampling: Frequently in marketing research, the sampling frame is in the form of a list. Lists of previous customers, registered users of a Web site, or members of an organization are all examples. Once the list is obtained, the first step is to remove any duplicates. Often, multiple lists that may contain some of the same respondents are combined in an attempt to include each member of the population in the sampling frame.

When the list is complete and clean, there are two methods for selecting random samples from it:

Simple Random Sample: The first and preferable method is to incrementally assign each respondent a number. Then, using a random number generator, select the desired quantity of random numbers from the range of numbers represented in the list. To create your sample, match the resulting array of random numbers with the assigned values given to respondents. This is a bit like pulling winning raffle tickets out of a fishbowl and finding the winner who has the matching ticket stub.

Unfortunately, matching a long list of random numbers with a long list of respondents can be a tedious task. An easier method is to select a subset of list elements (respondents) randomly, using a computer program. A program can easily be created in nearly any scripting language (perl or C) that contains a function to randomly select elements from an array. But for those of you who aren't code heads, there are also many commercially available programs for selecting random samples from lists.

For truly lazy individuals, like us, Microsoft Excel provides a simple function for selecting a random subset of elements from a list. Start with an Excel spreadsheet listing potential respondents and their contact information in individual rows. For each entry, copy and paste the =RAND() function into a new column. This associates each respondent with a random number between 0 and 1 extending to many decimal places. Now, create a randomly ordered

TABLE 5.2: Random sampling using Microsoft Excel

Step 1		Step 2	
Assign Random #		**Sort by Random #**	
Customer1	"=RAND()"	Customer2	0.003917684
Customer2	"=RAND()"	Customer4	0.015116449
Customer3	"=RAND()"	Customer9	0.066306771
Customer4	0.015116449	Customer5	0.201457305
Customer5	0.201457305	Customer8	0.214220037
Customer6	0.723519874	Customer1	0.256439743
Customer7	0.900010477	Customer10	0.410121555
Customer8	0.214220037	Customer3	0.686900022
Customer9	0.066306771	Customer6	0.723519874
Customer10	0.410121555	Customer7	0.900010477

Note: The text "=RAND()" will not show up in your Excel sheet; it will resolve to a random number between 0 and 1 after you type in into a cell.

list simply by sorting it by the random number in ascending order.[1] Once sorted, select the desired sample size, starting at the beginning of the list. Voila! A random sample in under a minute.

2. *Periodic Sample:* There are instances when selecting elements from a list entirely at random is excessively difficult. An example might be a list in nondigital format, such that random numbers would have to be matched by hand with list respondents. In this case, a periodic or *N*th sampling technique can be employed to draw a random sample. In this method, every *N*th list element is selected to be part of the sample. So, if the value of *N* is 10, every tenth element in the list becomes part of the sample. To obtain the value of *N,* simply divide the number of elements in the list by the number of desired respondents.

[1]Before sorting the list, be certain to copy the list of random numbers created by the formula and use the [Paste special] function to paste only values into the same cells (select 'Paste only values' on the Paste special menu). Otherwise, sorting the list will only cause the formula to rerun and select new random numbers. You'll know you've done this correctly when sorting by the random number column causes the random values to appear in ascending order.

Random Digit Dial (RDD): This sampling approach is used when there is no existing, all-inclusive list of the population in question. As the name implies, this method involves dialing random combinations of numbers until a valid phone number is reached and answered.

While the effect is annoying, random digit dial is one of the most reliable methods of collecting a random sample of U.S. adults. Nearly every household in the U.S. has a phone, and the random digit dialing technique does not exclude unlisted numbers.

The extreme randomness that makes RDD so representative also makes it ill-suited for certain techniques. If the population you're attempting to research is broad-based, like automobile owners or fast-food consumers, then RDD is an ideal sampling method. However, if the incidence of your population among U.S. adults is small, then collecting a large enough sample of users via RDD will be prohibitively expensive.

Assume, for instance, that a major online software retailer is interested in researching the receptivity of online software purchasers to downloading their purchases immediately as opposed to having them shipped. To be qualified to provide feedback on this topic, respondents would have to meet two criteria:

1. Have access to the Web.
2. Have made software purchases online.

Currently, approximately 50% of U.S. households have access to the Web; of these, suppose that 5% have purchased software online. Therefore, one in two calls would reach a Web user, and one in every forty calls would reach an online purchaser of software.

At this rate, to collect even a paltry sample of 100 software purchasers, we would have to call a minimum of 4,000 people, entice them to participate in a survey, and qualify them as online software purchasers by asking at least two questions. A sample of 100 is hardly ideal, as it can produce sampling errors as high as

±10%. Also, such a small sample would not allow for many types of basic and in-depth analysis of the respondents. A reliable investigation would require significantly more respondents, necessitating a huge number of calls.

As frustrating as RDD research is, it is the only way to contact a nationally representative sample of Web users. Luckily, some savvy research companies have devised methods for significantly reducing the legwork associated with collecting a targeted yet representative population of Web users. This tool, called a nationally representative Web panel, is discussed in the section titled The Consumer Panel.

Online Techniques of Random Sampling

One of the major benefits of studying online populations is the ability to cheaply and easily collect large samples of representative users from a given Web site. Online random sampling techniques are used when the scope of the research is limited to the population of a Web site or a network of sites that will allow their users to be sampled. These studies, termed *sitecentric research,* should be the center of a Web-based company's research strategy for a variety of reasons, including easy access to reliable samples.

Online random sampling is conducted via any number of basic scripting languages, like JavaScript, ASP, or Perl. The simplest scripts are comprised of a few lines of code that are simple to write, edit, and implement. On the opposite end of the spectrum are sampling scripts that perform a seemingly endless variety of tasks and span pages of code. For nearly all occasions, one of the simple versions will more than suffice.

All online sampling scripts perform two basic functions:

1. *Select a random subset of users:* This is accomplished by first creating a random number (typically between 0 and 1) that extends to multiple decimal places. This number is evaluated against the desired sampling rate. If the random

number is higher than the desired sampling rate, nothing happens. If the random number is lower than the sampling rate, the user is selected and moved to the next step.

TABLE 5.3: Simple random sampling

Random #	Sampling Rate	Selected
.3456	.15	No
.1234	.15	Yes
.1523	.15	No
.0221	.15	Yes

2. Once a user has been selected, the program *solicits the user to participate in the study.* This process can occur as a *random intercept,* whereby the entire page the user was attempting to access is replaced by a page inviting the user to participate. More commonly, users are *randomly solicited* to participate via a pop-up window floating over the page they were originally accessing. The solicitations contain text explaining that the user has been selected at random and that participation is important to the development of the site (see Chapter 7). Users are also offered a clear means of opting out of the study.

These two basic components of online random sampling make it the most preferred method of establishing a representative collection of respondents. First, determining which users will be solicited at random allows for the calculation of a known sampling error and instills confidence in the results. Additionally, this method has minimal impact on the total audience's user experience, because only a subset of users are interrupted and redirected from using the site.

Because each randomly sampled respondent must actively opt out of the solicitation, response rates for this type of sampling are quite high. The range of expected response rates depends on the type of site. Informational sites like search engines or shopping sites generally see smaller response rates (approximately 20% to 35%) than do content sites (approximately 25% to 50%). Users of information sites are more likely to be focused on a specific task or just "passing through," and are therefore less likely to take a survey than a user of a content site, who is apt to be involved in leisure activities or planning to stay at the site for a bit.

The combination of a random sample and high response rates makes for highly projectable data. To fully leverage this increased reliability, it is critical to make the solicitation very evident and engaging. For every user who opts out of participating in the survey, another user has to be interrupted. More important, the nonresponse bias increases, reducing the confidence level of the results.

JavaScript Sampling: This is the most common method of random sampling online, probably because it is easy to implement, creates no additional load on servers, and doesn't alter the user's experience. JavaScript is a client-side scripting language. This means that the code is downloaded to the user's browser where it is compiled and executed on their machine. Because of this, implementing a JavaScript sampling script on a site typically requires about the same amount of effort and expertise as fixing a typo on a Web page. Even a nontechnical person can easily insert a few lines of code into one or more pages of a Web site, and begin collecting a random sample of users.

Figure 5.2 a simple example of a working JavaScript that provides a pop-up solicitation (invite.html) randomly to 15% of visitors.

Placing this script on one page of a site selects a random sample of users accessing that page. Placing it on every page selects a random sample of those accessing the entire site. Many sites are comprised of hundreds or even thousands of pages, so collecting a random sample of site users by placing a JavaScript on each page is often too arduous a task. Typically, sampling scripts are placed on the major access points to the site, such as the front page. This

FIGURE 5.2: Simple JavaScript Sampling Algorithm (Also available online at www.sitecentric.com/handbook/javascript/.)

```
<html>
<head>

<script language="javascript">


//<!--
//the variables sLocation and sRate
//are set to the location of your survey and
//the desired sampling rate

var sLocation = "http://www.sitecentric.com/invite.html";
var sRate = .15;

  var sampled = Math.random();
  if(sampled < sRate) {
    window.open(sLocation,'sWindow','scrollbars,resizable');
    }

//-->


</script>

</head>
<body>

<!--content of tested page goes
 between the <body> tags-->

</body>
</html>
```

ensures that nearly all users are eligible to be sampled, while alleviating the need to place scripts on each page of the site.

Server-Side Sampling: As the name implies, this type of sampling occurs on the Web server itself. Often, these scripts are written in a server-side language like ASP and are very similar to JavaScript sampling in that they sample only users accessing a single page. On rare occasions, server-side sampling can be executed on the server itself, collecting a random sample of users accessing any page on the site or even a specific section of the site. While this type of sampling is ideal, the technical expertise required to implement and maintain it makes it seldom utilized.

Some researchers argue that server-side sampling is faster and creates less of an impact on the user experience. In most cases, this argument is purely academic: The time it takes a Web page with JavaScript to execute and load is a fraction of a second greater than the time it takes a server-side enabled page to load. In fact, both methods are imperceptible to the user who is not offered the survey. The added difficulty in implementing a server-side sampling solution is rarely warranted, and even then, only for sites with extremely slow load times and plenty of extra CPU (server processing) time. Why CPU time? Because while the users notice no difference, Web servers may choke when asked to execute a small program each time a user hits the front page (which could occur millions of times a day for some large sites).

User versus Usage Sampling: An interesting issue associated with sampling online is that the sampling script executes each time a user hits a page. Thus, users have an equal opportunity to be sampled regardless of whether it is their first or fortieth visit to the site during the study. Sampling using this method is called *usage sampling;* it creates an inherent bias in the results by overrepresenting heavier users of the site. A user who has crossed the page 40 times over the course of the study has 40 times more opportunity to be sampled than a user who only visited the site once. Typically, this is not considered desirable, since the goal of most studies is to accurately reflect the customers accessing a site.

To work around this issue, the sampling script can be enhanced with the ability to determine whether a specific user has previously accessed the site during the study. This is achieved by assigning users a persistent cookie (a unique identifier) the first time the sampling script runs. The script looks for this cookie each time it is executed. If it is present, the sampling script terminates, because it knows the user has already had the opportunity to be sampled. This process, known as *user sampling,* ensures that each visitor has only one opportunity to be sampled, regardless of how frequently the user accesses the site. It is a more reliable method for providing a representative subset of the visitors accessing a particular site.

Figure 5.3 (on the next page) shows an expanded version of the previous example, designed to check for the presence of a cookie called [SurveyCookie]; if the cookie is not found, to assign a cookie of the same name; then to run the sampling routine that provides a pop-up solicitation (invite.html) randomly to 15% of visitors.

CONVENIENCE SAMPLES (NONPROBABILITY SAMPLES)

As we have mentioned, one major factor affecting sampling error is the sampling method. Samples must be random for the central limit theorem to apply and in order for the calculation of sampling error to be made. Unfortunately, random samples are not always available or affordable. In these cases, the next best thing is a nonprobability sample. These samples, often called convenience samples, have no known probability for each member of the population to be included in the sample; thus, each sample has some bias associated with it. Because the bias in unknown and immeasurable, it cannot be corrected for.

Does this mean that data collected from convenience samples is worthless? Not at all. While we cannot make statements of statistical significance about nonprobability samples, we can evaluate the sampling method and use common sense to determine the type and severity of bias introduced.

Limiting Bias

When selecting nonprobability samples to use in research, the most important step is to make every reasonable effort to reduce bias. This is done by including in the sample all known types of people in the population.

FIGURE 5.3: User Based JavaScript Sampling Algorithm (Also available online www.sitecentric.com/handbook/javascript/.)

```
<script language="javascript">


//<!--
//the variables sLocation and sRate
//are set to the location of your survey and
//the desired sampling rate

var sLocation = "http://www.sitecentric.com/invite.html";
var sRate = .15;
var cookieName = "SurveyCookie";

 var cookieValue = getCookie(cookieName);
 if (cookieValue == null){
  setCookie(cookieName, "Sampled");
  var sampled = Math.random();
  if(sampled < sRate) {
   window.open(sLocation,'sWindow','scrollbars,resizable');
   }
  }

 function getCookie(Name) {
   var search = Name + "=";
   if (document.cookie.length > 0) { //
     offset = document.cookie.indexOf(search);
     if (offset != -1) {
     offset += search.length ;
     end = document.cookie.indexOf(";", offset);
     if (end == -1);
     end = document.cookie.length;
     return unescape(document.cookie.substring(offset, end));
     }
   }
 }

 function setCookie(name, value, expire, domainname) {
   document.cookie = name + "=" + escape(value)
   + ((expire == null) ? "" : ("; expires=" + expire.toGMTStr
   + "; path=/"
 }

//-->
</script>
```

Example

A new Web-based company is considering creating an online service designed to provide deeply discounted stock trades. To determine the need for such a service and to determine the ideal price point, the company decides to conduct a study of investors who trade online. Because it is just starting out, the company cannot afford to collect a random sample of online investors either through random digit dial or a nationally representative Web panel (discussed later in this chapter). Therefore, it decides to use other nonrandom means of inviting users to participate in the survey.

Perhaps the company has some reputable secondary research available, the findings of which identify different types of online investors and the level to which each type exists in the population. In order to limit the bias of the study results, our company should make every effort to ensure that each type of investor is adequately represented in the sample, preferably in the same ratio as they occur in the population. So, if the secondary research identified that $1/2$ of online investors traded 30 or more times a week, then our company will want to be certain that the sample includes a number of investors who traded at that level. Ideally, these users should represent $1/2$ of the total study sample.

Unfortunately, reliable population statistics are not always available to help guide the sampling. In these cases, the way to manage the bias is to be aware of the type of bias each sampling source introduces. Some sources may be biased toward one type of consumer or another. In our example, we knew that heavy online traders should only comprise $1/2$ of the sample. If we had tried to collect a sample solely by soliciting users from investment club discussion lists, which cater to heavy investors, our sample would have overrepresented these users. Even without knowing that only $1/2$ of our sample should be comprised of heavy investors, common sense would tell us that sampling only from investment club lists would bias our sample toward heavier investors. Ideally, we should collect our sample from multiple sources, selected to provide an array of heavy, moderate, and light online traders.

Interpreting Biased Data

Knowing the limitations of nonprobability samples is the key to extracting valuable data from them. Nonprobability samples, for example, can rarely determine the degree to which certain types of customers exist in the marketplace. A better application is to use nonprobability samples to understand the characteristics, behaviors, and affinities of different types of customers.

As we saw in our investment company example, it would be nearly impossible to accurately report what percentage of the marketplace made 30 or more trades per week. Nor could we reliably state what percentage of the market used more than three online investment services, had portfolios over $200,000, or were dissatisfied with their current online trading service.

While we would not want to extrapolate our sample to the entire marketplace, we might venture to cull other findings from the data. For instance, it would be more accurate to state that, *"Among heavier traders,* 40% use three or more online investment services, 60% have portfolios over $200,000, and 50% are dissatisfied with their current online trading service." This is a more reliable finding, because the number of trades people make is likely to have a greater impact on the number of investment services they use, the size of their portfolios, or their satisfaction with current investment offerings than the method by which they were sampled.

An even better approach is to use nonprobability data to compare the attributes of different groups, rather than to understand the degree to which specific attributes exist within a particular group. Reporting that 50% of heavier online traders are dissatisfied with their current online trading service is less likely to be accurate than stating that lighter traders are less likely than heavier traders to be dissatisfied with their current online trading service.

Types of Convenience Samples

List sampling is the most common type of convenience sampling. Often, in lieu of a random sample drawn from the entire population, companies opt to use less-expensive lists of consumers obtained from a variety of sources. Many of these sampling methods were covered in our discussion of qualitative research in Chapter 2. The major difference between using these sampling sources for qualitative versus quantitative research is that the former makes no pretense of being representative of the population; hence, the bias introduced by each source is irrelevant. When using these sampling sources for quantitative research, however, it is important to evaluate the biases and determine how they will affect the results.

Posting to newsgroups or email list groups: As we discussed earlier, newsgroups and a number of email-based or Web-based discussion lists (e.g., egroups.com or topica.com) provide researchers with access to highly targeted groups of potential respondents. Posting invitations to these lists to participate in online studies can be a highly effective means of soliciting samples that exhibit specific characteristics or behaviors necessary to the research.

The most important thing to keep in mind when posting to these lists is that it is considered poor etiquette to submit off-topic posts. It might be okay for our investment site to post carefully worded solicitations on investment-related lists, but doing so on a sports and recreation list would surely invite retaliation. The most successful solicitations pitch the surveys as a learning process and implore list members to help improve the product offerings in their area of interest by participating in the survey.

Beyond avoiding the wrath of technically-savvy Web users, it is critical to attempt to limit and understand the bias introduced into the study by sampling from these lists. Many of the lists are populated by highly involved people in the category they represent. A sample derived wholly from such a list would overrepresent the opinions of these highly involved individuals and ignore the likely larger population of lesser-involved individuals. If unchecked or unidentified, this bias can lead to erroneous findings and costly mistakes. A sample biased toward heavier investors, for instance, might result in future development of high-end investment tools that the vast majority of online traders may find irrelevant or confusing.

When sampling from lists, it is a sound practice to post to a variety of lists that cater to each type of consumer in the marketplace. Soliciting from both high-end and beginner investment lists would be a wise tactic to help ensure a more balanced sample. Additionally, building in a mechanism to determine which list the respondents came from will help you evaluate the type and degree of bias at work in your sample.

Finally, your survey should collect data on the characteristics and behaviors of the respondents who participate in the study to allow different types of consumers to be easily identified. Don't make the mistake of conducting a study among online investors and forgetting to ask the basics of trading frequency and portfolio size before asking respondents what they think about your slick new service.

Rental Lists: Also known as opt-in lists, these are composed of users who specifically stated that they were interested in being contacted to hear about certain topics. PostMasterDirect (www.postmasterdirect.com) offers easy access to large numbers of targeted consumers though such lists. We've used them with great success in both qualitative and quantitative recruitment. Similar to discussion lists, opt-in lists are likely to be biased. They are populated by people who are actively seeking additional information on a topic and therefore are typically biased toward being highly involved members of the category.

Banner and Link Sampling: One nonprobability method of obtaining samples online is though a hypertext link or advertising banner on a site that invites users to participate in a survey. While it may be straightforward and therefore tempting to solicit respondents in this manner, the technique results in highly dubious data. Links and banners are rarely noticed by users, and even when noticed are likely to be ignored in lieu of more engaging content.

Because these solicitations are so unengaging and lack text explaining the importance of the study, the response rates achieved with this type of sampling are extremely low—typically less than one percent. Recalling our previous discussion of nonresponse bias, we know that response rate is directly related to data validity, and that one percent is hardly high enough to instill the confidence needed to make critical business decisions based on the results.

Unfortunately, this type of sampling is prevalent in the online research world. This is partly because those executing the studies are not aware of the bias introduced by this method, or lack the technical skills to obtain a random sample. This book removes both of these excuses for its readers. Still, many companies opt for this method of sampling because it is their belief that users will become angered and alienated if their experience is interrupted with a request to participate in a study. This is simply not true. We've conducted hundreds of online studies across a vast array of sites. Even though we provide a clear means of contacting us, never have we received negative responses from more than .1% of those asked to participate. That means that fewer than 1 in 1,000 have been angered enough to click on an email link to tell us that they were annoyed. We do, however, receive plenty of positive feedback from dedicated and first-time users of sites, thanking us for the opportunity to provide their input and help improve the site for other users like them.

We hope we have dissuaded you from ever sampling via a link or advertising banner. However, we should mention a couple of situations in which doing so might prove the most effective method of sampling. Random sampling online requires that you have the ability to implement JavaScript or server-side code on a site. This means you'll probably only be able to collect a random sample on your own site or the site of a close business partner. If the population you're attempting to sample is not at your site, or you have no site to sample from, then soliciting respondents through a Web advertising banner may be a consideration. Keep in mind, however, that in addition to concerns about data reliability, this may not be a cost-effective option. The percentage of users who click on banners is typically around one or two percent and less for boring banners touting surveys. Therefore, you'll need to serve 100 banners to collect one survey response, and that's assuming (incorrectly) that each user who clicks on the banner fills out a complete survey. More likely, you'll end up serving as many as 40,000 to 100,000 banners to collect a measly 100 responses to your survey. If your study requires respondents with specific characteristics or behaviors, like students or online investors, then the number of banners can skyrocket—perhaps as high as a million or more. According to the most recent Online Advertising Report conducted by AdKnowledge, the average cost of serving a million banners is approximately $33,000. Cost aside, the response rate of .25% to .1% makes the potential impact of nonresponse bias loom large.

Quota sampling is a technique for sampling that strives to obtain predetermined quantities of respondents who have specific characteristics. It is typically employed to develop samples that mirror known proportions of specific characteristics in the population. Recall our example investment company that used reliable secondary research to determine what percentage of heavy online investors to include in its sample.

Quota sampling is also employed in business-to-business applications where the 20–80 rule may apply. When 20% of the population accounts for 80% of sales, quotas are designed to ensure the sample includes a representative base of these disproportionately valuable customers.

Snowball or referral sampling is used when the population being researched is difficult to reach or exists in very small numbers. The method relies on finding one respondent who fits the profile for the research, interviewing that person, and asking the person to provide other potential respondents who fit the profile. These potential respondents are contacted, asked to participate in the study, and in turn, asked to provide other qualified potential respondents. This technique, which is seldom used for quantitative research, is best suited for business-to-business studies that attempt to interview users of a specific product or service for which a customer list either does not exist or is not available for competitive reasons.

THE CONSUMER PANEL

Panels of consumers are designed to combine the projectability of the random sample with the efficiency of the convenience sample. As we have discussed, creating random samples of customers with specific characteristics can be a very costly proposition. If the characteristic you're sampling for exists in only 5% of the population, you'll need to contact 20 people randomly for every interview you conduct. If this is too expensive, the other option is to use a non-probability sample. Unfortunately, these convenience samples cannot be reliably projected to the larger population.

To address these issues, many marketing research companies have established panels of consumers who agree to participate in future research. Panelists are initially contacted randomly and asked to take a qualifier survey. This survey gathers a number of metrics to determine the suitability of the respondents for the panel. If they qualify, they are then asked to be part of a panel. If they agree, they are given an extensive study covering a variety of demographics, psychographics, and consumer behaviors. These respondents, along with their customer characteristics, are stowed away in a database until a research project comes along. When a client approaches the company with the goal of researching a specific population, the company can simply pull from the panel a random sample of respondents who match the needs of the study.

Because these panels allow for representative research to be conducted cost-effectively, they are very popular with marketing researchers. For a variety of reasons, panels are especially popular online.

Reliable Access to Populations: While Internet penetration is growing rapidly, still only half of U.S. households have Internet access, and far fewer use the Web regularly enough to be of much assistance in researching online topics. For instance, the number of calls required to collect a nationally representative sample of online investors is prohibitively high—perhaps as many as 40 or 50 calls for every qualified respondent. Imagine if the study design further required that the sample not only be comprised of online investors, but also those who have used three or more online trading services. The number of calls required might rise from 50 to 500 per qualified respondent. Online panels allow researchers to interview difficult-to-find populations, without sacrificing data validity by resorting to nonprobability samples.

Tracking and Behavioral Panels: Another prominent use of online panels is for behavioral and tracking studies. One of the most pressing issues for online businesses is understanding how frequently users are visiting different sites. Individual sites can certainly analyze their own Web server logs to determine these numbers, but knowing that their traffic has increased by 15% over the previous month does little to help a company understand how it is performing relative to competitors or the online industry as a whole. A 15% increase in site traffic could simply be the result of a 25% increase in the number of users with Internet access. In that case, the 15% increase would actually indicate an overall loss of market share.

To address this issue, research companies have developed panels of users who, in addition to taking an in-depth initial study, also agree to install software on their computers that tracks their Web usage—a sort of frequent shopper card for your computer. This information is periodically uploaded to a central database maintained by the research company. Clients of the research company can then use a Web-based tool to access the database and slice and dice the information.

This is an extremely valuable service for marketers, because it not only tells them how many users are at their sites versus their competitors', but the information can be interpreted to understand what types of customers (in terms of demographics, psychographics, etc.) each site is attracting.

Furthermore, these panels facilitate longitudinal research. Clients can use these panels to understand changes in their products or marketplace. Obviously, the ability to determine, for instance, that a major competitor has experienced a 20% increase in traffic, the majority of whom are males between 18 and 25, will go a long way toward helping to identify the reason behind the erosion of the same customer base at your site.

While commercially available online tracking panels can certainly be a marketer's best friend, sadly, only the largest online brands are in a position to benefit from them. Because the number of panelists being tracked is limited, only sites with the most traffic show up on the proverbial radar. Even in a very large online panel of 100,000 users, a major site with 100,000 regular unique visitors would be used by less than .1% of the sample. Smaller sites would disappear entirely, or not have large enough samples sizes to be reliably evaluated longitudinally in terms of audience composition.

Three of the best-known behavioral and tracking services are:

- *MediaMetrix* (*www.mediametrix.com*): This company uses highly representative RDD recruitment methodology to obtain panelists, then uses tracking software to monitor their Web usage.
- *Net Ratings* (*www.netratings.com*): This service is run by the folks at Nielsen, same company that monitors TV viewership.
- *PC Data Online* (*www.pcdataonline.com*): This company, which traditionally tracked computer hardware purchases, now also tracks the usage of more than 120,000 Web users.

Issues to Consider When Using Panel-Based Samples

Whether panels are used to conduct ad hoc research or leveraged to create a behavioral tracking product, there are a number of issues to weigh when evaluating which consumer panel is right for you.

Panels are not inexpensive. The costs associated with recruiting, maintaining, and surveying a panel are significant. Expect to pay in excess of $10,000 for the privilege of accessing a sample for an ad hoc research project, and more still to develop and conduct the study itself.

Good panels are built by large companies. Due to high panel development costs, nearly all panels worth using are owned and operated by large market research firms. Sometimes, dealing with large marketing research firms can be a trying experience, especially for smaller companies that frequently do not receive the same level of service as larger, and potentially more lucrative, clients.

Not all panels are created equal. A good panel needs a sizable sampling of respondents to reflect the entire group that it is attempting to represent. So a nationally representative panel (what most panels purport to be) should have the same relative share of men, women, students, users of search engines, online shoppers, and sports enthusiasts as would be found if the study were conducted independently via random digit dial methods.

Even though a panel may appear nationally representative, mirroring the population in terms of characteristics and behaviors, the similarities may be only skin-deep. The manner in which consumers are contacted, solicited, and enrolled in the panel can also affect its quality. For example, some research companies solicit panelists via nonprobability methods such as Web banners and other marketing-type approaches. As we have discussed, response rates to banner solicitations hover somewhere around one percent, so this "nationally representative" panel actually consists of the one percent of Web users who clicked on a banner with the sole purpose of becoming part of a panel!

RDD phone solicitation is the ideal method of recruiting panelists. Unfortunately, the multiple steps required to empanel Web users often result in massive levels of attrition. It is not uncommon for fewer than 5% of respondents who are called and asked to participate in a panel to actually fill out the Web-based questionnaire and become part of the panel. Knowledge of this unacceptable level of nonresponse bias might destroy our confidence in an otherwise apparently nationally representative Web panel.

Before investing in the use of a panel, ask yourself these questions:

1. How was the sample collected?
2. What was the overall response rate?
3. What measures have been taken to ensure that the panel proportions accurately reflect the actual population?

When selecting a panel to use, keep in mind your level of tolerance for error in the data. Extremely rigorous panels also tend to come with extremely high price tags. Conversely, less rigorous panels can be quite a deal, even though their data may be no better than that of a convenience sample and not projectable to the marketplace at large. Depending on your specific needs, budget, and the questions you're attempting to answer, each can be a valuable source of respondents.

Panels to Consider

- Greenfield Interactive (*www.greenfield.com*): This is an example of a panel built from less rigorous recruitment practices. Greenfield collects panelists via Web banners and other nonprobability methods. However, the size, diversity, and cost-effectiveness of this panel makes it well-suited for certain types of research projects.

- Intelliquest (*www.intelliquest.com*): Intelliquest maintains the largest technology panel in the research industry. While the panel is not nationally representative, the company offers to weight panel data back to U.S. Census data to provide more accurate results.

- Millward Brown (*www.mbinteractive.com*): This leader of branding and online advertising research offers a panel collected via both highly representative phone RDD methods and less rigorous convenience methods such as sitecentric samples.

- NFO (*www.nforesearch.com*): This traditional research company has developed an online consumer panel called Net.source that, while not collected via RDD methods, is balanced back to data collected from an extensive nationally representative study.

- NPD (*www.npd.com*): The NPD Group Inc. maintains a panel that is demographically representative of the Web population.

CHAPTER 6

Data Collection

Data collection is one of the central challenges in any research project. It is the process through which the opinions of customers are collected and categorized, and by which your hypotheses are proven or overturned. There are many methods of collecting data. Traditionally, researchers have conducted interviews in person, via the phone, or through the mail. Online, however, respondent information can be obtained through either email or Web-based questionnaires. Each method has its strengths and weaknesses, and each is more or less suited to specific research applications.

The cost associated with conducting respondent interviews can be substantial, and the implications of poor data collection extreme. Traditionally, the bulk of research costs and imprecision occur in the data collection stage. With online research, however, automation of the collection process can significantly reduce the cost of data collection as well as eliminate human error, which can compromise the data's integrity.

To fully appreciate the power of online interviewing techniques, it is important to have an understanding of traditional methods of data collection. While this book focuses on online research, a knowledge of off-line strategies will prove useful when collecting data online is not advisable or efficient. Therefore, in the first portion of this chapter, we briefly discuss some of the methods, merits, and drawbacks of off-line data collection.

Next, we turn our attention to online data collection. As you'll see, not only is this new medium less expensive and more accurate, but it allows for many exciting new applications of research. As honest researchers, we're obliged inform you of our obvious bias toward collecting data online. We hope this discussion will leave you as excited about conducting online research as we are.

To conclude the chapter, we introduce a few of the commercial products for conducting surveys online. So, let's begin by taking a look at where the market research profession has its roots.

TRADITIONAL METHODS OF DATA COLLECTION

In-Person

Before telephones were ubiquitous in U.S. households, nearly all marketing research was conducted in person, by interviewers who went from door to door surveying consumers in their homes. This is, in fact, where the common marketing research term *field,* used interchangeably with the term *data collection,* originated. While door-to-door interviewing is still the dominant technique in some foreign countries, it has been almost entirely replaced by phone methods in the United States.

One driving force behind the transition to phone surveying is the difficulty of selecting good random samples by going door to door. It is simply not feasible to preselect households across the United States at random, then fly interviewers halfway across the country to conduct a single interview in Podunk, Nowhere, then have them rent a car and drive two hours to The Middle of Nowhere to conduct the next interview. To work around this problem, those who conduct in-person interviews use a sampling method called *stratified sampling* that selects a number of areas at random in which the interviewing will take place. Stratified sampling can still provide reliable results, but it is far more complex to execute and, in the end, still inferior to simple random sampling.

In addition to sampling logistics, the dispersed nature of in-person data collection makes it difficult for researchers to monitor the quality of the interview process. Questionnaires may include awkward portions that are troublesome for the interviewers to administer. Interviewers themselves may not strictly follow overly challenging sampling or screening procedures. In some rare cases, interviewers may even be dishonest and falsify data, by submitting "complete" surveys that were never administered or completing surveys that were terminated early.

Concern for the personal safety of interviewers is another deterrent to conducting in-person interviews in the United States. It is an unfortunate reality that we live in a dangerous society; there are some neighborhoods where it would be irresponsible to send people randomly knocking on doors. The implications associated with this issue do not affect consumer research, which is better conducted via phone or alternate methods of data collection.

In-person interviews are, however, extremely relevant to one of our most important political processes—the U.S. Census. The difficulty of conducting interviews in impoverished neighborhoods causes these populations to be underrepresented in the U.S. Census. This is a major social issue, as the Census is the primary tool used by government agencies to determine allocation of congressional representation and many other resources. The U.S. Census Bureau has long advocated the implementation of rigorous random sampling techniques to help determine and correct for the bias introduced by underrepresenting impoverished communities. Unfortunately, the current Republican majority in Congress has nothing to gain by ensuring the accurate representation of these traditionally Democratic populations. As a result, efforts of the Census Bureau to implement corrective sampling techniques have been blocked aggressively.

Phone

This is currently the most prevalent method of data collection. As we discussed in Chapter 5, sampling via phone is a highly representative means of conducing a study, due to near-ubiquitous phone penetration levels and the ability of random digit dial techniques to contact households with unlisted phone numbers. On the other hand, phone research is slowly becoming impractical, as response rates drop dramatically, and utilizing RDD samples to research populations that are not prevalent in the population becomes prohibitively expensive.

Despite the limitations, we concluded that phone research is still useful for some online applications, such as testing consumer awareness levels of online brands that were advertised on television, determining the level of penetration of Internet use and the composition of the Internet-using population, and recruiting nationally representative Web panels.

Beyond sampling, however, other issues present themselves when we actually attempt to use the phone to conduct interviews. The issues arise from the fact that phone interviews lack any visual component to assist the interviewer in conveying the issues and the respondent in understanding them.

Unlike other interviewing methods whereby respondents are provided either paper or electronic questionnaires to fill out, phone interviews are administered orally. Thus, interviewers must read aloud each question and its corresponding answer choices. Respondents are expected to sit patiently though all this on the other end of the phone, recall all the answer choices, carefully consider the answer, and then respond to the question. Unfortunately, not all respondents have photographic memories, and some quickly become confused and frustrated when asked to recall long lists of answers. This severely limits the length and complexity of the question and answer choices that can be used in phone research. In addition, the interview process can take considerably longer than would be the case with written surveys (online or paper), and that limits the amount of data that can be collected in an interview.

Another limitation of conducting research via the telephone is the inability to show products or visual cues to respondents. To assist in the formulation of opinions, it is sometimes helpful or necessary to provide respondents with physical samples or accurate representations of the product in question. In-person, mail, and online data collection methods all provide means of doing this. Phone research, however, is limited to using descriptions that the interviewer can read to the respondent. In many instances, a simple recitation of product descriptions or concepts is insufficient to engage the imagination of respondents and allow them to provide meaningful responses.

One benefit of phone-based data collection is that it can be conducted from a centralized location that facilitates quality control measures. Processes can be implemented to help ensure that awkward elements in a questionnaire or other oversights by the researcher are identified and dealt with before they introduce major errors into the data. Many of these processes are directed toward limiting the human error introduced by poor interviewing techniques. Most interviewers who conduct large consumer studies are not trained researchers. While study design and analysis may be managed by a skilled researcher, the actual data collection in phone surveys is nearly always outsourced to a third party or a separate department within a research organization. Sometimes (as in the case of a business-to-business study), the interviewers are highly qualified and well trained in administering interviews. But in consumer studies with larger sample sizes, data collection is typically executed using low-paid and poorly trained interviewers. It is not uncommon for these individuals to inadvertently introduce error into the data.

Mail Surveys

Paper-based questionnaires that are sent and returned through the mail make up another common data collection technique. This method eliminates many of the negative issues associated with phone interviews, but it introduces a whole new set of challenges.

A benefit of mail surveys is that they do not require an inter-viewer to find or contact a respondent at home. Mail surveys are therefore effective at reaching respondents who are rarely at home or otherwise difficult to research. Active young adults, for example, are very difficult to find and survey via phone-based methods, but receive and read mail regularly.

Unfortunately, simply reaching a potential respondent is not always enough to convince them to participate in a survey. This is especially true when conducting mail surveys. In-person, phone, and some online methods require potential respondents to actively decline a survey. This additional pressure causes a greater number of people to participate than would otherwise be the case. Mail sur-veys are passive, and easily ignored by potential respondents. Additionally, respondents must take the time and make the effort to mail the survey back. Both issues can result in very low response rates. Response rates for mail surveys vary dramatically, depending on the level of involvement a respondent has with the subject. A survey about Cheeze Whiz sent to randomly selected U.S. house-holds would receive a pathetic response rate. Conversely, a survey about binoculars sent to a sample of bird-watchers would probably be completed and returned by the majority of respondents.

Incentives are often provided in mail surveys to increase the probability that individuals will take the time to complete and return the surveys. The incentives usually differ from those used in other types of research, in which the respondents receive an incen-tive only if they complete the study. In mail surveys, it is common practice to include actual cash with the questionnaire in an attempt to guilt individuals into completing the study. Typical amounts range between $1 and $10; however, some research has been done that indicates that $2 bills are the most effective in terms of a cost-to-response ratio.

Unlike phone surveys, which require respondents to listen to and recall questions, mail surveys allow respondents to carefully consider questions and answer choices. As a result, mail surveys can include more complex questions and answer sets. Paper surveys can be designed and laid out on the page to enable easy scanning and readability. This feature can keep respondents from becoming frustrated or tired and enables the collection of more data than would typically be possible over the phone.

One severe limitation of mail surveys is that the linear and static nature of text does not facilitate the execution of dynamic study designs. It is often helpful in research to customize or skip questions based on a respondent's previous answers. Given the opportunity, for example, we would not interview young adults under 21 about their brand preference for alcoholic beverages. The seamless use of skipping or substitution techniques is quite effective in a phone or interactive survey. Mail surveys, however, have no feedback loop to enable real-time customization of future questions, and require long and often confusing instructions to guide respondents through skips and substitutions.

Mail surveys also tend to require a significant investment of labor. The preparation of the mailing lists, stuffing of envelopes, posting, and mailing usually take a few days for a staff person to complete. Additionally, as we once discovered, the process of obtaining a thousand $2 bills from the local bank can cause the bank teller a great deal of distress (and delay your study another day or two).

Getting the questionnaires to respondents is only half the battle. Receiving and processing the surveys once (and if) they're returned can be a monumental and monotonous task. In most cases, the paper surveys need to be converted into digital format. This is usually accomplished by laboriously keying surveys, one by one, into a spreadsheet program like Excel or another specialized analysis package. Some packages, such as Inquisite (discussed later in this chapter), support optical character recognition (OCR) and eliminate the need to key in survey data. In any case, even OCR surveys require additional time for scanning and processing. Depending on the size of the study and the degree of automation, this process can add a significant amount of time and cost to a mail-based research project.

ONLINE METHODS OF DATA COLLECTION

Now that we're familiar with the major types of off-line data collection and the issues associated with each one, we turn our attention to online data collection, the method that is so well-suited to marketing research.

Online data collection can occur either through email or over the Web; but only Web-based interviewing truly leverages the power of the interactive medium. Using email to conduct interviews is analogous to conducting paper-based mail surveys, but without the ability to design the questionnaire to be easily scannable. The only reason we can think of to conduct a survey via email is if the population you're surveying has access to email but not to the Web. An instance of this might be a job satisfaction survey at a company that provides their employees interoffice email, but not Web access (a medieval practice that we hope the study results would suggest ending). Though some might argue that an email-based survey eliminates an additional step associated with a Web survey (opening a browser and going to the survey's Web address), we contend that the less user-friendly experience of completing an email survey will discourage more respondents than it saves.

Even if the sample must be contacted via email (as opposed to random-intercept sampling, for example), we hold that a survey itself is more easily and better conducted via the Web. This is accomplished by including a URL link to a Web-based survey in an email solicitation. Nearly all email clients treat URLs as hyperlinks, so users can simply click on them to automatically launch the Web browser and the survey. Otherwise, users can copy and paste the URL into a browser location window. Either way, interviewing Web-enabled consumers via email is a waste of time for both you and your respondents.

Online research that is conducted via the Web combines the strength of mail surveys with the dynamic nature of a phone survey. Like mail surveys, online studies allow respondents the ability to carefully consider well-designed questions without the need to recall all the answer choices from memory. Like phone surveys, however, the interactive nature of online surveys provides the ability to customize questions and answer choices based on a respondent's previous answers.

For instance, a survey for an auto manufacturer's Web site might begin by asking respondents if they were visiting the site to a) Research a car they were considering buying, or b) Find services for a car they already own. An online survey can fully leverage the value of each respondent by branching off distinct segments of users and obtaining different information on each one. It would not be relevant for us to ask current owners about the types of models or competitive brands they were considering, or about the desirability of purchase decision enabling tools like virtual 3D models or pricing information. Similarly, it would be inappropriate to survey nonowners about their current usage of post-purchase online services such as maintenance reminders or online repair manuals.

The Web is a rich multimedia environment and, as such, allows the inclusion of pictures, sounds, video, and any other imaginable descriptive content you may wish. Studies about packaging design, for instance, could have respondents rank order images of different package designs. Even more effective might be to use an animation tool like Macromedia's Flash to create 3D replicas of the different packaging designs for respondents to rate.

Traditionally, obtaining feedback on products or prototypes means incurring the often prohibitive expense of creating, producing, and distributing physical examples to respondents. Often, this severely limited the number of different product executions to be tested. Online, however, a variety of prototypes can be created and presented to consumers for comparatively little expense. These prototypes might be for online products, such as Web site mockups, or for off-line products simulated in the online environment via photos, computer animation, story boards, and so on.

Beyond providing an easy way to of depict products for respondents, online data collection greatly simplifies the implementation of powerful research methodologies. Experimental research designs are an excellent example. In these studies, a representative sample is randomly shown one of two potential Web interface designs, then asked to rate the designs on a variety of attributes (e.g., perceptions of speed, hip-ness, usage intent, etc.) that the design attempts to optimize. The ratings of the tested interface can then be compared to determine the relevant differences between the two Web site designs. One design, for instance, may rate higher for speed and the other for hip-ness.

Experimental designs like the one described are extremely powerful research techniques that allow for precise measurements by holding all other variables constant. These designs are often used in medical research to compare the effects of a drug in one test population against a control group that is given a placebo. In later chapters that focus on specific applications of online marketing research, we present an extensive discussion of the use of experiential designs to aid online product development, advertising and branding effectiveness, and other common issues faced by Web sites and marketers.

The type and complexity of study designs that can be implemented online are limited only by the researcher's imagination and programming skills. The proliferation of online interviewing techniques has enabled the commercial application of many powerful methodologies that, due to their complexity, were previously limited to the academic realm. One example is adaptive conjoint analysis, a research technique in which respondents trade off different product or service attributes against each other to arrive at the ideal feature set for a specific product.

Active Research, Inc. has leveraged conjoint analysis along with a variety of other research techniques to help consumers determine which brands and models of products are most likely to suit their needs. The company has built an interesting product called Active Buyers Guide (*www.activebuyersguide.com/*), which applies these techniques to assist consumers in the selection of

FIGURE 6.1: Experimental design evaluating two possible Web interfaces

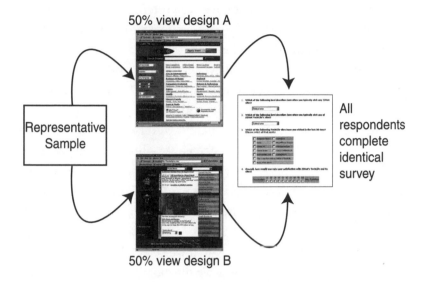

50% view design A

Representative Sample

All respondents complete identical survey

50% view design B

consumer goods like computers, sporting equipment, and even food and drink.

Using interactive research methodologies to recommend products to consumers has appeal beyond the satisfaction of matching people with products they're likely to enjoy. The real power and profit of online product decision enablers is that once a decision has been made, users can immediately purchase the product (in many cases cheaply) directly from the manufacturer. Decision-enabling companies can strike deals with manufacturers to receive a referral fee or percentage of the purchase price. In addition, the process by which consumers go about determining their best product fit yields an enormous amount of knowledge about factors driving the decision-making process, which can then be sold to manufacturers and marketers within that product category.

Eventually, decision-enabling sites will implement more advanced techniques, like neural networking software. This software uses information not only about your preferences, but also about your satisfaction with past recommendations, to vastly improve its ability to suggest products and services you'll enjoy. Furthermore, neural nets combine your preferences and past experience with those of others like you, and so provide you with the ability to leverage the trial and error of others.

Given these increasingly powerful methods of recommending products and services to consumers, it is not difficult to imagine an online economy that consists entirely of reliable third-party purchase decision sites and product manufacturers. This book is not a futurist text, but what's an Internet book without a few general, sweeping statements about new economic paradigms? Obviously, the convergence of interactive interview techniques, e-commerce, and database technology will dramatically change the way we shop for and purchase goods. What is not so obvious is how that convergence will affect the ways in which we select the movies we see, the books we read, the restaurants we dine at, and many of the other decisions we make every day.

Beyond enabling diverse, dynamic, and descriptive study designs, online research offers three other key attributes that you'll love: It's cheap, quick, and easy.

It's Cheap: Unlike phone and in-person data collection techniques, the actual process of collecting interviews online is completely automated. Online questionnaires are administered through HTML pages that are controlled by a back-end script (manually written or generated by a survey package). When the researcher has finalized the questionnaire, it is programmed either into a commercially available survey package or by hand into a series of HTML form pages (discussed in Chapter 7). Next, a survey package or a programmer converts this into an automated script to run on a Web server, guiding respondents through the survey process.

The automation alleviates the incremental cost associated with paying interviewers to conduct each survey individually. If you consider that phone interviewers earn at least $7 an hour, and can conduct approximately 5 interviews per hour, this translates to $1.40 per interview in labor alone. Then, add on the cost of telephone centers, telephone bills, and the administrative support necessary to keep the process running.

By contrast, nearly all of the costs of conducting online research studies are incurred before the first respondent is interviewed. This near-elimination of incremental costs allows (and encourages) the collection of larger sample sizes than would be feasible using phone or in-person techniques. As we discussed in Chapter 5, sample size directly affects the reliability of the data and the depth of analysis that can be conducted. Off-line, collecting data is a constant source of hand-wringing, compromise, and complex statistical processes to deal with paltry sample sizes. Online, it is a simple matter of determining the ideal sample size, padding it a bit for good measure, turning the study on, and watching the responses roll in! It is common to conduct studies with samples of 2,000 or more users randomly sampled from a Web site's population. We've collected samples of more than 20,000 for a few complex study designs—a number unimaginable in traditional research.

In addition to the cost savings realized during a single study, another appealing aspect of online research is the reduced cost of conducting multiple fields of the same study, or even the implementation of a tracking study. Thus, longitudinal techniques for evaluating business success that were once affordable only for the largest of brands are brought within reach of the smallest online venture.

It's Quick: Another advantage to automated interview processes is that they enable quick turnaround times. Typically, the longest phase of a research project is the data collection phase, often taking upward of two weeks to complete off-line. (That's assuming, of course, that you don't have to wait out a backlog of other studies currently taking up the resources of the phone center.)

The number of interviews that can be collected off-line over a certain period of time is limited; but computers can collect tens of thousands of interviews each day.

The timeline for conducting traditional research is added to by the necessary back and forth between the researcher and the data collection agency—often a different organization specializing strictly in field work. This lag time between needing an answer and actually *getting* the answer limits the ability of research to be leveraged spontaneously to address pressing business questions that arise unexpectedly. Therefore, most companies use research only to assist in the decision-making process for long-term projects. Online, however, the turnaround time for simple studies, from conception to actionable findings, can be as short as a single day.

The affordability and speed with which online research can be conducted enables marketing research techniques to be applied to an entire new range of extremely time-sensitive business problems. This enables a new data-driven and customer-centric approach to conducting business online, an approach we describe in Part II.

It's Easy: While off-line techniques may require teams of people, online projects can be conducted end-to-end by a single person. Beyond the teams of people needed to administer phone studies or mail out questionnaires, the work off-line does not end there. The data still needs to be processed and input into a data analysis package. This can be an expensive and excruciatingly monotonous task. As we discussed with mail surveys, Paper surveys must be opened by hand and, often, manually keyed into a computer. This task is typically conducted by poorly paid individuals who have little or no interest in the accuracy of the study results. Unless rigid quality control methods are implemented, the data can be riddled with inaccuracies.

Many automated processes have been designed to reduce the work associated with inputting, scanning, coding, cleaning, and checking the data. Few have eliminated this process altogether; those that have are extremely costly and therefore possessed only by professional research companies. Online, however, survey data is always in electronic format. This greatly reduces the work, cost, and time involved in arriving at relevant results, because data from online studies can easily be converted for use in an analysis package. The automated script that runs the Web survey stores answers in a database or text file. The researcher simply turns the survey on and goes to the spa until the target number of respondents is reached. Upon returning, the researcher opens the results file in Excel or another analysis package and begins the analysis—simple as that! Most online surveying packages, in fact, provide built-in analysis tools that provide you with real-time results from your survey. So, instead of going to the spa, you can sit and watch the responses roll in. We personally recommend the spa, however.

ONLINE SURVEYING TOOLS

We hope we've managed to impart to you some of our excitement about online marketing research. Perhaps you're considering conducting a study of your own. Before we move on to cover some of the basics of questionnaire design and provide you with specific methodologies for understanding issues that face online projects, we introduce some of the tools available for conducting Web research. It's important to begin thinking about which tools meet your needs now, because as we continue through the book we'll evaluate the ability of these tools to perform the different tasks and methodologies we introduce.

When we first began conducting online research, the few tools that existed enabled only the most rudimentary of studies—and that's putting it nicely. As a result, we decided to build our own survey system. The process involved obtaining a working knowledge of Perl (a server-side scripting language) and some Unix to interface with the Web server. While the initial stages of this process were quite painful, we ended up with an incredibly flexible online survey package that enabled us to leverage the full power of the Web when creating study designs.

Thankfully, those skills are no longer needed for most studies. The commercial appeal of online research has spurred a number of software companies to create packages and services that allow online research to be conducted by those with minimal (if any) technical know-how. Some have succeeded more than others, and there are a couple that we recommend. We first cover two products that would meet the needs of a beginner or intermediate researcher. For advanced online researchers, we still recommend learning to create and field studies using Perl and Unix. The scope of this text does not permit us to teach Perl or Unix; however, we discuss some excellent resources that will quickly get you up to speed on these topics. Our goal is to provide cost-effective and simple options for conducting basic surveys, along with more expensive approaches for advanced techniques. Each tool or approach covered, therefore, represents a different level of cost, flexibility, and complexity.

Beginner Level

The first tool is SurveyBuilder, an innovative product from Informative Inc.

www.surveybuilder.com

www.informative.com

SurveyBuilder is simple. The primary advantage of this surveying tool is its accessibility for beginning marketing researchers. It requires no specific technical skills to set up or execute. This is because SurveyBuilder is a *hosted* solution, meaning that the survey itself is hosted on a third-party Web server. This eliminates a great deal of the underlying effort of setting up and maintaining a Web server, or installing application software to collect and process responses. In addition to hosting the survey, the processes of sampling, authoring, and analyzing the survey itself are conducted entirely, start to finish, via the Web through relatively straightforward tools.

The researcher who wishes to conduct a survey using this product goes to *www.surveybuilder.com,* establishes a user account, and clicks on "new survey" to begin creating the study. The process is divided into five parts:

1. Survey setup
2. Questionnaire design
3. Testing
4. Study field
5. Analysis

Survey Setup: Informative has greatly reduced the effort and technical know-how required to set up a survey. The process begins with a series of wizard-style Web pages that ask the researcher a variety of questions to help determine when the survey will be conducted, what incentive will be used, the type of sampling to be employed, the number of respondents to be surveyed, and so on. SurveyBuilder allows you either to conduct your own sampling by providing a URL to direct respondents to; or, more interestingly, to use the information gathered during the setup stage to create a customized sampling script. The script is very similar to the JavaScript sampling scripts in our discussion of random sampling techniques. The JavaScript itself, however, resides on the SurveyBuilder server and is included virtually[1] on the tested page, thus simplifying the sampling process even further. SurveyBuilder's approach to obtaining reliable random samples of your Web site is one of the most appealing and innovative aspects of the product.

Questionnaire Design: After competing the setup phase, you'll proceed to a Web-based questionnaire design application. You begin by electing to create a survey from scratch or to edit one of SurveyBuilder's prewritten studies. The prewritten questionnaires

---

[1]A Web-serving technique whereby the client's browser receives the JavaScript source code from a different server.

FIGURE 6.2: SurveyBuilder's innovative setup wizard

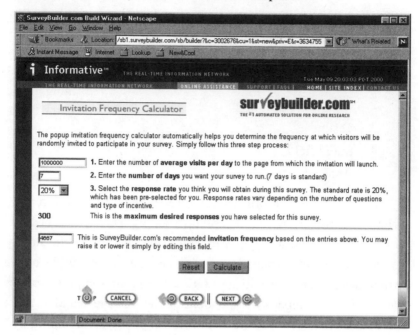

cover a variety of areas, from basic demographics to customer satisfaction with content or product offerings. Additionally, there are a
number of question sets dealing with consumption habits of specific
consumer categories, such as automotive, travel, or finance. These
can be especially helpful to the beginning researcher who may be
unfamiliar with the types of questions typically asked when
researching these areas.

The survey design process walks you through defining a number of elements such as the background color, font type, and head-
er images. By using template designs provided by SurveyBuilder or
by linking to external images, you should be able to create a survey
design that will reflect the look and feel of your Web site. After
these initial steps, SurveyBuilder provides an intuitive interface for
building and editing the actual questionnaire. Question types are
selected from lists and then customized to meet your specific needs.
SurveyBuilder provides you with access to most of the common
types of questions (e.g., select a single answer, select multiple

answers, etc.) used in marketing research. We discuss question types in detail in Chapter 7 on questionnaire design. While editing the question text and answer choices in SurveyBuilder is relatively straightforward, the Web is not ideally suited to editing content. You'll quickly become frustrated waiting for changes to be submitted to the server and for the page to reload, confirming those changes. Furthermore, depending on your caffeine intake, the occasional Net outage can leave you twiddling your thumbs or pulling your hair out.

Testing: Before long, your efforts will result in a completed questionnaire that can be previewed on a Web browser. To thoroughly test the survey and the data collection systems, however, you'll need to contact someone at Informative to enable the survey in testing mode. We consider this requirement a major drawback to this product; as we'll see, you'll need to call the folks at Informative to discuss other aspects of the project as well. In the testing mode, the study can be distributed throughout your organization for review and approval by all key staff involved in the project. Additionally, the study can be submitted multiple times to create a sample data set. Armed with this data sct, you can explore the analysis capabilities of SurveyBuilder, and ensure that your analysis plan (which, of course, you'll have carefully developcd) can be executed within the confines of the tools provided by the program.

Study Field: Once the questionnaire is approved by the primary decision makers involved in the project, and you're convinced that the structure will allow for relevant and actionable analysis, another call to the SurveyBuilder staff clears the database of test results. Now the survey is ready to receive actual respondents. This process is started either by including the sampling script on the tested Web page, or by inviting respondents to participate in the study via other means, such as email. During the field of the study, you can visit the SurveyBuilder site to check on the progress of the survey and to view preliminary results (also called *marginal results*). SurveyBuilder continues to interview respondents until the

desired sample size is reached. At this point, the folks at
Informative will notify you, via email, that the survey is complete
and that the JavaScript can be removed from the tested page.

Analysis: With the data collection process complete, you can
now perform basic analysis on the data using Web-based tools provided by SurveyBuilder. These tools allow for the review of frequency data (e.g., 40% of the sample is malc) and the calculation
of bivariate cross-tabs (e.g., 40% of men have college degrees versus 50% of women). Tools are also provided for creating basic
graphs and charts of the frequency data. To conduct any further
analysis on the data, you'll need to download the raw data to Excel
or another statistics package.

Limitations of SurveyBuilder

More Expensive: Unlike most survey tools whose costs are a
factor of the software purchase price, SurveyBuilder charges by
project. The cost of a project is based on the number of respondents
to be surveyed. We consider this a questionable pricing model,
because the incremental costs of conducting research online are
nearly nonexistent. However, many researchers are likely comfortable with this structure, since it is common in traditional forms of
research.

One problem with this pricing model is that conducting subsequent surveys does not result in increased savings. Every study
conducted through SurveyBuilder is a unique project and is priced
independently. While the ease of executing online research with
SurveyBuilder makes it a good product for conducting a single
study, any researcher who plans to conduct even a few studies a
year would be better off using the intermediate or advanced solutions we outline. While the initial learning curve for the alternate
options may be steeper, the cost savings will be dramatic.

Pricing is another aspect of the SurveyBuilder process that
requires interaction with an Informative employee. Nowhere on its
site does Informative post the pricing for using its product. This is
obviously an annoying factor when attempting to determine the

best product for conducting your online survey. Currently, their pricing is about $2 to $4 dollars per respondent.

Limited Functionality: If the cost of conducting multiple studies through SurveyBuilder is not a deterrent, eventually its lack of flexibility will be. As your study and questionnaire design skills become more advanced, you'll want to conduct research beyond the current capabilities of the SurveyBuilder product.

Limited Question Library: Creating questionnaires in SurveyBuilder consists of selecting either predefined questions or question types from a library. Once selected, the question and answer text can be customized to better suit your needs. While this library does contain most of the common research question types, you'll eventually become frustrated with the inability to create more complicated custom question structures.

As we discussed, one of the powerful aspects of conducting research via the Web is the ability to design intuitive questionnaires that enable the collection of more data from respondents. One method for doing this, as we'll see in Chapter 7, is by consolidating questions together into grids. SurveyBuilder, unfortunately, does not support the custom development of complex grid questions. Without custom grids, many online research approaches will be less feasible, as the questionnaire would span many, many screens and result in tired and frustrated respondents.

Troublesome to Implement Survey Logic: The ability to customize future questions based on respondent's previous answers is an intrinsic aspect of interactive research. Questionnaire *branching* or *skipping* is the first advanced survey tool you'll reach for as your knowledge and ability expand. This functionality is a prerequisite for any respectable online survey package. SurveyBuilder does, in fact, support survey logic, but unfortunately its implementation is rather difficult. To include skips in a survey, you are yet again required to pick up the phone and call a customer support person at SurveyBuilder. In our opinion, this is not an acceptable implementation of skips and branching in a survey package. In reality, you will experiment with different survey logic before settling on the best method, and having to call someone at SurveyBuilder every time you want to make a change will quickly become annoying. For this reason alone, we would recommend against using this product for all but the most basic studies.

No Advanced Survey Designs: As we have discussed, Web-based research designs are limited only by the researcher's imagination. This is not the case if the researcher is using SurveyBuilder. Complicated survey designs, such as experimental designs and conjoint analysis, require extremely flexible surveying tools. Conducting these types of study designs using SurveyBuilder is either impossible or accomplished only through a kludge of awkward workarounds. Some of these advanced research techniques, such as experimental designs, are really quite simple to conduct and provide invaluable ways of understanding customers and their behaviors. In Chapter 12, we cover methods of conducting them (however ungracefully) using any survey package.

Limited Built-In Analysis Capabilities: The frequency and cross-tabular functionality implemented in SurveyBuilder are sufficient for basic data review and analysis. Limited access to the data itself, however, will likely necessitate exporting the data into a specialized data analysis package. In most studies, you will desire to combine a number of variables together to create a new variable for analysis. Single mothers, for instance, is a combined variable made up of the marital status, parental status, and gender of respondents. SurveyBuilder's analysis capabilities, unfortunately, do not allow you to combine questions in this manner. A well-thought-out analysis plan could save a researcher using SurveyBuilder the trouble of exporting data to another analysis package. Those who knew in advance that their analysis would be conducted among single mothers could ask this question specifically (e.g., "Are you a single mother?").

Standardized Surveys: Recently, SurveyBuilder has established an area of its site that offers standardized survey methodologies. As this book goes to press, there is only one such methodology available. Dubbed the Site Exit Survey, this methodology uses a bit of JavaScript trickery to sample users as they exit (as opposed to enter) a site. Respondents, therefore, have the site experience fresh in their minds as they answer the survey. This enables them to provide informed feedback on specific aspects of the site, such as design, navigation, product offerings, and so forth.

This is a powerful methodology in many respects. Most important, however, it allows marketers to understand one of the largest and most elusive populations of Web consumers—those who visit a site once, but never return. Nearly all Web sites experience large levels of attrition from customers who are swayed by marketing to visit a site, but to whom the site does not immediately convey its value proposition. Frustrated or disinterested, these trial customers leave the site, never to return. Conducting research to determine who these consumers are and why they're leaving is critical to the success of any Web site.

SurveyBuilder is planning to release more standardized studies in the future. We strongly recommend that readers check the site (*www.surveybuilder.com*) to see what new, innovative approaches to online research the company has developed.

Intermediate Level

The next tool is Inquisite from Catapult Systems Inc. *(www.inquisite.com)*. We've chosen Inquisite as our intermediate research option because in our opinion it has struck the best balance between price and functionality. It differs from SurveyBuilder in the following ways:

Self-Hosted Solution: Inquisite can function as a hosted survey solution like SurveyBuilder for those who do not have access to or do not wish to run surveys on their own Web server. As with SurveyBuilder, however, the downside of this approach is that you'll pay per respondent surveyed. In addition to a hosted solution, Inquisite can also be purchased outright for use on a private Web server. Currently, Inquisite offers two survey packages. The first, and the one we cover here, is dubbed the Professional edition and retails for $1,500. The second is the Enterprise edition, which retails for $6,000. The Professional edition enables up to four studies running simultaneously and allows for unlimited respondents to each study. With the Enterprise edition, there is no limit to the number of studies you can conduct at one time. Beyond this, there are few differences between the two products. One notable exception is that the Enterprise edition is compliant with a variety of high-end databases like Oracle and Sybase; but for the vast majority of us, this additional functionality does not warrant the price difference.

Inquisite is especially appealing as a self-hosted solution because it can be installed on either a Unix-based or Windows-based Web server. The Inquisite program runs as a CGI (Common Gateway Interface) script, eliminating the need to set up from scratch or even install any new software on a Web server. This means that researchers with a shell account on a Web server can execute online studies without soliciting the assistance of a network administrator. To further simplify the process of creating survey directories and implementing the CGI script, Inquisite provides a handy Web-server configuration utility.

Desktop versus Web-based Application: One of the greatest advantages of Inquisite over SurveyBuilder is that it uses a desktop application (running locally on your machine) to develop surveys. While the Web is certainly a powerful tool, it cannot match the flexibility, functionality, and control of a desktop application. Inquisite's desktop survey development scheme provides you with all the power of a Windows-based operating environment, such as copy and paste, dragging, and many other features that greatly reduce frustration when developing questionnaires. If you want to move a question from one part of the study to another, you can simply use the cut and paste feature, instead of deleting the question and recreating it from scratch in the new location.

Inquisite also uses a WYSIWYG (what you see is what you get) editor to create questionnaires. This allows you to create aesthetically pleasing and intuitively designed online questionnaires without any knowledge of HTML. Questions can easily be set side by side or stacked to maximize screen real estate. Additionally, familiar Windows methods for changing text characteristics, alignment, or including images are employed to greatly ease the creation of questionnaires. The end result is a higher-quality experience for your respondents and better quality data for you.

Most important, however, is the speed and reliability of the desktop application over a Web-based application. You will not require a speedy Internet connection to create questionnaires, nor worry about sporadic Internet access outages jeopardizing a project deadline.

Built-In Logic Support: Beyond design and aesthetics, the desktop application also enables more complex functionality. Inquisite puts the power of creating skip and branching patterns directly in the hands of the researcher. For Web-based studies, Inquisite uses a method of survey logic called page branching. This means that decisions take place when a respondent completes and submits a page of questions—a fairly typical and thoroughly annoying aspect of the Web. Assume that you want to ask respondents first how often they've visited a Web site and then, based on their answers, ask repeat users to rate site content while asking first-timers where they learned of the site. The survey structure to do this requires that the usage question be asked first, on a page 1, along with a number of demographic questions to be asked of all respondents. Once respondents finish these questions, the survey would be submitted to the CGI. Based on a respondent's answer to the usage question, the CGI would display either page 2a, containing the content questions, or page 2b, with the source of awareness question.

Response Validation: Another useful feature of Inquisite is the ability to check the validity of data submitted by respondents or to require that specific questions be answered before the respondent is allowed to proceed to the next page. Generally, it is not advisable to force respondents to change answers to questions, because they become fatigued and often opt to discontinue the survey altogether. In some cases, however, it is necessary to validate or require input.

FIGURE 6.3: Questionnaire branching based on previous answers

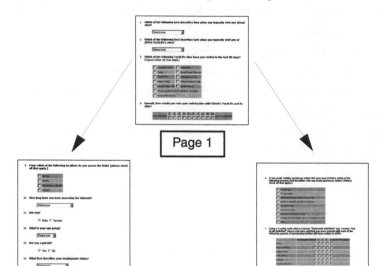

The previous branching question is a good example, because the survey cannot continue if respondents neglect to answer the first question about how often they use the site.

Data Analysis: The built-in data analysis capabilities of Inquisite assist in some of the basic tasks of reviewing frequency tables, creating cross-tabs, and making charts and graphs.

The frequency and cross-tabular functionality in Inquisite is far superior to that available in SurveyBuilder. Inquisite allows you to filter the answers from many disparate questions, effectively creating new variables to be used for cross-tabulation purposes. For example, to investigate single mothers, you would filter the data set by unmarried respondents, then by women, and finally by parents. There is a graphical interface for performing this task that is otherwise typically performed using arduous regular expressions[2] or

[2]An extensive set of special characters that enables the definition of very powerful pattern matches.

complicated if–then statements. This key functionality will go a long way toward easing analysis and avoiding the need to export a data set into a separate analysis package.

Inquisite's most enticing analysis feature is the ability to *filter* data by the date it was collected. This apparently small feature adds a great deal of value to the product, as it enables longitudinal tracking studies to be implemented easily. Using Inquisite, you can continuously sample and interview customers on your Web site. Then, using the date filtering option, you can run monthly, weekly, or even daily profiles of the customers visiting the site. Custom reports can also be run to investigate the before-and-after effects of specific promotional or feature changes.

The graphing functionality of Inquisite will be familiar and useful to most people, because the developers chose to use Microsoft Excel's graphing utility. You can to easily create many common types of charts and graphs (bar, pie, area, column, scatter, etc.). Because the charts are already Microsoft compliant, you can simply use the copy and paste feature to include charts created in Inquisite into Microsoft documents like Word, Excel, and PowerPoint. The downside of Inquisite's graphing implementation is that it does not provide any of the respondent filtering tools necessary for the creation of frequency or cross-tabular reports. This severely limits the usefulness of graphing, since it is unlikely that you will always be charting unfiltered or non-time-series data. In most cases, you will have to create charts by inputting tabular output into another program with graphing capabilities, like Excel.

Limitations of Inquisite: While Inquisite certainly represents a significant improvement over SurveyBuilder, it does share a number of limitations that are, as far as we can tell, problems shared by the majority of survey packages.

Limited Questionnaire Libraries: Inquisite's questionnaire library is an improvement over SurveyBuilder's. This is mostly because it provides a tool to facilitate the easy creation of two-dimensional grid questions. Grids are a necessary part of any advanced survey design, because they enable the collection of a great deal of data by maximizing the use of screen real estate. Unfortunately, Inquisite stopped a step short by not implementing enhanced grids (covered in Chapter 7 on questionnaire design).

No product developer can ever anticipate all the question types and formats you may wish to include in a survey. Even if they could, implementing them in a commercial survey product would be unprofitable and likely make the core product more complicated to use. The question types provided by Inquisite are sufficient to meet the needs of the vast majority of survey projects. However, in those cases where it does not meet the needs, you will have to resort to ungraceful workarounds.

No Dynamic Word Replacement: Often, in addition to page branching, it is necessary to change the question text, but not the answer choices, based on previous questions. An example of this is a competitive positioning study that first asks respondents to select their favorite Web sites and then uses this information to customize subsequent questions about the respondents' usage and attitudes concerning their favorite Web site.

Page branching could be used to accomplish this by creating a unique page for each possible site. This approach might be manageable for four or five competitors, but what if there were 15 to 20 competitors? What if the researcher wanted to add more flexibility by allowing users to type in their favorite Web sites? Yikes! Word substitution is a common survey practice; the lack of it may be one limitation of Inquisite that sends advanced researchers looking for different solutions.

No Advanced Methodologies: Similar to SurveyBuilder, Inquisite is not flexible enough to enable advanced survey designs like conjoint analysis, and experimental designs.

No Random Rotation: Displaying answers to questions or sets of questions themselves in random order is another common surveying technique. We discuss the reasons for this in Chapter 7 on questionnaire design. For now, it is sufficient for you to know that researchers who wish to implement randomization in their studies need to look beyond Inquisite or SurveyBuilder.

No Query Strings: A query string is a method for passing additional information to the survey by appending variables to the end of a URL. Any information preceded by a "?" is passed to the Web server as a variable and can be used to influence the way a survey is presented to a given respondent, or can be passed into the data set as a new variable. For instance, a survey might sample respondents from multiple locations on a site (e.g., the home page, product pages, review pages, etc.). By using a query string, you can send all respondents to the same URL, changing only the query string to pass the sampling location as a variable into the survey:

www.sitecentric.com/client/survey.cgi?homepage

www.sitecentric.com/client/survey.cgi?product

www.sitecentric.com/client/survey.cgi?reviews

Once passed into the data set, these variables can be further leveraged to customize the question text or even the types of questions asked in the survey. Having access to the query string in survey development is necessary for the execution of many advanced study designs. Unfortunately, neither SurveyBuilder or Inquisite provide this functionality.

No Cookies: We defined cookies earlier as unique identifiers used to track customers over time. Cookies can also be used to store information about consumers. Common examples include how often consumers visit a site; what sections of the site they access; or whether they have made a purchase from the site. The ability to assign, read, and update cookies is a valuable tool for researchers to have at their disposal when creating and conducting online marketing research. Without cookies, your ability to conduct studies that require you to field several surveys to the same respondent over a period of time or to link survey data to behavioral data will be severely limited.

Advanced Level

At the advanced level are custom-built surveys using Perl and Unix. The two survey packages we have already covered are likely to meet the needs of most online research projects. They fall far short for those advanced marketing studies that require precise control and necessitate the use of advanced tools like cookies, query strings, or advanced survey logic. To run advanced studies, a researcher could purchase a high-end survey package like Market Tools (*www.mar-kettools.com*), which can cost from $200,000 to $500,000. Market Tools and products like it are geared toward research firms and are quite robust in their functionality. The costs of these products is the limiting factor. In most cases, you would fare better by hiring a third-party research firm to conduct custom research, than to incur the large up-front cost of purchasing a high-end product. Spent wisely, $200,000 buys a lot of quality online research.

Assuming you're not Mr. or Mrs. Money Bags, and you don't want to farm your complex studies out to a third-party vendor, the other option is to invest some time in learning Perl and Unix, and use these skills to field your own surveys. We won't deceive you by saying this is an easy process; but honestly, it's not very difficult.

The reason we suggest Perl and Unix over some other options like ASP (Active Server Pages) or Tickle is that the latter tools require you to set up and manage a Web server on a Windows-based system. The Unix and Perl option, however, can be executed entirely via a $30 Internet account from any major ISP that allows both shell access (Unix) and scripting (Perl). So for $30 a month, you not only get powerful surveying capabilities, you also get an extremely reliable and fast network or Web server to field them from. If that's not enough, you get a free dial-up account to boot. In many cases, for a small additional fee, the ISPs will register and host a special domain name for you to use for your surveys, and will provide you with an email address to help manage respondents.

Once you have a Unix shell account established, you'll need to learn a little about Unix and Perl. In our opinion, the best resource for introductory information is created and maintained by our friends at Wired Digital. They've put together a site called Webmonkey (*www.webmonkey.com*) containing useful and easy-to-understand tutorials on all things Web.

Here are the Webmonkey tutorials we recommend:

Unix

- "Enough Unix for Your Résumé
- Introduction to vi
- Unix Reference Guide

Perl

- CGI Scripts for Fun and Profit
- Intro to Perl for CGI

Webmonkey is a good starting point if you want to understand the basics about Perl and Unix. In addition to tutorials, Webmonkey maintains links to many helpful online resources. In our meandering, we've stumbled across a few online resources ourselves:

Unix

- O'Reilly's listing of Unix books (*unix.oreilly.com/*)
- Unix is a four letter word (*www.linuxave.net/~taylor/4ltr-wrd/*)—An approachable guide to Unix.
- Unix man pages (*www.ntua.gr/cgi-bin/man-cgi*)
- Unix reference desk (*www.ntua.gr/cgi-bin/man-cgi*)

Perl

- CPAN (*www.cpan.org/*)—The acronym says it all: Comprehensive Perl Archive Network.
- O'Reilly's listing of Perl books (*perl.oreilly.com/*)
- Perl.com (www.perl.com)—The Web site for all things Perl.
- Picking Up Perl (*www.ebb.org/PickingUpPerl/*)—A freely redistributable tutorial on Perl.

CHAPTER

7

Questionnaire Design

The ability to design effective questionnaires is an essential skill you'll need to conduct quality marketing research. Because everything flows from the questionnaire, advanced statistical analysis and high-quality sampling techniques will be of limited value if your data has been biased by poorly worded questionnaires or if you obtain a low response rate because the survey was awkward and difficult to complete.

This chapter takes you through the process of writing a good questionnaire, and focuses on the do's and don'ts of constructing that questionnaire for use online.

SURVEY LIMITATIONS

Respondent Fatigue

Unlike behavioral tracking methods or other observatory techniques, a survey requires effort (often considerable) from the sample you hope to measure. Surveys, especially those dealing with a broad range of issues, can easily require 10 to 15 minutes to complete. Surveys may ask respondents to recall past behavior, provide opinions, or offer input on new concepts. As the survey wears on, patience can wear thin—and the attention and consideration given to subsequent questions wanes. In many cases, respondents give up altogether, and you lose their valuable feedback.

The potential for respondent fatigue forces you to achieve a delicate balance between:

- trying to capture all the information you'd love to have, while running the risk of discouraging respondents;

or

- trimming down your line of questioning (perhaps saving some for a later survey) in favor of a better response rate and more considered answers.

The latter option is preferable in most cases, and is not necessarily a bad thing. The need to focus the survey additionally serves to focus the research effort on answering the most critical, action-oriented questions.

Measurement Bias

Measurement bias is the difference between the true state (behavior, perceptions, social status, etc.) we want to measure, and the measurement we obtain through our measurement tool (observation, survey, in-depth interview, etc.) Some techniques, like passive behavioral tracking (e.g., frequent shopper cards), introduce little measurement bias. Little bias is introduced by querying a database, counting the number and types of products purchased, and perhaps developing some trending analysis based on the data. Correctly implemented, Web site usage tracking is also minimally subject to measurement bias: Scan the server logs, run some database queries, and provide an accurate picture of reality.

Surveys, on the other hand, can be subject to significant amounts of measurement bias. This can come from two primary sources. First, the act of asking respondents a question can influence the way they perceive their reality, or at the least, what they'll tell you about it. Survey respondents obviously know that they are being evaluated; this knowledge can influence the way they answer questions, particularly when the questions involve some sort of socially loaded trait. For example, most everyone realizes that exercise is an important part of staying healthy. When asked about their exercise habits, people's natural tendency is to overstate—perhaps not so much to make the researcher feel good about them as to make them feel good about themselves.

Second, the way a question is asked can lead a respondent toward answering in a certain way, somewhat like the way a lawyer might ask a leading question of a witness. Though both are unavoidable limitations of surveys, questionnaire-induced bias can be significantly minimized through close attention to the questionnaire structure, design, and wording.

TYPES OF INFORMATION COLLECTED IN A QUESTIONNAIRE

The information you can collect in a questionnaire can be broken into three major areas:

Classification:	Who you are.
Behavioral:	What you do.
Attitudinal:	What you think.

Classification Data

Classification data encompasses personal attributes like demographics and socioeconomics, and includes familiar survey topics such as:

- age

- gender
- income
- occupation
- education
- company size
- position in organization
- marital status
- parental status
- geographic location (Zip code, state, country, etc.)

Most classification questions are pretty straightforward and easy to answer from the respondent's point of view. Because they focus on simple personal characteristics, they are not generally subject to much questionnaire-induced bias. Assuming they are not trying to mislead with deliberately erroneous responses, a respondent will typically provide accurate classification data.

Though straightforward, some classification questions might be considered sensitive to the respondent. In consumer surveys, for example, respondents may be uncomfortable answering questions about certain personal issues like age, income, net worth, or investment portfolio valuation. In business surveys, data like annual sales, profit levels, or future strategy may be confidential to the company, and the respondent may not be at liberty to disclose such information. In such cases, options should always be provided for respondents to opt out of answering the question, rather than risk respondents' terminating the survey altogether.

There is the possibility that the choice to opt out of a particular question is linked to other key factors. However, this occurrence is not randomly distributed throughout the population. In other words, the nonresponse can skew your perspective. To keep nonresponse to a minimum, we suggest ways to encourage respondent participation to sensitive questions later in the chapter (see Questionnaire Writing Tips).

Behavioral Data

Behavioral data encompasses a broad range of metrics that define your consumer. While classification data involves asking respondents about who they are, behavioral data probes into what consumers do with their lives or, at the least, how they spend their time and money. Here are a few examples of behavioral data:

- leisure activities engaged in
- time spent watching television in the past seven days
- Web sites tried or used on a regular basis
- styles of music listened to in the past six months
- home electronics products currently owned
- number of magazine titles currently subscribed to
- money spent on takeout food in the past month
- exercise habits
- brand of toothpaste currently used

Obviously, behavioral data can cover a wide range of topics; you will find yourself asking behavioral questions frequently in your surveys.

Providing behavioral data in a survey requires more effort on the respondents' behalf than providing classification data, because they'll need to assess their personal habits and past actions in order to answer your questions. The more detailed the required response and the farther into the past you are probing, the more work the respondent is required to do. Both respondent fatigue and simple lapses of memory can limit the level of accuracy of the data you can obtain on a behavioral survey that is extremely detailed or that asks about occurrences far in the past.

Respondents are apt to overstate or understate their answers to behavioral questions. Most people think they should work out more, eat better, or save more money; but life has a way of interfering with these genuine ambitions. When respondents are asked to recall their behaviors, they tend to alter their reporting to more closely mirror their ambitions.

In many ways, this bias is unavoidable. One convenient aspect of it, however, is that everyone tends to fib in the same direction. For example, few people overstate their consumption of junk food. So, while behavioral data obtained in surveys may not be exact, the relative differences between respondents should be consistent. Another aspect to be aware of when phrasing behavioral questions is that longer timelines encourage more bias. We are more likely to admit that we didn't eat well this week than we are to admit that we ate badly all year. The former answer allows me to consider all the elements that lead me to eat poorly (e.g., working late, the poker game, pizza with friends), whereas the latter makes me feel like a loser.

Attitudinal Data

Attitudinal data captures opinions, preferences, or perceptions as opposed to reporting concrete facts. Attitudinal data can include things that are based on personal beliefs, such as positions on social issues, or self-image. It can also encompass a wider range of topics that share a common characteristic: They are driven by the consumers' cognitive and emotional processes. Such issues include:

- brand preferences
- brand perceptions
- advertising response
- future anticipated behavior
- product requirements
- lifestyle and values

Attitudinal data is used to understand subtle issues that drive consumer behavior; it can provide rich insight into the mind-sets of your customers. It is marketing research's attempt to reduce the incredibly complex thought processes of the human brain into concise, easily modeled bits of information. There is a catch, however: It isn't easy to break down the human mind into pie charts and bar graphs. Just ask anyone who's tried to figure out what's going on in the head of a spouse or friend.

Attitudinal questions deal with very subjective material; hence they are typically the most difficult for respondents to answer. By the same token, they are the most vulnerable to questionnaire-induced bias. Unlike the bias associated with behavioral questions, attitudinal bias is introduced in the design of the questionnaire. Even the slightest difference in question wording can have measurable effects on the way a respondent answers the question.

Accurately collecting this type of information is so critical to product development and marketing strategy that most of the R&D in marketing research has gone toward creating sophisticated analytic and questionnaire-writing techniques that are designed to draw out attitudes, and then separate the truth from the artificial impacts of the questionnaire.

QUESTION TYPES

Before we plunge into questionnaire writing, we need to spend some time defining the different types of data gathered in a questionnaire.

The function of a questionnaire is to ask a standardized set of questions of a large number of people to enable you to summarize the population. The questionnaire is a collection of measurement tools, much like a yardstick, bathroom scale, or gas gauge. Each question or combination of questions can be thought of as a distinct measurement tool. In the measurement of physical attributes, there are appropriate and inappropriate tools for the job. A yardstick might be quite effective for determining the length of a piece of wood, but would be useless for measuring its weight. The same principles apply to the questions in a questionnaire.

Open-Ended Questions

The most obvious way to gather data in a survey is to ask a question and then provide respondents a way of writing in their answer, like the box in Figure 7.1.

The advantage of open-ended responses is that they allow for all types of answers by not restricting the respondent to choosing from a predefined list. Similar to qualitative research, open-ended questions can provide very rich, contextual results. Their nature makes these questions ideally suited to investigating the issues that surround a research topic.

But these advantages can become problematic if you want to summarize the data. To be more than an interesting read, this type of data must be converted into some kind of numerical format before you can do anything very useful with it. This process is called *coding*. Depending upon the size of your sample, coding can be merely annoying and time-consuming, or completely excruciating. Large marketing research firms that deal with verbatim data contract out coding work to people who do the work at home and send back the summarized results. If you've ever seen an add offering you the "opportunity to make hundreds, even thousands of dollars per week working out of your house," you may have seen an ad for marketing research coding. Needless to say, if you can avoid free-response data in your survey, you can save yourself a lot of

FIGURE 7.1: Open-ended question

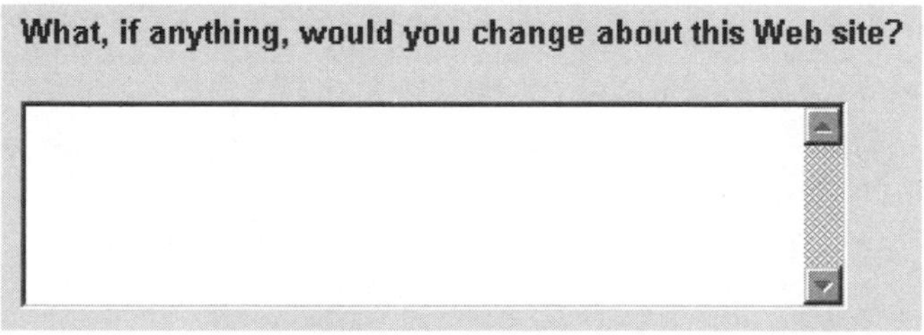

What, if anything, would you change about this Web site?

headaches. A single free-response question that captures any other comments your respondent might have is fine, as long as you'll only be reading through the data for more contextual feedback. For other applications, multiple-choice questions are usually the best option.

Multiple-Choice Questions

Because open-ended questions make analysis time-consuming and difficult, researchers typically use multiple-choice questions to understand how respondents relate to an issue. Multiple-choice questions are especially relevant when researchers understand the major issues surrounding a research topic and are mostly concerned with quantifying the degree to which those issues exist with respondents.

Instead of writing in answers (e.g., "I want to see more news sources"), respondents are asked to select single or multiple items that apply from a list. The list items correspond to precoded numeric values that are stored in your data set. This conversion makes the final data set much smaller (critical when you have thousands of respondents), allows your data processing program to summarize the data more efficiently, and allows advanced statistical procedures to be run.

In hearing this, your first reaction might be, "My customers are people, not numbers!" That's an appropriate reaction. Just as

FIGURE 7.2: Multiple-choice question

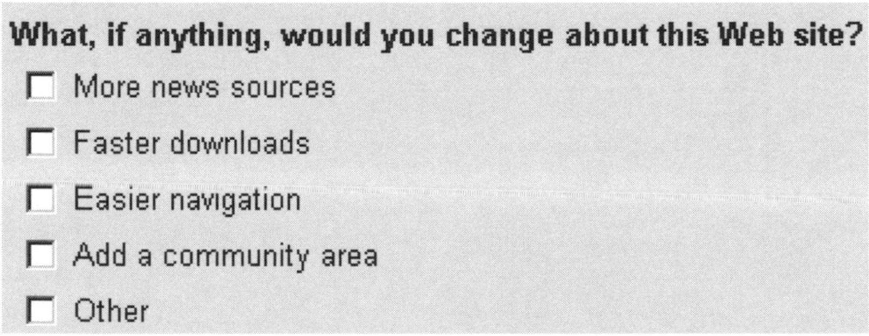

What, if anything, would you change about this Web site?
- ☐ More news sources
- ☐ Faster downloads
- ☐ Easier navigation
- ☐ Add a community area
- ☐ Other

freeze-dried coffee doesn't always taste like the real thing, trying to reduce the nuances of human behavior into a finite list of responses can distort your view of the issues at hand. But, by following the guidelines in the rest of this chapter, you can ensure that the distortion introduced is minimal and will be greatly outweighed by the ability to summarize responses into relevant findings.

DATA TYPES

Measurement theory concerns itself with how real-world ideas and issues convert into tidy, easily graphable sets of data. We won't go into detail here (see *www.measurementdevices.com/mtheory.html* if you find yourself with a few spare hours), but briefly discuss how measurement theory deals with the types of data different survey questions provide.

The answer choices for your multiple-choice questions will use one of several formats, known as *scales*. Different scales result in different data types, and each data type has significant implications for your ability to summarize and analyze that piece of data. Because of these implications, you need to design and write your questionnaire with your intended analysis in mind. Otherwise, you may find out, too late, that a particular analysis (e.g., determining the most receptive demographic for your new product concept), or conclusion (e.g., XYZ.com customers spend an average $127 more on household cleaners than the typical American) is not possible because of the way a particular question was asked in the survey.

Keep in mind how you will be using the data before you choose how to write a particular question. If you want to learn all there is to know (and then some) about scales and statistics, check out the excellent resources at HyperStat (*www.ruf.rice.edu/~lane/hyperstat/intro.html*).

There are four types of scales typically used in a survey: nominal, ordinal, interval, and ratio.

Nominal

Nominal measurements allow you to determine whether respondents possess certain characteristics, but no judgment is made about whether one characteristic is ranked above another, or whether one respondent has more of a particular characteristic than another. Results are pretty black and white as far as data goes. Variables measured on a nominal scale can also be referred to as categorical or qualitative variables.

Permitted Analysis: Nominal data is limited in terms of analysis. Frequency distributions, cross-tabulations, and calculation of the mode (most frequently occurring answer) comprise the whole of it. Means (averages) and medians (the midpoint of the distribution of the range of answers) cannot be calculated on nominal data, if you use these variables correctly. We should point out that

FIGURE 7.3: Nominal Data

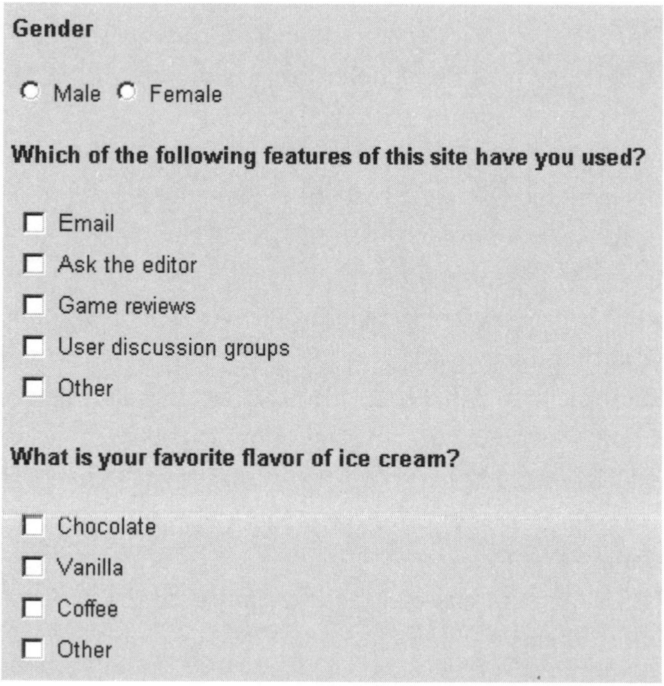

statistical analysis packages don't know one type of data from the next. They have no idea how the question was asked, so they are quite happy to provide a wide array of meaningless statistics about your nominal data. Because the packages don't distinguish data types, it is up to the researcher to decide which types of analysis are appropriate to the data type.

Ordinal

Ordinal data implies a hierarchy in the answer choices, but does not imply a set amount of distance between each choice. For example, a survey might ask users how much of the time they wear a seat belt when in an automobile. The question might ask users to characterize their level of usage as:

Always
Sometimes
Rarely
Never

Because there are four options on the scale, it may be tempting to assume that the distance between each choice is constant, as in this example:

Always   =   100% of the time
Sometimes   =   75 % of the time
Rarely   =   25% of the time
Never   =   0% of the time

The problem is, the respondent might not be making that same assumption! Those who, by their nature, are wary of saying they "always" do anything might choose "sometimes" even though they wear their belts 99% of the time. Likewise, someone who chooses "sometimes" might only wear the belt three or four times a year. Indeed, three or four times a year does qualify as "sometimes." As a result, you cannot (rightly) make any assumptions about the distance between the choices on the scale. All you know is that the order of the choices represents an increase in the level of the attribute measured.

To think of it another way, when you go to the movies, you have the option of purchasing a small, medium, or large popcorn. Aside from eyeballing the bag, you have no idea how much more popcorn you'll be getting by buying a large over a small (or over a medium, for that matter). All you know is that you'll be getting more (and paying more).

Permitted Analysis: Because we cannot quantify the distances between answer choices in the scale, we can only perform limited analysis and summary on this data. As with nominal data, frequency distributions, cross-tabulations, and calculation of the mode (most frequently occurring answer) are the only correctly applied procedures. In practice, the calculation of averages and

FIGURE 7.4: Ordinal data

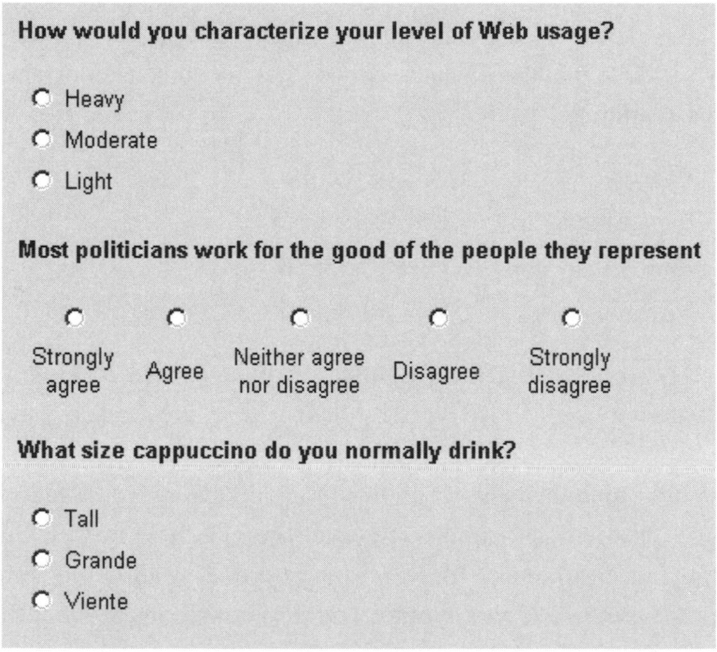

How would you characterize your level of Web usage?

○ Heavy
○ Moderate
○ Light

Most politicians work for the good of the people they represent

○ Strongly agree   ○ Agree   ○ Neither agree nor disagree   ○ Disagree   ○ Strongly disagree

What size cappuccino do you normally drink?

○ Tall
○ Grande
○ Viente

other techniques are applied to ordinal data by making assumptions about the distances between answer choices. Sometimes these assumptions are acceptable; at other times they can be misleading and dangerous. A good rule of thumb is to consider whether another person might interpret the meaning of the scale differently than you did, and if so, by how much. If it seems that there is a lot of room for error, stick to the simplest types of analysis and summary, or rewrite your question to capture a more precise type of data.

Interval

Interval data improves upon ordinal because we explicitly define the distances between answer choices. Using ordinal data, we can only state that one answer choice is greater or less than another. With interval data, we can quantify the size of the difference. A good example of precise interval data would be temperature in degrees Fahrenheit. We can say that the distance between 40 and 60 degrees is the same as the distance between 60 and 80 degrees.

In marketing research, it is common to use interval scales that are noncontinuous in the form of response bands, or ranges of answer choices.

> *How many times in the past month have you shopped at XYZ.com?*
> *None*
> *1–4 times*
> *5–9 times*
> *10–19 times*
> *20 times or more*

The ordinal question about seat belt use could be modified to provide interval data if we state what we mean by each of the answer choices, as in this example:

> *How often do you wear a seat belt when riding in an automobile?*
> *Always (75%–100% of the time)*
> *Sometimes (50%–74 % of the time)*
> *Rarely (25%–49% of the time)*
> *Never (0%–24% of the time)*

To take a more accurate measure, more points can be added to
the scale (e.g, "nearly always", "hardly ever", etc.); or the nature of
the question could be changed to be more data-oriented, as in this
example:

What percentage of the time do you wear a seat belt when riding in
an automobile?
   100%
   99%
   98%
   and so forth ...
   2%
   1%
   0%

Using continuous scales obviously provides very precise data,
assuming respondents can accurately report on their behavior to
that level of detail. In practice, humans are rarely able to achieve
that level of detail. Instead, respondents tend to group their answers
around more manageable chunks. About 10 chunks is the maximum level of detail most people prefer to consider; structure questions to reflect this, as in Figure 7.5.

FIGURE 7.5: Response ranges

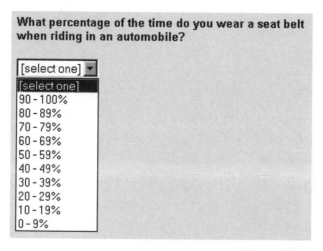

This type of question is familiar to anyone who's ever taken a survey. Those of you who have been paying close attention to the definitions of each type of data might argue that we really don't know how far along the scale each point is from the next, because each point can represent a number of true values. A person who checks 90–100%, for example, could use seat belts 90%, 91%, 92%, 95% … well, you get the idea. How is a question like this one considered to provide interval data?

Technically, it doesn't. But, thanks to a simple assumption, we can treat it as such and get on with the business of conducting research. The assumption we make is that, within a given answer band (e.g., 90–100%), the true values of the population (e.g., 90%, 91%, 92%, etc.) who chose that answer will be evenly distributed throughout the range. In other words, if 100 respondents selected the 90–100% choice, 10 people's true value was 90%, 10 people's was 91%, 10 people's was 92%, and so forth. In most cases, this is a pretty fair assumption to make. In some instances, however, users' responses may cluster toward one end of the range, especially if the answer bands are very wide. A rule of thumb is that the larger the bands, the larger the chance for error. Try to keep your answer bands to a reasonable size and ensure that they reflect any knowledge or hypothesis you have about the distribution of the values among the population.

Here's an example to clarify the issue. Suppose you wanted to gauge the average price paid for airline tickets by the population. You chose to provide these ranges, and received these results:

Range	% Selecting
$1–$99	30
$100–$199	30
$200–$299	20
$300–$399	10
$400–$499	5
$500 or above	5

Calculating an average on this data involves multiplying the percentage for the range by the value of the midpoint of the range. Why? Because we assume that the true values are evenly distributed across the range, we can also assume that the average of all these values is equal to the midpoint of the range. Multiplying the percentages by the midpoint values gives us an average for the question. But is it the correct average?

Consider the $1–$99 range. Assume, again, that 100 people answered the question and that 30 people fell into the $1–$99 range. By calculating an average, we're assuming that one person paid $3.30 for a ticket, another paid $6.60 for a ticket, and so forth. While airline tickets have certainly come down in price, chances are that most were not purchased for much less than $50. More likely, the real average for this range is $75 or $80, not the $50 we are calculating the average from. Again, this problem can be remedied, to some extent, by keeping your ranges small enough so that the effects of nonequal distributions are minimized.

Permitted Analysis: Interval data allows a wide range of analysis and summarization, because we know the amount of change in the measured attribute that is indicated by a change in the answer choice. Calculation of the mean, median, and mode are all possible, as are more advanced correlation techniques and regression models designed to identify linkages between variables or groups of variables.

Ratio

The fourth and final type of data is called ratio data. We're not going to cover this type of data in depth, because for all practical purposes, it is identical to interval data. The only difference between the two data types is that ratio data has an absolute zero point. Remember our initial example, using temperature in degrees Fahrenheit to define interval data. The Fahrenheit scale does not have an absolute zero point (as those who live in cold climates are painfully aware). Therefore, we cannot make the statement that 80 degrees is twice as warm as 40 degrees. Height and weight are good examples of ratio scales, since they each have an absolute zero point. It's quite possible to be twice as tall or weigh half as much as another person.

Permitted Analysis: There is little difference between the types of analysis you'll be able to conduct using ratio or interval data. Averages, correlation, and regression will work with both. If you're considering doing more advanced analysis than that, consult another source to learn about the subtle differences between these two data types.

RATING SCALES

Rating scales are the most popular approach for probing into respondents' thoughts, opinions, and beliefs. All rating scales offer the ability to measure attitudes; but different types of scales involve tradeoffs in terms of the effort required on behalf of respondents, the accuracy possible in measuring the attitude, and the types of analysis you can perform on the data.

Numeric Scales

Numeric scales are what they sound like: The respondent rates the attribute with a number according to a defined range (e.g., 1 to 10). To instill the rating scale with meaning, anchor words or phrases are typically placed at either end of the scale.

Advantages of Numeric Scales

1. *Allow a varying number of answer points for various degrees of granularity in the data.*

If you believe that very small differences in a particular attribute may be significant, you can break up a numeric scale into as many points as you think are necessary. Typically, numeric scales are either 5, 7, or 10 points wide. Some researchers prefer 5 points, because the smaller number of choices makes it easier for

FIGURE 7.6: Numeric Scale

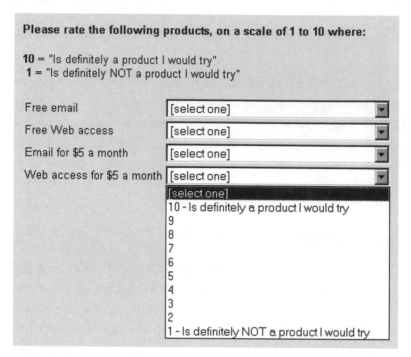

respondents to discriminate and quicker to answer. Others prefer 7 points, to gain a bit more granularity. Still others use a 10-point scale, which provides the most granularity (assuming respondents can discriminate between the choices down to that level) and also facilitates calculation of indexed means. The 10-point scales, like lesser-used 4-, 6-, and 8-point scales, are even-numbered. As a result, there is no middle answer, forcing respondents to lean one way or another. This is a useful strategy to get at the opinions of those who would otherwise straddle the fence.

2. *Avoid loading the answer choices with semantic meaning.*

Most other rating scales associate each point along the scale with a term (e.g., "Agree somewhat"). The perceived meanings of these terms may not be consistent from person to person, and that can introduce measurement bias into the data. Theoretically, numbers mean the same thing to all people, and each point along the scale should be interpreted by the respondent as equating to an equal change in the attribute.

Disadvantages of Numeric Scales

1. *Difficult to complete without visual reference.*

If there is no visual reference (in telephone interviews, for example) a disadvantage of numeric scales is that the lack of ability to see the actual numbers on the scale and visually assess how far apart a 1, for example, is from a 5, respondents can have difficulty accurately scoring the question. Online, however, this is not an issue. When conducting research on the Web, numeric scales work quite well because they are able to be seen and assessed by the respondent, and also take up very little screen real estate in the survey.

Likert Scales

Named after their originator, Likert scales are the "Strongly agree, Agree Somewhat, Neither Agree nor Disagree, etc." scales you've probably encountered if you've ever been surveyed in a phone interview. In a Likert-scaled question, respondents are asked to agree or disagree with a series of statements that address the issues on which the researcher seeks information.

FIGURE 7.7: Likert Scale

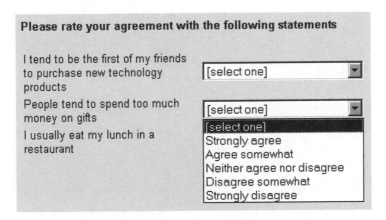

Advantages of Likert Scales

Likert scales have the advantage of grounding each point in the rating to something tangible to the respondent, as opposed to the numeric scales. Because of the word association, Likert scales tend to work better than numeric scales for telephone research, when visual cues are absent. Online, they work well also, having the added advantage of continuously displaying the available answer choices to the respondent, as opposed to having a telephone interviewer repeat them continuously.

Disadvantages of Likert Scales

As mentioned in the discussion of ordinal versus interval data, a disadvantage of the Likert scale is the fact that respondents may not all place the same value on each point in the scale, or the distance between one point and the next. For example, respondents tend to cluster their opinions around the center of the scale (Somewhat agree or disagree, or Neutral) on most issues except the ones they feel very strongly about. In scales with fewer rating points (5-point, for example), there is a reasonable possibility that the increase represented by a jump from 4 to 5 (Somewhat agree to Strongly agree) is significantly more than the jump from 3 to 4 (Neutral to Somewhat agree). As a result, consider the Likert scale more of an ordinal measurement than an interval scale. That said, plenty of analysis is done in marketing research by treating Likert scales as Intervals, assuming that each step along the scale represents an equal change in the attribute measured.

FIGURE 7.8: Semantic differential scale

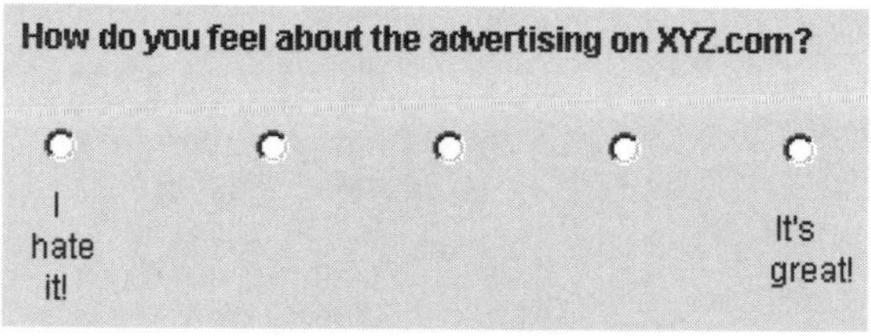

How do you feel about the advertising on XYZ.com?

○   ○   ○   ○   ○

I
hate
it!

It's
great!

Semantic Differential

A variation of the Likert scale opposes two adjectives (or phrases) at either end of the scale. Respondents are asked to choose the adjective most closely representing their feeling on the issue. The scale may be as simple as a 2-point scale, but more often it has several points to choose from.

Other Rating Scales

Ratings scales can be created for almost anything you can conceive of. Here are some common applications:

Customer Satisfaction

Satisfaction with various aspects of your product or service's performance is an important metric that rating scales can provide. Furthermore, by using the same scale over time, improvements (or lack thereof) can be monitored.

FIGURE 7.9: Numeric satisfaction scale

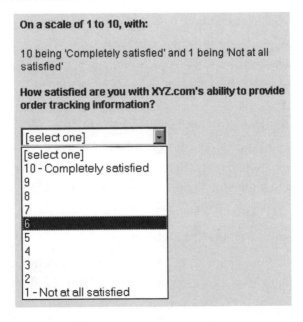

FIGURE 7.10: Verbal satisfaction scale

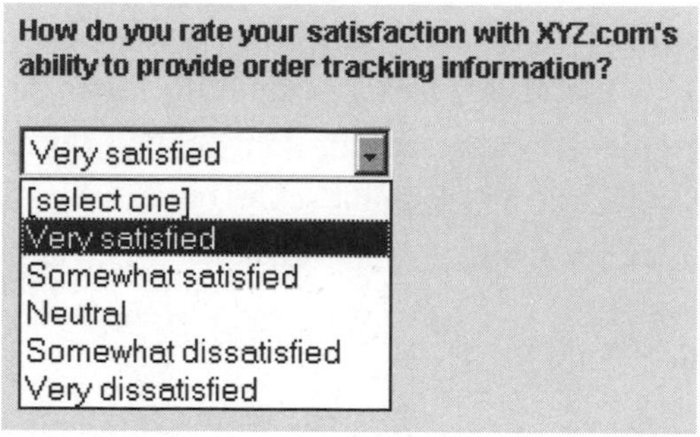

How do you rate your satisfaction with XYZ.com's
ability to provide order tracking information?

| Very satisfied |
| [select one] |
| Very satisfied |
| Somewhat satisfied |
| Neutral |
| Somewhat dissatisfied |
| Very dissatisfied |

FIGURE 7.11: Simple product performance scale

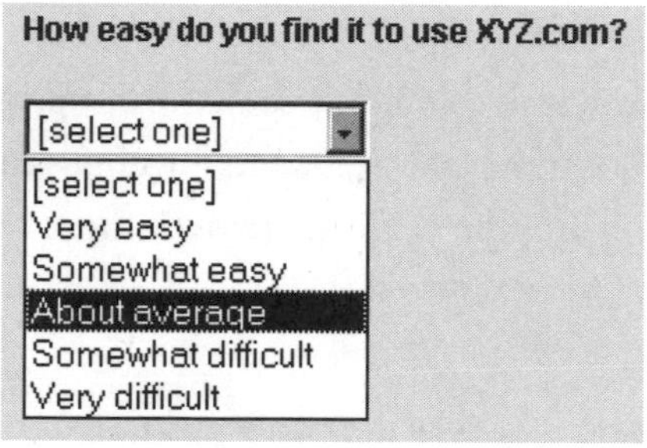

How easy do you find it to use XYZ.com?

| [select one] |
| [select one] |
| Very easy |
| Somewhat easy |
| About average |
| Somewhat difficult |
| Very difficult |

Product Performance

Scales can provide feedback on specific areas of product or
service performance—a key area to focus on when considering
future development work or enhancements. Rather than gauge satisfaction, the scale can probe specifically into the level of performance on an attribute.

Because perceptions of performance often have more relevance in a competitive context (e.g., how your product stacks up
against the competition's), the scale can be modified to provide
competitive context feedback.

Issue or Attribute Importance

Ratings scales are frequently used to determine the importance of issues (for strategic planning work) or the desirability of
specific product attributes (for tactical product development
research).

FIGURE 7.12: Competitive context performance scale

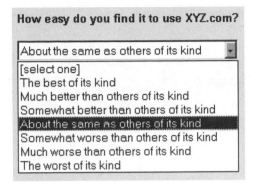

FIGURE 7.13: Issue importance scale

How important are the following issues in your choice of an Internet service provider?		
Customer service	[select one]	▼
Low prices	[select one]	▼
Consistent connection quality	[select one]	
	Absolutely critical	
	Extremely important	
	Very important	
	Important	
	Somewhat important	
	Not very important relative to other considerations	
	Not at all important relative to other considerations	

A fundamental issue with importance ratings is that consumers tend to rate all attributes as extremely or very important. This is problematic, because these types of questions are typically employed to help decision makers develop strategy and allocate limited resources to achieve the most bang for the buck. To compensate, there are several approaches to analysis and question writing that help draw out the most desirable attributes. These methods are covered in detail in Chapters 10 through 14.

Boolean Scales

Boolean scales are simple "Yes or No" or checkbox questions that are used to get feedback quickly on a large number of items. Obviously, only a limited amount of granularity can be obtained with Boolean data (it's either selected or it's not); but it is a very

FIGURE 7.14: Boolean scale

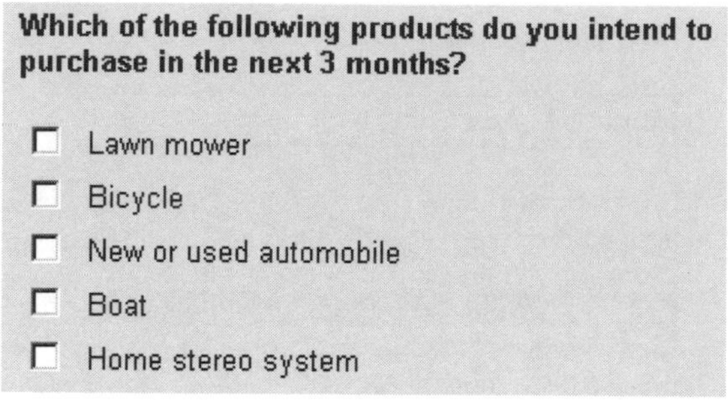

Which of the following products do you intend to purchase in the next 3 months?

☐ Lawn mower
☐ Bicycle
☐ New or used automobile
☐ Boat
☐ Home stereo system

effective way of gathering key data when there is a lot of ground to cover. Boolean scales typically provide data that is nominal in character.

ELEMENTS USED IN CONSTRUCTING AN ONLINE SURVEY

Now let's review the elements used to gather data in online surveys. The designers of Web browsers must have had marketing research in mind when they wrote the specifications for their software. In addition to text and graphical images, browsers provide the ability to embed a number of data collection elements (known as form elements) into a Web page to allow the implementation of any type of commonly used survey question.

Radio Buttons

You've already seen examples of radio buttons in this book, and have no doubt encountered some while surfing the Web. Radio buttons are used when you want respondents to select only one option from a list, commonly known in market research as a "single punch" or "choose one" question. In a radio button question, the variable can take one of an array of values, each value corresponding to the answer choice selected by the respondent.

FIGURE 7.15: Radio button

Pulldown Menus

Another means of asking "choose one" questions is the pulldown menu. You've already seen examples of these throughout this chapter. In a pulldown menu, the answer choices are hidden until the respondent clicks on the menu box. The desired selection can then be highlighted.

Pulldowns are very useful in online surveys because they keep the screen from becoming cluttered with answer choices and make for a less intimidating survey (which can result in higher response rates). The downside to the hidden answer choices is that the respondent has to click on the pulldown menu to access the choices, which could conceivably increase respondent fatigue. If there are a large number of choices (more than 7 or 8), the pulldown menu will prevent all options from appearing on the screen; to minimize order bias (addressed later in this chapter), another answer format may be more appropriate. Despite the drawbacks, pulldown menus are important tools in the construction of visually appealing, manageable surveys.

FIGURE 7.16: Pulldown menu

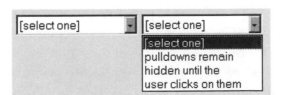

Checkboxes

Checkboxes allow you to ask questions for which the respondent can choose more than one option (known as "multipunch" or "choose many" questions in the marketing research field). In online surveys, each checkbox has its own variable associated with it, and each variable can have one of two values (checked or unchecked). Online, this is the most common implementation of the Boolean scale. Multipunch data is an extremely useful research tool, because it enables respondents to provide rich information about their behaviors and attitudes. In a single multipunch question about investment habits, for instance, a respondents could inform us that they trade securities and mutual funds, but not bonds and options. Because the data type delivered in a multipunch question is nominal in character, the type of data analysis that can be performed on multipunch questions is in some ways quite limited. In other ways, however, these questions enable us to classify groups of consumers based on their behaviors and characteristics. Therefore, they are very useful for segmentation, regression, and clustering analysis.

FIGURE 7.17: Checkbox

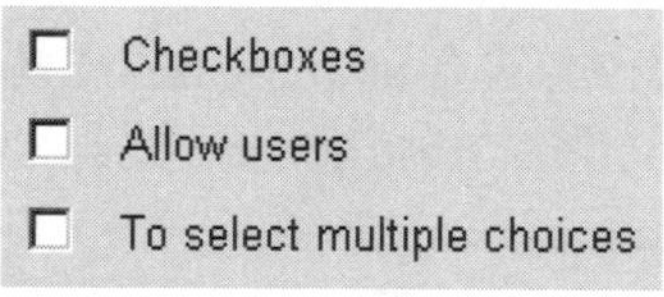

Selection Menus

Another means of allowing respondents to answer a "choose many" question is to use a selection menu. The main advantage of using a selection menu is that the answer choices appear in a box that is scrollable, which allows you to provide a long list of options without creating an enormous (and intimidating) grid of checkboxes. The drawback of using selection menus, and the main reason we don't often employ them, is that they require the use of multiple keys (typically the [CTRL] key) in order to select multiple options that apply. As a result, there is a large chance that less technically

FIGURE 7.18: Selection menu

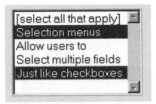

savvy respondents won't be able to answer the question. We've personally observed lower completion rates for this type of question, despite providing explicit instructions.

Text Fields

Text fields are input areas that allow respondents to write in short, one-line responses. They are typically used when including an "Other—please specify" answer option to provide a means of capturing response possibilities that weren't included in the multiple-choice list.

FIGURE 7.19: Text field

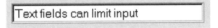

A text field can be set to a specific length and to a maximum number of characters allowed as input. This can be useful when leveraging these fields to collect numeric data like Zip codes or birth dates. However, without data validation at the time the survey is taken (either on the server or locally via JavaScript or another client-side scripting language) to make sure the input is in the correct format, lots of back-end cleaning of the data may be required in order to make use of the input.

Text Boxes

If you seek extended comments from a user, you might use a text box to obtain multiline responses. We often use text boxes as a final question in surveys, to collect any other comments the user might

FIGURE 7.20: Text box

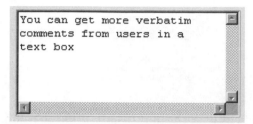

have that were not covered in the survey. Respondents tend to appreciate this wrap-up question, as it represents an opportunity for them to provide feedback pertaining to their personal needs, but not necessarily those of the study.

This type of data is even more difficult to validate or analyze than the single-line text field data, and is typically used in a verbatim format. Including several text box questions is usually superfluous, because respondents tend not to limit their open-ended thoughts to the question at hand, but rather include all their comments in the answer to the first open-ended question they come upon.

Question Grids

A final element of Web surveys is the question grid, or table. A question grid combines the various form elements already described in a two-dimensional grid. The grid allows the researcher to maximize screen real estate and enhance the survey flow when several types of information are desired about the same attribute. For example, the question grid in Figure 7.21 is used to determine brand trial, repeat purchase likelihood, and favorite brand.

Though they can speed up survey taking, grids can be visually intimidating. It is important to use visual cues, such as alternating row colors, to avoid discouraging the respondent. Another drawback to the grid is that some respondents may skip over some of the questions unless data validation techniques (such as alerting respondents if they did not complete part of the grid) are employed. Questions that are broken out into their constituent parts tend to have slightly higher completion rates.

FIGURE 7.21: Question grid

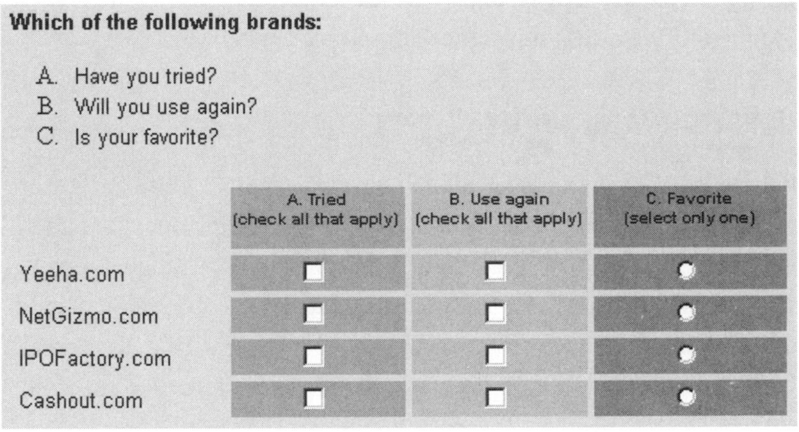

Which of the following brands:

   A. Have you tried?
   B. Will you use again?
   C. Is your favorite?

	A. Tried (check all that apply)	B. Use again (check all that apply)	C. Favorite (select only one)
Yeeha.com	☐	☐	○
NetGizmo.com	☐	☐	○
IPOFactory.com	☐	☐	○
Cashout.com	☐	☐	○

FIGURE 7.22: Enhanced question grid

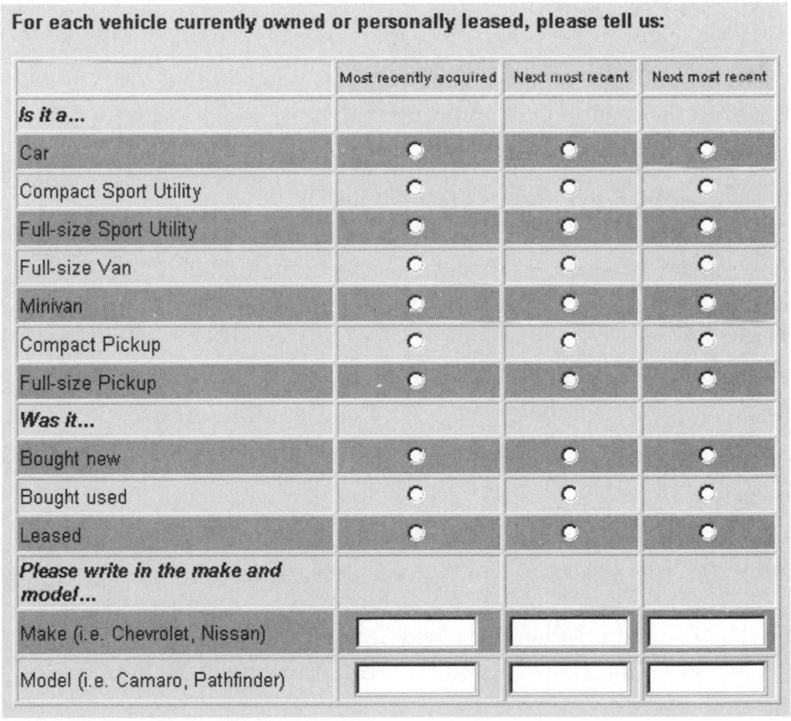

For each vehicle currently owned or personally leased, please tell us:

	Most recently acquired	Next most recent	Next most recent
Is it a...			
Car	○	○	○
Compact Sport Utility	○	○	○
Full-size Sport Utility	○	○	○
Full-size Van	○	○	○
Minivan	○	○	○
Compact Pickup	○	○	○
Full-size Pickup	○	○	○
Was it...			
Bought new	○	○	○
Bought used	○	○	○
Leased	○	○	○
Please write in the make and model...			
Make (i.e. Chevrolet, Nissan)	[ ]	[ ]	[ ]
Model (i.e. Camaro, Pathfinder)	[ ]	[ ]	[ ]

Despite the drawbacks, grids can be an important part of creating a visually appealing page of questions that gather large amounts of data in a minimum amount of time.

QUESTIONNAIRE WRITING TIPS

Online or off, many of the guidelines for writing a good survey are the same. Remember that the overall objective of the questionnaire is to obtain accurate data while minimizing respondent fatigue, increasing completion rates, and keeping respondents involved and interested enough in the survey to provide you with quality data. To this end, here are some tips to help you write better, more effective surveys.

Keep It Short and Simple

As much as we hope they will pay close attention to every nuance of a questionnaire, respondents tend to quickly scan through the question and answer choices. Subtleties are likely to be lost on respondents, so your questions should be as clear and concise as possible. Compound sentences force your respondents to juggle too many ideas in their heads. If there is a critical element to the question that the respondent might miss (Murphy's law applies to surveys too), be sure to highlight that element, either through the use of color, bold type, italics, or all capital letters.

Don't Be Negative

Try to use positive statements (Which of the following brands have you heard of?) rather than negative ones (Which of the following brands haven't you heard of?). You can get the same information, and reduce the risk that the respondent will miss the meaning of the question.

Write for the Lowest Common Denominator

A survey is not the place to impress with artistic writing or esoteric vocabulary. Questions should be written using simple terminology and avoiding technical jargon, unless you are dealing with a very specific population who are sure to understand exactly what you are talking about. By the same token, the use of vernacular or slang should be avoided, unless you are certain that everyone in the population will be able to relate to it. Use a professional tone in your surveys; that will encourage respondents to put the same quality of thought into their responses as you put into the questions.

Say What You Mean

Vague questions are of little value to you, in keeping with the garbage in, garbage out principle. Write your questions with your analysis plan in mind. Subjective terminology, such as "frequently," "often," and "rarely" can, and will be interpreted differently by different respondents. In addition to confused respondents, decision makers will struggle with the meaning of these vague terms when you report them in your analysis. Instead, ground the question in specific examples.

If you are trying to gauge the usage of your competitors' sites, why ask:

"Which of the following sites do you use frequently?"

What does frequently mean to you, or to the respondent? Instead, ask:

"Which of the following sites do you use more than twice a week?"

Now you both have a common understanding of the metric to be provided.

Act Like Switzerland

A good researcher and a good questionnaire should be unbiased. It is all too easy to bias your results by the way you ask a question. Avoid influencing the respondent by refraining from writing questions that imply a correct answer or otherwise push respondents toward answering on one end of a scale or the other.

Biased:	"How much do you love our site?"
Unbiased:	"What is your opinion of our site?"
Biased:	"Company XYZ has one of the highest customer satisfaction ratings in the industry. How satisfied are you with our level of customer service?"
Unbiased:	"How satisfied are you with our level of customer service?"

Provide Respondents an "Out"

Some questions may put respondents in an uncomfortable position, causing them to skip the question or answer dishonestly. For example, issues like exercising, or spending time with your children may alienate respondents who don't feel up to par. To get the best possible data and keep the respondent involved in the questionnaire, approach such issues as follows:

> "There are many reasons why parents can't spend as much time with their children as they'd like to. Work and other responsibilities can sometimes leave too few hours in the day. How much time do you get to spend with your child each week?"[1]

Questions having to do with personal issues, such as age, income, and personal habits and that may be sensitive to some members of the population should include a "Decline to answer" option. It is better to lose data on one question than to alienate respondents and risk losing them from the survey altogether.

Make Answer Choices Exhaustive, Not Exhausting

Nothing frustrates respondents more than not finding the answer choice that corresponds to their situation. A Coke drinker would be annoyed by this question:

[1]If you've been paying attention to the tips, you'll probably notice that we are breaking our earlier law about keeping the question as simple as possible. In this case, we justify spending more time on a longer question rather than risk having respondents give dishonest answers or skip the question.

What is your favorite soft drink?
>Pepsi
>7Up
>Sunkist
>A&W Root Beer

Often, the list of possibilities is too broad to include all choices in the list. When this situation occurs, be sure to provide an "Other" option (and perhaps a text field to capture the respondent's choice) so respondents aren't left feeling that their opinions don't matter. In the analysis stage, pay attention to the share of people who checked "Other" and note their fill-in responses. You may be missing an important category.

Scales that deal with money, time, or consumption levels should have an unbounded choice at the upper end of the scale, as illustrated in these examples:

How much do you spend on cosmetics each month?
>Under $100
>$100–$199
>$200 or more

How many times have you visited Site XYZ?
>This is my first visit
>1–3 visits
>4–6 visits
>7 visits or more

Make Answer Choices Mutually Exclusive

When writing questions involving ranges, don't let the categories overlap. Data can be compromised if the respondent could have more than one legitimate answer. In this example, a respondent who earns $50,000 a year could correctly choose either option 2 or 3. This is an easy mistake to make—double-check your work!

What is your annual pretax income?
>Under $25,000
>$25,000–$50,000
>$50,000–$60,000
>More than $60,000

The ranges should be structured to provide only one option for someone who earns $50,000 per year:

> Under $25,000
> $25,000–$49,999
> $50,000–$59,999
> $60,000 or above

If They Don't Know, They Don't Know

For some questions, respondents simply may not have enough knowledge of the issue to give an informed response. In such cases, provide a "Don't know" answer choice. We recommend against using this option too frequently, as some respondents tend to take the easy way out on every question. Nonetheless, if a respondent can't provide quality data, it is better to know that they can't, rather than introduce random error into the data set (especially if you intend to do any advanced statistical modeling).

Avoid Order Bias

In long answer lists in which respondents are asked to provide information on awareness, attitudes, brand association, and the like, the answer choices nearest the top of the list tend to get higher

FIGURE 7.23: Logical ordering

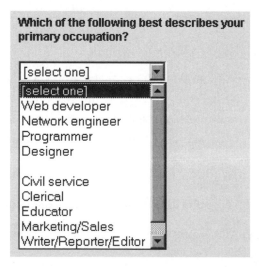

scores than those near the end of the list. This phenomenon, called order bias, can be eliminated in online research (and to some degree in telephone research) by randomizing the answer choices presented to any given respondent. As we mentioned in Chapter 6, a regrettable drawback of most affordable survey packages currently on the market is their inability to support randomization. It is one of the primary reasons we have continued to use our in-house tools for survey fielding, rather than using an off-the-shelf package. Perhaps by the time this book hits the shelves developers will have taken notice and added this simple functionality to their products.

Put Behavioral or Classification Questions in Logical Order

The major drawback to randomization is that it makes it more difficult for respondents to locate specific answer choices they may be considering. In behavioral or classification questions, respondents are more likely to be scanning for specific answers, and it's unlikely the order of the answer choices will change the choices they make. You can make these questions easier to complete by keeping responses in some type of logical order. Alphabetical order is one obvious choice. Another effective way to order choices in behavioral questions is by grouping them logically, placing the most commonly selected choices near the top of the list.

For example, if we were surveying a population that we expect to have a large concentration of Web professionals, we might group Web-related jobs together and place them near the top of the answer list. Other choices would be available following the Web jobs, in standard alphabetical order.

GUIDELINES FOR CONSTRUCTING QUESTIONNAIRES

Now that you have a good idea of how to create questions, it's time to put them all together in a questionnaire. Here's a process we recommend.

Begin with a questionnaire outline.

In Chapter 1, we took you through the research process. At that time, you should have determined your research objectives and written a research objective statement that encapsulated these issues. Go find that now, or turn back to Chapter 1, reread it, and write an objective statement now. You'll refer to it as you construct your questionnaire outline.

It is very tempting to simply dive in and begin writing a questionnaire. Developing an outline may seem like a waste of time, especially when deadlines press your development schedule. However, you will find that putting some up-front effort into the outline will make writing the rest of your questionnaire go more smoothly, and very likely save you a lot of time in revisions further down the road.

Rather than getting bogged down in the specific wording of your questions, start by writing an outline that sketches out the type of questions you will be asking and provides a description of how the information will be collected and used in later analysis. For example:

Gender
- Pulldown menu
- Determine gender breakdown of audience; will be used to analyze male and female segments.

Usage frequency of XYZ.com
- Pulldown menu
- Will be used to determine usage frequency of site, calculated into first-time, light, moderate, and heavy users. Analysis by breakout of this variable will allow us to examine differences between first-time users and repeat visitors. Heaviest users represent our core audience and will be studied carefully to understand their characteristics.

As you write your outline, consider how each question relates back to your original research objective statement. If it does not contribute to the overall goal, leave the question out. It is very easy to let your questionnaire balloon out of control and to end up with an unmanageably long survey that has little focus and is likely to receive a poor response rate.

When you write each question in your outline, be sure to write down how you will use each piece of data, and what other pieces of data will be used in the analysis of this question. Sometimes you will notice the need for an additional question or modification of an existing one in order to perform your desired analysis.

When your first draft of the outline is finished, circulate it throughout the organization to make sure you've covered all the critical metrics, and incorporate any feedback into the next revision.

Consider the flow of the questionnaire.

You can go a long way towards making your survey interesting and engaging to respondents by considering the flow of the questionnaire and the way you turn their attention to new topics. A good questionnaire helps respondents tell a story about themselves, rather than being a hodgepodge collection of data points with no apparent logic behind it.

Questionnaires typically require respondents to address a wide variety of issues in the course of the survey. To keep things manageable, follow these guidelines:

Kick off the survey with easy questions that will arouse interest. Unlike telephone interviews, online surveys give respondents the opportunity to see what they are getting themselves into. Start off the survey with some interesting but easy-to-answer questions that will get respondents involved without intimidating them. The start of a survey is not the place for extensive multipart grid questions that involve long lists of possible answer choices or very detailed thinking.

Cluster questions on the same topic. This serves to focus respondents on the topic and stimulate their thinking about the issues that surround that topic. Respondents may already have considered the answers to a question before you got around to asking it.

Questions on a topic should flow from general to specific. This tip is based on the idea that you want to ease respondents into more difficult questions gradually, instead of hitting them with the hard stuff right away. It is very easy for respondents to terminate the survey if they decide it is more trouble than it's worth; a gradual buildup of the questionnaire's complexity is important for maintaining involvement.

When addressing a topic, ask behavioral questions first, and then move to attitudinal questions. Behavioral questions (What do you do? What have you done?) are typically easier to answer than subjective attitudinal questions (What do you think? How do you feel?). Asking behavioral questions early on in your treatment of a topic will help respondents warm up to the topic and make it easier for them to zero in on their attitudes later in the survey.

Suppose, for example, that part of our survey dealt with automobiles and attitudes toward the purchase process. Specifically, we wanted to understand:

- satisfaction with specific aspects of the purchase process,
- overall satisfaction with the last purchase experience,
- type of vehicle last purchased, and
- type of purchase (new, leased, or used).

Rather than ask respondents to provide attitudinal feedback on their last purchase right away, it is advantageous to warm them up with the behavioral questions (type of vehicle last purchased and whether it was a new, leased, or used vehicle). When answering behavioral questions, respondents will recall other aspects of that experience, such as the salesperson's personality or how they felt about the deal they got. Answering the attitudinal questions will then be much easier, since some of the requisite thinking has already occurred in the background.

Place "easy" questions, such as demographics, near the end of the survey. By the time respondents have spent 15 minutes on your survey, they will start to burn out and put less and less thought into each subsequent question. The end of the questionnaire, therefore, should contain the easiest questions. Typically, demographic questions are placed at the end, because they require little thought to answer accurately.

If you must ask about them, place sensitive topics at the end of the survey. Questions that have the potential to alienate should be placed at the end of the survey, where they can do the least damage. If you approach touchy subjects early on, you risk the possibility that respondents will terminate the survey before they submit their data. Remember to provide respondents a way to opt out of answering a particularly sensitive subject.

DESIGNING AN ONLINE QUESTIONNAIRE

Once you've gotten all the kinks worked out of your questionnaire and have a final version, you can turn to the task of putting it on the Web. We've already discussed some of the effective tools for conducting online surveys. This section focuses on maximizing their use.

Multipage versus Single-Page Surveys

Online surveys can consist of a single page, whereby a respondent completes all questions before submitting the data; or they can have multiple pages, whereby a respondent completes a portion of the survey, submits the data from that page to the server, and moves on to the next set of questions.

There is no established rule for deciding whether to make your survey span multiple pages; but based on our experience, we've established some guidelines.

Short surveys that contain two screen-lengths of questions should be placed on a single page, unless there is an important reason why the respondent should not see subsequent questions in the survey. Reloading pages takes time—sometimes a lot of time, if the respondent's connection to the Internet is slow. The delay interrupts the survey flow and increases the risk of losing the respondent due to unforeseen server-related or Internet traffic-related problems. In addition, we've found that respondents are more likely to complete a short questionnaire when they can see for themselves how short it is. Multiple pages make the overall length of a survey suspect.

Longer surveys can benefit from being broken up into multiple parts. First, with longer surveys, it is likely that some respondents will drop out at various points. Of those who start the survey, 98% may complete the first page, 85% the second page, 80% the third page, and so forth. If your surveying system allows you to capture data from the intermediate submits (most do), you can compare the data common from the first page to see if any relevant nonresponse patterns exist that may bias the data (e.g., heavier, more loyal users may see the survey all the way through, while first-time users may drop out early).

A second benefit to breaking up longer surveys is that the load time for survey pages can be relatively long. The HTML elements that make up a survey can be extensive. Loading several screen-lengths of questions at once can take more time than many respondents may be willing to wait.

If you decide to break your survey up into multiple pages, we recommend that you choose your break points in a logical fashion. First, try to save your break points for when the survey needs to change dynamically based on prior input, or when it is important that respondents not see subsequent questions before answering the current set (critical in branding research or advertising effectiveness studies).

Maximize Screen Real Estate

An effective survey leverages the horizontal as well as vertical screen space to display questions and accompanying text or images. It is simple to choose a vertical format, in which all questions align at the left of the screen and every element of the survey appears on a new line; but bear in mind that the respondent will have to continually scroll down the screen to get to new questions. This has the potential to increase respondent fatigue and impact response rates. Creative use of screen real estate allows the respondent to answer more questions and see more information before having to scroll down. This approach, of course, must be balanced against creating overcrowded, difficult-to-read pages that are intimidating or confusing.

FIGURE 7.24: Maximizing real estate

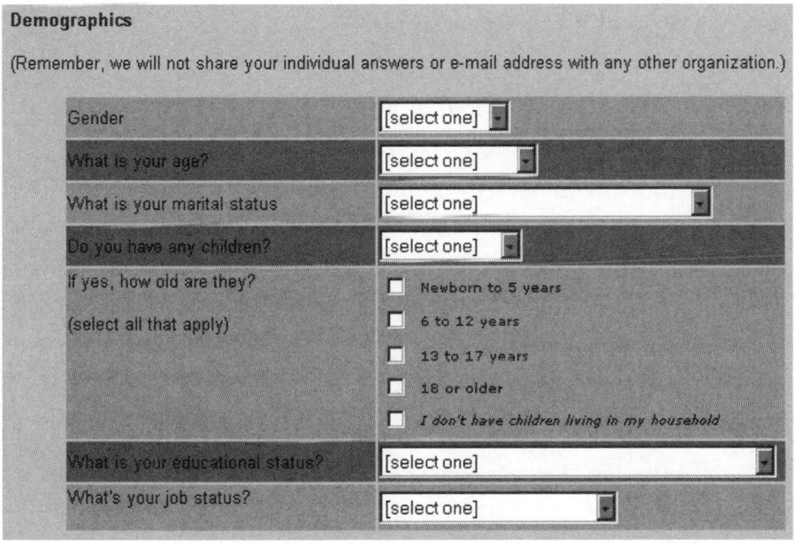

Design for the Lowest Common Denominator Screen Size

This is a tip taken from Web developers, and should be heeded by online researchers as well. Just because you have the luxury of developing your survey using a 19-inch monitor with 1024×768

resolution, that doesn't mean that everyone you survey will have the same benefit. If a survey is designed to take up all the screen room on your giant monitor, people using laptops or smaller screens with lower resolution will be faced with an unusable survey. Try to design your survey at a resolution of 800 × 600 or lower, so that nearly all users on the Web can see the survey as you intended them to. A quick and easy way to make sure you design at the right resolution is to change your screen settings. Go to Start → Settings → Control Panels → Display → Settings and change your resolution to 800 × 600 when you design your survey. If you'd prefer to develop at your current resolution, at least take the time to preview your creation at various screen resolutions to get an idea of what is in store for others.

Use Logical Questionnaire Routing

A major advantage of Web-based surveys over email or postal questionnaires is the ability to ask different questions, variants on a common question, or different sets of questions based on the respondent's previous answers. You can shorten the overall length of a questionnaire considerably if you use skips to jump over questions that don't apply to a particular respondent. A respondent who indicates she is currently in college can be asked about her grade level and area of study, while those who are not in school can be skipped past these questions. Nearly all major survey packages offer some ability to implement skips in Web-based questionnaires. Email surveys are static, and so are obviously not as flexible in terms of how the survey is presented. Skips in these situations are typically handled with instructions to the respondent to skip to the next appropriate numbered question.

Response Piping

Piping allows elements of previous responses to be incorporated into upcoming questions. Suppose, for example, you presented a long list of automobile makes and asked respondents to check which ones they'd be most likely to purchase for their next vehicle. A respondent indicated that he'd be most likely to consider purchasing a Saab for his next vehicle. Using response piping, you could ask follow-up questions about Saabs that identify the attributes most responsible for driving the respondent to consider that brand. Piping is often used in branding research; respondents are first asked to identify brands they are aware of; then, among those, which brands they've tried; and finally, among those, ratings of their satisfaction with each of the experienced brands.

Random Rotation of Question Sets

Another useful approach is to randomly rotate entire sets of questions into the questionnaire. When questionnaires are very long, this enables a survey to be cut down considerably from the respondent's perspective, while still providing the researcher with the necessary set of data. See Figure 11.4 for an illustration.

Because a set of questions is served to a population at random, the subset of respondents who complete it can be projected across the entire population: It is a random sample within a random sample. To confirm that there are no statistically significant differences, a survey will typically ask a set of independent variables of the entire population before moving on to the randomly-rotated sections. This allows the composition of the population who completed each of the random sections to be compared, confirming that systematic bias was not introduced.

Random rotation fields questions only to a subset of the total sample, so the overall sample size may need to be increased to provide statistically stable base sizes for the rotated questions. If we required a minimum of 200 respondents to answer a given question for an acceptable margin of error, and we had 5 randomly-rotated sets of questions, we would need to have an overall sample size of 1,000 respondents for the questionnaire (200 × 5 = 1,000). If we had only 200 respondents take the survey, and then split those respondents up over 5 sections, the sample size for a given set of questions would only be 40 persons, which is lower than we'd need for the required level of statistical confidence. This limitation is not typically an issue in online research, however, because the incremental cost of gathering additional respondents in an online survey is extremely low.

If you choose to use random rotation, you must pay particular advance attention to your analysis plan. Questions that are asked in one rotated set cannot be combined with data in other sets. As such, data points that will be used to drive cross-tabular or multivariate analysis should be gathered from the entire sample. The questionnaire should be structured to include all necessary cross-tabular variables in nonrotated sections, with the rotated sections containing the dependent variables.

Aesthetic Guidelines

A survey doesn't have to have a boring appearance in order to be effective. In fact, a pleasing design will keep respondents more interested and increase response rates. Use background colors, fonts (make sure they are universally supported on all Web browsers), or images to help the survey along. But be sure not to overcrowd the page. If you are conducting a survey for a Web site with an established brand identity and feel, you can usually copy the background image and a few branding elements (logo, icons, etc.) into your survey to quickly give it a professional look that is complementary to the site it represents.

Again, make sure the survey looks acceptable on various screen sizes and resolutions. It doesn't hurt to test the survey on a variety of platforms and configurations as well, just to be sure that you aren't creating a survey that is distorted by the quirks of your own particular setup.

Keep the overall file size of your survey pages to a minimum. Remember that on average Web users can download your pages at a rate of around 4K per second. That means a page that is 50K in size will take about 12 seconds to download into the computer. Though images can definitely make the survey more visually appealing, they greatly increase the size of your file. Respondents may cancel the load of the page if it taxes their patience, or if they think the survey is malfunctioning because it's taking so long to load.

Testing

Once your questionnaire is constructed and online, you should triple-check your work. A good solid proofreading for spelling and grammatical errors is essential. It is amazing how many misspellings can creep into your survey in the course of revisions and programming. If your surveying package doesn't check spelling, you can easily copy the text of the survey from your browser and paste it into a word processing application.

Reading the questionnaire out loud is a good way of assessing the clarity of questions and overall flow. Another invaluable step is to have the decision makers in the organization give the survey a once-through in its final online form. Pilot test the survey with a small sample of people who are not familiar with the project to gain feedback on the overall length of the questionnaire and to identify any issues that may pose problems in the actual field of the study.

Finally, check the data that comes back as a result of the pilot test. Make sure that all the data points come back as you expected. Even with survey packages, it is possible to make errors that will result in the loss of critical data points, so try to do a data processing dry-run before you officially begin taking real respondents. Finding a mistake after the survey is completed will do you little good; now is the time to catch any problems.

Solicitation Page

Whether you execute a Web-based or email-based study, create a solicitation or introduction to your survey that will encourage respondents to begin answering questions. After all the time you've spent creating the perfect survey, it may seem like a minor consideration, but please heed our advice! All the work you've put into the rest of the process will be for naught if the response rate to the survey is unacceptably low. Your solicitation has the power to drive people to the survey.

Have a clear, concise message in your solicitation. It might help to think of it as a direct marketing exercise: Get the user's attention, convey a message, and motivate action. Here are some things that should be included in the solicitation:

- Convey that the respondent is one of only a select few who have been randomly chosen to participate (if appropriate).
- Impart that this is an important study that will benefit the respondent and others. Provide specifics.
- Inform the respondent of the time commitment required.

FIGURE 7.25: Solicitation page

ZDNet TECH LIFE

We interrupt your normally scheduled browsing for this important announcement:

Welcome to ZDNet Tech Life--and congratulations!

You are one of a handful of users randomly selected to participate in the ZDNet visitor survey-- and receive a shot at winning $100. (Chances of winning are 1 in 250 for eligible respondents)

Please help us out by filling in the following questionnaire. It will take less than 10 minutes. Your answers will be kept in the strictest confidence, and we promise not to distribute any of your information to any other Website.

Your help is very important to us, whether you're a ZDNet first-timer or a regular user.

But if you'd rather not participate, click I'm outta here to be returned to your originally scheduled programming.

Thanks in advance for helping!

On to the Survey

- If an incentive is used, mention the incentive and the odds of winning (assuming they are attractive odds!).
- Include an image of the incentive, if appropriate. (Keep the file size of the image below 10K.)
- Ensure respondents that all information will be kept strictly confidential (and stick to this promise).

Completing surveys is voluntary. As such, your solicitation should always provide a clear means of opting out of the survey if the respondent doesn't care to participate. Of course, it goes without saying that they should have an even clearer means of opting in!

Online solicitations are often delivered via a pop-up window that launches on top of the main screen of the site where sampling occurred. The page that loads into the pop-up must have a short load time in order to be noticed before users move on. It is tempting to spend a lot of time designing a graphically elaborate solicitation page; but if it can't convey its message because the user has moved on before it loaded, it will be of little use. Make it interesting, but make it small!

A word on incentives: Incentives are small payments or other compensation for respondent participation. They can play a major role in the response rate you are able to achieve with your study. Originally, online research was so novel that most people would take a few minutes out of their surfing to participate in a study. As Web usage has become more and more commonplace, respondents are rightfully coming to expect some sort of compensation for their input.

While it is possible to offer a small incentive to every person who fills out your survey, we have found the costs and trouble of distributing such incentives to be prohibitive for all but the smallest studies. Instead, we recommend the use of a lottery-style incentive: A small number of higher-value prizes or cash awards are given out to winners who are drawn at random. In order to be appealing, the odds of winning should be kept as high as possible while balancing the cost constraints of the study. We have enjoyed great success offering $100 cash prizes with odds of winning set at 1 in 250. This amounts to a per-respondent cost of $0.40, which is extremely reasonable by marketing research standards.

In some cases, a prize that has particular appeal to the population can yield an even better response rate at a lower cost. One noteworthy example involved giving away early releases of a new video game console system to a group of dedicated gamers. Response rates exceeded 50% and the cost per respondent was less than $0.25. There is a risk in using an incentive other than cash, however. If the incentive appeals to only a specific subgroup of the population, you may bias the sample toward those who place high value in the product or service. Cash, on the other hand, has universal appeal. Lottery-style incentives involve a degree of legal exposure as well. Contests and lotteries can be viewed as gambling by some state governments; consult an attorney to determine the legality of your proposed incentive scheme.

PART

Applications

ROADMAP TO PART II

In Part I we focused on the tools of online market research. Like a skilled carpenter, the researcher needs to understand both the tools of the trade and when to use them. The online researcher may not exclusively use online tools. There may be instances in which an off-line approach can get the job done more efficiently or cost-effectively. In some cases, it may provide the only available solution.

In Part II, we discuss the practical application of the tools we introduced in Part I. The benefits of online research lie not only in the opportunities it presents for professional market research practitioners, but also in its ability to empower individuals in large or small organizations to conduct their own research and approach the business process from a data-driven perspective.

Though this book concerns itself largely with online topics, it is important to remember that the online world is only a subset of the larger global marketplace. Rather than a world unto itself, the online world is best thought of as another vehicle used to deliver marketing messages, communicate with consumers, sell products, and provide services.

Much of the information we use to make key business decisions about online products must be obtained and understood for both online and offline markets. In this spirit, in the first chapter of Part II we discuss different *measurement spheres*. We coined this term to describe the divisions between the primary groups of consumers you seek to understand through research. Measurement spheres include:

- the overall market,
- the Internet,
- the intersection of the Internet with the overall market (the online marketplace), and
- your existing online customer base.

In many cases, the metrics and concepts you'll want to understand in each measurement sphere will be quite similar. Each sphere may have particular research approaches that are most efficient at gathering this information, but the underlying concepts will be nearly identical. We address these issues separately in the next three chapters:

- Chapter 8: Market Research: Understanding the Market
- Chapter 9: Segmentation: Developing Target Markets
- Chapter 10: Competition: Assessment and Positioning

After presenting the fundamentals of key information objectives, we turn our focus to elements specific to your online product:

- Chapter 11: Existing Online Products: Audience Composition and Performance Testing

MEASUREMENT SPHERES

Now that you have a road map to the second part of the book, let's return to the issue of measurement spheres. In other words, what groups of consumers do you need to understand, and how will you understand them?

As an online marketing research consulting firm, the majority of the projects we execute focus on a very specific part of the marketplace: the online marketplace for our clients' products and services. This focus, as illustrated in the accompanying diagram, is comprised of the intersection of the overall market for these types

FIGURE II.1

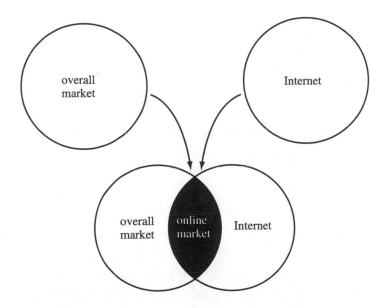

of goods and services (both online and offline) with the total population of everyone who currently uses the Internet.

Sphere 1—The Overall Market

Before we dive into the online market, let's take a few minutes to discuss the overall market—that is to say, *the total potential base of customers and competition for your goods or services, both online and off.* The overall market can be thought of as the layer that underlies everything that impacts your business opportunity, the competitive environment, and the strategy that will enable your success.

Remember that your online market is only a piece of the big picture. As an online venture, you might be tempted to ignore anything offline, because it doesn't appear to directly impact your business. But the fact remains that issues impacting the real world will eventually impact the online world—sometimes disproportionately. Further, as adoption continues to grow toward ubiquity, online markets will look much like the market at large. Understanding the big picture can actually give you a crystal ball insight into your future. Consider the fortunes of America Online: While doomsayers decried America Online's simplistic interface and collection of novice-targeted services, AOL recognized the mainstreaming potential of the Net early on. Through a skillful combination of product, positioning, and distribution, it positioned itself to be the preeminent destination and service provider for newbies across the nation. Other content and connectivity services that concentrated on the early adopters have enjoyed success among only a niche audience.

Far too often, however, new businesses or strategies are launched with only a cursory understanding of the market it will service. It's understandable; most businesses are launched by individuals highly familiar with the field, who tend to trust their instincts. Many times, these instincts are right; sometimes, they're dead wrong. Like a house of cards, a faulty foundation will render later efforts weak and ineffectual. So before you go building the next "killer Web application," it pays to spend some time *understanding* the market you are about to corner.

The challenge in obtaining a thorough understanding of the market is a major reason why many opt to rely on hunches and intuition, rather than substantiate theory with data. Ideally, you could go to a library, type a request into a search engine, or order a syndicated report to find out everything you need to know. Unfortunately, there isn't any all-in-one magic resource or approach to finding all the answers. Obtaining information about the overall marketplace often involves weaving together bits from disparate data sources, along with some assumptions and common sense. All your effort will be rewarded, however, with a much more informed foundation upon which to base later decisions.

Sphere 2—The Internet

It almost goes without saying that the Internet is a unique business and marketing environment that holds great promise and many pitfalls for the companies that venture into it. While the Net continues to move toward the mainstream, e-commerce and e-media still exhibit many differences from conducting brick-and-mortar commerce.

It is beyond the scope of this book to discuss the many differences in online consumer culture and good business practice; we urge those who are new to the field to take some time to familiarize themselves with the learning that has been gained over the past several years of experimentation. There are a number of overarching issues that impact all organizations doing business on the Internet. Understanding the experience of your predecessors will help you avoid the costly mistakes that they made, and more important, enable you to emulate their success.

Some of the hot issues are:

- advertising response and advertising models,
- business-to-business e-commerce,

- business-to-consumer e-commerce,
- customer support,
- niche marketing,
- real-time personalization and customer relationship management (CRM),
- pay-for-use revenue models,
- price sensitivity,
- privacy, and
- product shipping and delivery times.

Numerous books have been published with extensive case studies, and journals and magazines that chronicle the growth of this new medium are widely available. A quick surf of Amazon.com or any of the major Internet news sources (News.com, ZDNet, Wired News) should demonstrate that there is no shortage of resources to choose from.

The Internet is changing so rapidly it makes little sense to include current trends and theories in this book; they will likely be obsolete by the time this book hits the shelves. Instead, we suggest you turn to the rapidly growing subindustry of marketing research that is devoted to tracking the current state of the Net and its future prospects. The Web is currently one of the most analyzed and documented mediums in the world; finding information is less difficult than the task of sifting through and making sense of all that's available.

Putting a face to the average Web user is not nearly as difficult as it once used to be. Numerous Web-wide studies are conducted on a regular basis. Some of them are available for purchase by the general public; some are available on a subscriber-only basis; and others are used to drive more focused syndicated products that concentrate on specific markets (e.g., ISPs, B2B commerce, etc.).

CyberDialog (www.cyberdialog.com) conducts the American Internet User Study (AIUS), an annual, nationally representative

RDD (random digit dialed) survey of U.S. Web users. Topics of common interest such as demographics, Web usage habits, and e-commerce activities are detailed and trended over time to identify shifts in the online population that will change the playing field for e-businesses. Intelliquest (www.intelliquest.com) offers the Worldwide Internet/Online Tracking Service (WWITS); and Nielsen Media Research, in association with CommerceNet (www.commerce.net), conducts its CommerceNet/Nielsen Internet Demographic Survey. Jupiter Communications (www.jup.com) also conducts an annual Web survey, in conjunction with NFO Interactive (www.nfoi.com), which is available only to subscribers to packages of specific information services.

In addition to continuous tracking studies like those mentioned, numerous specialty research firms have focused their attention on analyzing and forecasting the Internet's development. Forrester Research (www.forrester.com), Jupiter Communications, and the Yankee Group (www.yankeegroup.com) have extensive catalogs of prewritten analysis and position papers that can quickly get you up to speed on a multitude of Web and Net topics.

Beyond paid for professional analysis, an abundance of free resources is available to the intrepid surfer. Some of our favorites are:

- *News.com (www.news.com)*

  CNET's online news service covers the gamut of technology topics, with a heavy concentration on e-business.

- *Wired News (www.wired.com) and Wired Magazine (www.wiredmag.com)*

  These were the original sources of information and commentary about technology trends and· culture. While no longer owned and operated by Louis Rossetto, the magazine's new owners have carried on the tradition of providing high-quality information about Internet trends and technology in an aesthetically pleasing package. *Wired*

News offers intelligent and tech-savvy Net news with a nod toward its antiestablishment origins.

- *The Industry Standard (www.thestandard.com)*

  The Industry Standard is a weekly print magazine full of feature-length articles on the latest issues to face online businesses. The content is timely, well-written, and perceptive. Its online site offers a host of searchable archives and useful statistics.

- *Iconocast (www.iconocast.com)*

  This is an informative and entertaining weekly email-based newsletter strongly targeted at interactive marketers, often providing insightful tips about using email marketing to establishing ongoing customer contact. It's also a good place to pick up the latest e-business gossip, if you're interested in that sort of thing.

- *Business 2.0 (www.business2.com)*

  A slick print monthly with a counterpart Web site, *Business 2.0* tends to have lengthier, more in-depth feature articles and a bit more entertainment value than *The Industry Standard*.

- *CyberAtlas (www.cyberatlas.com)*

  This is a compendium of useful Net statistics and excerpts from published syndicated reports on the development of online markets.

Sphere 3—The Online Marketplace

For most online ventures, this is the area you will realistically pay the most attention to as you develop short-term tactics and longer-term strategy. Within the Internet exists a subset of the consumers from the total market for your product or service. In some cases, penetration may be nearly 100%. Cisco Systems, for example, manufactures and sells high-speed Internet and intranet networking solutions. Nearly all of its customers are involved in and actively use the Internet. As a result, Cisco is able to structure sales channels to drive a tremendous amount of business (an astonishing 84%) through a Web-based system.

In other cases, current penetration of Internet usage may be low. A firm wishing to wholesale plumbing supplies through the Web might find that Internet usage among plumbing contractors is very low.

Depending upon the level of Internet penetration, the characteristics of your online market may vary widely from the general marketplace. Both the customers and the competition will present a unique set of challenges that will demand a strategy informed by research.

FIGURE II.2: Cisco online marketplace penetration

FIGURE II.3: Plumbing supplies online marketplace penetration

To further complicate matters, there are multiple measure-ment spaces within the Online marketplace. The star diagram illus-trates the areas you will seek to understand.

This diagram is quite simplified, but it serves to show that there are several distinct spheres to understand:

Overall Online Marketplace: First, consider the overall online marketplace for your goods and services. What do the con-sumers look like? What motivates them? Where can they be reached with marketing messages? What are their buying patterns in your category?

Much like the overall market, understanding the online mar-ketplace requires a creative mix of information and intuition. The specifics are discussed in Chapter 8.

Direct Competition: Next, consider the direct online compe-tition. What do they have to offer? What is their strategy? What is

Figure II.4: Areas of research inquiry

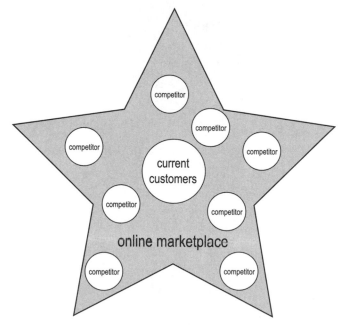

their market share? Who have they targeted and appealed to? What are their strengths and weaknesses?

Understanding the competition is almost an entire field unto itself. Competitive intelligence consultancies reap handsome fees for providing in-depth information on what the other guy is up to. Short of hiring specialists, powerful tools are available to online ventures to gain ample knowledge for product development and marketing or positioning efforts. Understanding the competition is discussed in depth in Chapter 10.

Current Customers: Finally, consider your relationship with your current customer base (if one exists). Many organizations spend outlandish amounts of money designed to win market share without taking an introspective approach to understanding, retaining, and maximizing the value of their existing customers. What has been successful? What has failed? What types of customers have found the most value with your current offerings? Who has visited but failed to return? Before embarking on a quest to dominate your industry, be sure to maximize the value of the customers already in your hands. Your current customer base is an invaluable source of information for fine-tuning your approach before embarking on a multimillion-dollar marketing campaign.

Beyond the fact that a comprehensive knowledge of your current customer base is a powerful ally, conducting research within your customer base is typically the most feasible and has the most favorable cost–benefit relationship. You will have the greatest control over these sitecentric studies with cheap access to a quality sample and the ability to execute flexible study designs— otherwise impossible when researching the broader issues we mentioned earlier. We devote the last six chapters of the book to the use of sitecentric studies to squeeze all the value out of your current customers.

8

Market Research: Understanding the Market

W hether researching the overall marketplace or focusing on the online space, the metrics collected on the road to enlightenment will be quite similar. For this reason we treat both areas simultaneously, noting areas where resources or approaches differ from one measurement sphere to the other.

In this chapter we review key pieces of market data that should be obtained (or at the least, estimated), and provide examples of collecting and tailoring the available data to meet your specific needs.

DEFINING YOUR MARKET

Before you can understand your market, you must first define what it is and what it isn't. Simply put, your market is the group of consumers or businesses to whom you will provide your product or service. You undoubtedly have some hypothesis of who these consumers are. But how detailed or actionable is your current hypothesis? Take some time to revisit your target market definition. Try to be as specific as possible, as this definition will assist you in narrowing your search for market information down the road.

After determining your ideal target market, you may be quite satisfied with and attached to the definition you created. But as your understanding of the market grows, you may discover that your initial target was too small, too broad, or not lucrative enough to pursue. By the same token, you may discover previously unconsidered opportunities. Both scenarios suggest that you remain open to revising your initial definition.

Presumably, if you are reading this book, you are building a strategy for an online product or service. Many may already restrict their definitions of the marketplace to include only online customers and competition. We've discussed the dangers of ignoring and the merits of including the overall marketplace, but we'll say it once again for good measure: *Online products and services do not exist in a vacuum, and your thinking should reflect this fact.* Customers consider both online and off-line alternatives to satisfy their needs; and as online penetration continues to grow toward ubiquity, customers who are outside your target market one day could be in it the next.

Given limited resources and time pressures, obtaining a comprehensive understanding of both online and off-line markets might seem unrealistic. But the development of innovative approaches to providing research data for the small business customer has made this goal more attainable than ever before.

WHAT SHOULD YOU LEARN ABOUT THE MARKETPLACE?

Market Size

The market size is the total number of potential customers for your product or service. This may not seem like a particularly useful metric, aside from being able to say "five million people could possibly buy our product!" But when combined with other data (or estimates) of consumption or expenditure levels, market size will drive an estimate of the market's total value. The metric is of particular interest to investors who want revenue forecasts to determine whether a concept and market are worth pursuing.

How to Get This Information

Secondary sources (see Chapter 2) can provide the majority of the research you'll use to find information on the marketplace. Because a market can be very large (perhaps even global), it is usually prohibitively expensive to conduct custom primary research. Fortunately, the same factors that prevent you from doing the work yourself have encouraged other firms to execute large studies that are sold, or syndicated, to a large number of clients.

Because syndicated research uses the "one size fits all" approach, chances are slim that an existing syndicated study will estimate the size of the precise market you have in mind. This is particularly so if you are researching a new or ill-defined market. In 1990, for example, 3COM would have been hard-pressed to find a syndicated study that explicitly measured the potential market for PDAs. But a study doesn't have to directly address your market in order to be useful.

By arming yourself with the available data and some carefully thought out assumptions, you can usually approximate the market size. If your search through secondary sources fails to yield any information that directly addresses the market you have envisioned, determine the size of a related, established market that would be an obvious adopter of your product or services. You can then scale your estimate up or down from that point.

Size of the Target Demographic

Another approach to estimating market size is to determine the size of the demographic who would potentially be receptive to the product or service. Obviously this will not be completely accurate, since some percentage of the target demographic will be uninterested in the category (not all 25-year-olds listen to cutting-edge music), and other potential customers will fall outside the demographic (lots of 60-year-olds are interested in fashion magazines). But by estimating the level of interest within the category, a reasonable approximation of market size can be computed.

A business catering to the information needs of young single mothers could size its market using the following metrics:

- female,
- not married,
- under 35 years of age, and
- parents.

Using a nationally representative demographic study, you can determine the number of U.S. consumers who satisfy the requirements. Data from the U.S. Census (www.census.gov) is an ideal resource for estimating the largest potential customer base for the product. Bear in mind that this number will likely overstate the actual market size, since demographics don't typically tell everything there is to know about purchasing habits or product requirements. Consumers have numerous other traits that impact purchase behavior. Demographics alone won't give you the whole story, but they're a good start.

To evaluate online markets, you'll need to determine what share of *Web users* fit the target demographic profile. Here, a resource like the U.S. Census will be of minimal use, since the demographics of the Web aren't representative of the nation (yet!). Instead, turn to one of a variety of studies that accurately profile the demographics of the Web. Some notable ones available from companies like CyberDialogue and Intelliquest are listed in the introduction to Part II.

Again, a simple computation of the size of your target demographic will not yield an entirely accurate prediction of the true market size. If possible, obtain the following supplemental information to round out your perspective.

Category Penetration

This metric refers to the share of consumers who currently purchase or use the types of products or services you will offer. This is an important consideration, since the lowest hanging fruit are those who have already incorporated similar offerings into their lifestyle. It is far easier to market a new mountain bike to those who already participate in the sport, for example, than to those who haven't been on a bicycle since their childhood years. So, while there might be 50 million people who fit the customer profile demographically, perhaps only 5% of those (2.5 million people) are realistic prospects.

How do you obtain category penetration metrics? If you are entering a relatively established market or one that has received recent attention and new business development, you can often find existing research with the data you need. A good starting point is to comb through related trade journals or search general press archives to see if useful data points have been included to support articles. Nearly all major print news sources have online archives, and searching through back issues is easier now than it has ever been.

Trade or industry associations provide another good source, and often compile statistics aimed at answering exactly this type of question. If you are dealing with a larger industry that involves publicly traded companies, investment analysis sites are good free sources of information. Investors are obviously interested in the market size and growth prospects for their investment opportunities, so you may discover exactly what you're looking for with no more than a few mouse clicks.

The availability of up-to-date metrics for online markets is especially good. Creators of new syndicated research products who are battling for recognition often publish excerpts of their recent studies on the multitude of sites dedicated to chronicling the commercial explosion of the Web.

Beyond free sources, you can turn to a growing industry of research resellers who slice and dice high-quality syndicated studies into affordable bits so that you pay for only the data points you need. USADATA (www.usadata.com), mentioned in Chapter 2, is a good resource for obtaining market penetration data, as well as a host of focused information about your target market. You'll see it referenced several times throughout this chapter. Specific data points (e.g., 20% of U.S. households own downhill skis) and smaller reports cost as little as $150, making them cost-effective resources for a variety of applications when you need nationally representative data about the overall marketplace. A nice aspect of using USADATA is that you can also narrow your focus to include only online users, thereby giving you the same data for your online market.

It is more difficult to find made-to-fit data for products or services that are innovative or launching into ill-defined markets. Syndicated market research is seldom ahead of its time, and only covers topics that have clearly demonstrated demand. Many Web ventures find themselves in uncharted territory and have to make creative use of the resources available. Look for the closest comparison to your new concept, and work with assumptions from there.

For example, while there might not be any existing market (or market research) for a new form of online music distribution, there is plenty of existing research about the packaged music industry to draw upon. Tailoring this information to your specific situation requires making some inferences about the relationship of the new market with the larger, established category. You can make these inferences based on hypotheses, or you can conduct some of your own informal primary research (such as a small survey of a convenience sample) to inform your assumptions.

Another way to understand the size of a market for which little formal research has been done is to look at the experience of pioneers or bellwether examples in the field—especially if they've been highly publicized or documented. The number of downloads through MP3.com and Liquid Audio might be good reference points if you were looking into the adoption of online music distribution, for example. By assuming how large a slice these competitors have captured, you can derive the total size of the pie as well.

You have probably gathered that this stage of research will require you to be creative with the resources you have on hand. After all, we're basically saying that there are lots of places you might look to find market size information, and half the time, you'll be making educated guesses to fill in the gaps. But the bottom line is that any concrete understanding you gain about the marketplace will be an improvement over what you had before.

To round out this section, here is a theoretical example of the process we've been discussing:

Suppose we're considering launching a Web site to sell car parts online. Specifically, we intend to sell commonly used and hard-to-find parts to motorists who work on their own vehicles.

Though working on one's own car is certainly not a new idea, it's rather unlikely that a great deal of syndicated research has been done on the online auto parts buying habits of automotive do-it-yourselfers. Our first stop is USADATA, where we perform a search to see what questions have been asked that deal with automobile self-repair. We discover that just such a question has been asked in one of the nationally representative studies that USADATA resells.

Specifically, the study asked the question:

"Who is primarily responsible for the maintenance on your most recently purchased vehicle?"
Answer choices were "Myself" or "Someone else."

Knowing the share of people who answered "Myself" (say, 20%) would give us the total potential market for the consumer sale of auto parts in the U.S. If we were looking to understand the overall market for direct-to-consumer auto parts, we'd be done. However, we are more concerned with the universe of online customers.

USADATA allows us to discover the Internet penetration level among do-it-yourselfers. Because these types of people probably spend more time tinkering with their cars than surfing the Net, let's suppose this penetration level is 30%. The service goes one step further by actually projecting out this penetration level to national levels, leaving us with the potential market size. Since there are about 250 million people in the U.S., suppose the total number of Web-using self-repairers numbers around 15 million persons (250 million × 20% × 30%).

The cost for this information, thus far, is $250. The Internet usage report that comes with this information also tells us the types of Internet-related activities our target engages in, which will facilitate development of an online marketing strategy.

So, 15 million people might represent the maximum current potential market size for our new company. But we need to consider that, just because people work on their own cars and use the Web, that doesn't necessarily mean that they'd be interested in purchasing car parts online. Unless there is information out there that explicitly studied this issue, we'll need to make an educated guess.

A good predictor of purchase probability is whether these consumers have made any other online purchases in the past. Those who are familiar and comfortable with buying online will be more likely to give this new service a try. USADATA provides the percentage of your target who have used the Web to "go shopping." It's not exactly what we're looking for, but it's included in the $250 price tag, so we'll make do with that. Suppose this number is 30%. Now we're down to 4.5 million customers (15 million × 30%). But not all shoppers have made purchases. Suppose only half have, leaving us with 2.25 million customers (4.5 million × 50%). So, we're going to estimate that perhaps 2.25 million customers might use our service.

Of course, we're not taking into account the fact that some types of products are better suited to e-commerce than others. Books and music, for example, are staples of online consumer sales. Auto parts? Perhaps not. Our total potential market size will probably be less than the 2.25 million we've estimated thus far. We might make a wild guess as to the share of the potential market that would consider buying auto parts online; or we could inform our estimate with a bit of primary (perhaps informal) research.

We might spend a few weekends outside of auto parts stores, asking customers if they use the Web and would be interested in buying auto parts online instead of at the shop. It's clearly a biased sample, because we're only going to have the opportunity to talk to a tiny share of the U.S. parts-buying public; but it's better than nothing, considering our time and cost constraints. Suppose that, out of the 100 Web-using customers we talk to, only 30 say they'd consider buying parts online. We might scale back our estimate of potential market size to 675,000 customers (2.25 M × 30% = 675,000). The decision to pursue this market will be influenced by the type of revenue you might expect to generate from each of the customers and the share of the total base you could expect to convert into customers.

Consumption and Usage Intensity Levels

Along with an estimate of market size, an estimate of consumption levels for the product or service is a main component of the overall value of the market. In its most basic form, the relationship is expressed by the following equation:

$$\text{Market Size} \times \text{Consumption} = \text{Market Value}$$

We've determined that approximately 675,000 consumers are in the target market. If we know that the typical consumer spends approximately $100 per year in the category, we could hypothesize that the market value is about $67.5 million per year. Of course, this ignores issues such as the growth rate of the market and the possibility that different groups of consumers have different consumption patterns. Both issues are addressed further in this chapter and in Chapter 9 on segmentation.

How to Get This Information

We recommend spending a little bit of money in exchange for the time you'll save with some professional help. Claritas, Inc. offers a product called DataMart on America™ (www.claritaexpress.com/tar/index.htm), which provides market penetration data and spending projections for more than 500 consumer product categories, 100 financial service products, and 60 insurance types. Pricing schemes start at around $250, and are dependent upon the geographic area you wish to cover and the level of detail you require. USADATA (www.usadata.com) again comes in handy with it's Data To Go™ service, which offers usage intensity reports in a wide variety of product categories.

Syndicated summary reports like those available from Jupiter (www.jup.com) or Forrester (www.forrester.com) typically have some degree of this information as well; but if all you're looking for is one or two data points, you're better off searching out more targeted information.

If you choose to watch your pennies and go the free route, numerous options exist, though you should be prepared to spend some time doing detective work.

The U.S. Bureau of Labor Statistics conducts the ongoing Consumer Expenditure Survey (CEX). Free reports are available at www.bls.gov/csxhome.htm. The CEX reporting on product categories in these free reports is not very granular; many types of products end up being lumped together in the "miscellaneous" category.

Industry bodies sometimes conduct high-quality primary research for their membership that may be available or for free or for a small membership fee. A list of major industry associations is found at the end of Chapter 2. If you don't find what you are looking for there, check out *The Encyclopedia of Associations— National Organizations of the United States* (Gale Research). This is an excellent resource for those who want to pick up the phone and do some investigation. Most major public and university libraries have this book in their reference collections. If you have an overwhelming desire for a monster-sized copy of your own, or an aversion to libraries, you can purchase one for around $500 at their Web site (www.gale.com). Two other online resources, Association Central and the American Society of Association Executives, were mentioned at the end of Chapter 2.

Again, the investment world chronicles major trends and statistics about the market. Market analysts write market opinion papers that are based on high-quality primary research. We listed some of our favorites in the Resources section at the end of Chapter 2. Looksmart (www.looksmart.com) provides an expansive list of online investment information sources, many of which provide analyst commentary and market sector facts and figures. It will be a hit-or-miss process, however, so you may end up paying more in labor costs than you'd spend purchasing the information.

What If I Can't Find It Anywhere?

If, after searching, you still can't find the average consumption of latch-hook rug kits among Internet users, you'll need to improvise. Ideally, you'd have a $100,000 research budget to conduct your own nationally representative study and obtain every metric you need. Because there are a few things standing between you and that budget, here are a few alternatives:

Guesstimate: Informally, ask some people in your target market about their consumption levels in the category and make your best guesstimate from here. Try to ask as diverse a group as possible so one or two oddballs don't lead you to a distorted picture.

Conduct some qualitative research: We've already discussed the reasons why qualitative research is a dangerous way of getting hard data, and as far as projectability goes, this is about the same as making a guesstimate. At least you'll have the opportunity to do some probing and gain more insight into the factors underlying consumer behavior. To put it another way, if you're already doing some qualitative research and don't intend to do anything more, you might as well get market information out of it as well. But be aware of the potential bias that the nonrepresentative sample will carry.

Conduct your own scaled-down quantitative research: Assuming we are still focusing on Web users, we can gather data on consumption levels by executing a Web-based survey. The potential for bias will depend upon the source of our sample.

Ideally, you will be able to gather participants from a source that contains a good cross-section of the target market and attempt to construct a sample that represents each type of customer you expect to target. The issues associated with gathering a sample were discussed extensively in Chapter 5; review that information if you plan to execute your own primary research.

One way to limit the potential for a distorted perspective is to avoid using nonrepresentative samples to describe the overall market size or consumption levels. Instead, perform your analysis by first segmenting the market and then investigating the characteristics and behaviors of the segments independently. Doing so can provide results that are reasonably projectable to the segment. Segmentation can be a powerful way of getting usable information out of a less-than-optimum sample. Methods of segmentation are discussed in detail in Chapter 9, but here is a simple example:

> We want to find category consumption metrics for the online auto parts store introduced earlier in the chapter, but we find ourselves needing to use a nonrepresentative sample (for any of a variety of reasons). Rather than give up altogether because we can't be confident of the data's projectablity to the total marketplace, we perform an a priori segmentation of the data.[1] We believe there exist three distinct groups of auto parts buyers in the market, and their characteristics are going to have the most impact on the consumption levels of the consumers in the auto parts field:
> - *Oil Changers:* Perform general maintenance tasks like oil changes, filter replacements, and windshield wiper upgrades.
> - *Goodwrenches:* Perform intermediate repairs such as brake jobs, clutch work, carburetor cleaning, and minor exhaust and electrical work.
> - *Customizers:* Looks at the vehicle as a hobby, upgrading drivetrain and suspension components for performance, adding customized exhausts, and performing body enhancements.

[1]See Chapter 9.

In our survey, we ask a set of questions that allows us to assign each respondent to one of these groups. The process is detailed in Chapter 9. We also ask some questions about spending levels in the auto parts category. When we do our analysis, we simply look at the spending level data within the segment.

In our example, the data might look like this:

Segment	Oil Changers	Goodwrenches	Customizers
Average yearly spending on auto parts	$75	$400	$2,100

If we are confident in our segment definition, we can obtain an understanding of all the other pertinent characteristics that describe each segment (such as consumption levels).

Further, if we have a way of obtaining the relative sizes of each segment in the overall marketplace, we can reverse-engineer a decent estimate of the overall market's consumption levels.

If you choose to conduct some research with a nonrepresentative sample (using a segmentation-driven analysis plan like the one in the example), a good, cost-effective means of obtaining a sample and quickly fielding a study is Greenfield Online's QuickTake service (www.quicktake.com). This service enables you to construct a survey entirely online (similar to SurveyBuilder) and then field it to a sample size you designate. The sample is gathered via an interesting ad banner solicitation approach, so response rates are quite low, and obviously sample quality is compromised. But the service is cheap—often below $2,000 to field to 500 respondents—so it is an interesting and viable alternative to more rigorous approaches.

Utilize a nationally representative panel or omnibus survey: Panels and omnibus surveys (see Chapter 2) exist to study both online and off-line markets. With an omnibus, you can pay to include a few targeted questions in a larger survey fielded to a nationally representative sample. The data is then tabulated and returned to you shortly thereafter (typically less than two weeks after the end of surveying). To estimate the market value for an online auto parts store, you could include the following questions in an omnibus study:

> *Do you currently use the World Wide Web?*
>
> *Who is primarily responsible for the maintenance of your most recently purchased vehicle?*
>
> *How much did you spend in the past year on parts for your vehicle that you installed yourself?*

The catch to using an omnibus survey is that you are charged by the number of questions asked and the number of respondents the question is fielded to. Typically this is in the range of approximately $400 to $1,000 per question per thousand respondents. If the area of inquiry is likely to have a low incidence (e.g., do-it-yourself auto repairers), you may not get a reliable sample size for your key metric (spending on auto parts) within the 1,000 respondents. To survey a statistically stable number of respondents, you may need to stay in field for a longer period (and incur additional costs). In our example, we would need to find approximately 60 people in 1,000 who purchased auto parts and used the Web. Investigating a topic with a more specific target population could end up being quite costly and warrant the use of a panel instead.

Panels, discussed in Chapters 2 and 6, offer the advantage of being able to target your questioning to a group of consumers who are preselected to meet your market definition. Panels are built from large groups who have agreed to be surveyed from time to time and have completed extensive background questionnaires. This background information enables you to ask detailed questions among a group of consumers who are qualified to address the topic at hand. Panels are very costly to build and maintain, so you will pay a premium to talk to panelists. There is not generally a set pricing scheme to access most panels, as the panel research company often attempts to sell additional consulting services and research along with panel access. Even for a small number of questions, expect to pay in excess of several thousand dollars to talk to a panel.

Market Growth

Your market is not static. It is constantly changing. Some will be on the rise while others have topped out and are fading. The astronomical valuations of e-businesses illustrate that growth prospects are especially pertinent to investors. New ventures are frequently called upon to demonstrate the near- and long-term growth potential of their markets. It's a reasonable request: The market's growth impacts market size down the line, and ultimately, your company's bottom line as well.

How to Get This Information

As we have mentioned, the investment community is a great resource for this type of information. It has a huge vested interest in predicting the prospects of industries and industry sectors. The personal investing craze has led to the development of dozens of investment information portals that offer vast amounts of industry and company-specific analysis. After conducting some searches of these portals, you will discover that there is plenty of fluff out there as well. To cut to the chase, use services like Dialog (openaccess.dialog.com/business) that enable you to conduct granular searches for previous research and analysis on your topic of interest. Dialog and other subscriber information services like Lexis-Nexis index market research studies, industry and market analysis reports, news sources, and the like. If you find an abstract for a useful report, you can usually purchase the full article or report for a marginal fee ($2 to $3 for most information).

Online, the two most prominent e-strategy and research firms, Forrester (www.forrester.com) and Jupiter (www.jup.com), periodically issue industry spotlight reports on a variety of established and budding online business sectors. In addition to discussing the major players and issues, these reports also forecast growth. The projections are based on a combination of current spending levels and modeling that uses primary research to gauge anticipated spending in future years. DeepCanyon (www.deepcanyon.com) also offers links to and previews of syndicated studies from a wide range of vendors (typically focusing on high-tech topics), and will alert you if a new study matching your criteria comes out.

In your search, don't discount articles published in the general or business press. Frequently, coverage is given to industries that are growing rapidly or in decline, with potentially useful data points included as supporting evidence. Authors frequently pull this information from primary research—typically from syndicated studies available for purchase. For example, articles on e-commerce liberally quote sources like Jupiter and Forrester as evidence to support their thesis.

Customer Characteristics

Finally, and perhaps most important, you should seek to profile the consumers who make up your marketplace. Are they men? Women? How old are they? What do they do for a living? Are they concentrated in urban areas or scattered throughout the countryside?

Whether you are researching the overall marketplace, the online marketplace, or your own customer base, being able to put a face to and get inside the mind of your target consumer is arguably the most basic and most valuable application of marketing research. It will shape the development of your product, drive your attempts to reach the customer with marketing, suggest the messages that will be most likely to motivate them to trial and purchase, and spur ideas for customer loyalty strategies designed to improve retention of your hard-won market share.

An almost virtually infinite range of facts is available about your customer. Each market has its own unique defining characteristics, but in general, they fall into seven major categories:

1. demographics and socioeconomics;
2. Webographics;
3. corpographics;
4. attitudes, values, and lifestyle;
5. consumer behavior;
6. brand relationships; and
7. media consumption.

Demographics and Socioeconomics

Demographic and socioeconomic data offer the most basic understanding of who your customer is. You already have a conceptual idea, but this information will ground the hypothetical. Perhaps its most powerful application is the elimination of any discrepancies that exist within the organization about who the customer is. Putting everyone on the same page increases the efficiency of the group and the quality of the product.

Demographics

- Age
- Gender
- Geography or region
- Household or family size
- Marital status
- Parental status
- Race, nationality, or ethnicity
- Religion

Socioeconomics

- Education
- Employment status
- Income
- Home ownership

Webographics

Webographics is a term coined for data that describes a consumer's relationship to online media. It is vital to site development strategy, content tone, and marketing efforts. Webographics encompasses:

- Access locations
- Browser or computer platform[2]

---

[2]Browser and some computer platform data is typically captured in Web-server access logs and can be reported on using any of a variety of third-party activity reporting packages. These types of questions are generally omitted from surveys unless the analysis plan calls for collecting this type of data.

- Connection speeds
- Internet service provider
- Popular online activities
- Web experience level
- Web usage level

Corpographics

Sometimes referred to as *firmographics*, corpographics describe a consumer's work life. This information is particularly critical to businesses who seek to sell products or services to other businesses (also known as B2B). Corpographics includes:

- Employer size
- Industry
- Occupation
- Organizational role

Attitudes, Values, and Lifestyle

Demographically, many consumers look similar. Beyond the top-line statistics, however, lie vastly different lifestyles, world-views, and personalities that can dramatically impact purchase behavior and brand preferences. Factors include:

- Personality self-descriptors
- Opinions on social issues
- Participation in social activities
- Recreation, hobbies, and interests
- Political party affiliation

Consumer Behavior

The crux of many a research inquiry, consumer behavior focuses on issues key to anyone seeking to sell or market products: What do consumers buy? What are they in the market for? How much do they spend? Where do they do their shopping? Data encompasses:

- Products shopped for or purchased
- Sales channels used
- Consumption patterns and spending levels

Brand Relationships

This data largely drives analysis of the competitive environment (see Chapter 11). It includes:

- Brand awareness
- Brand perceptions
- Brand preferences

Media Consumption

Advertising is the primary means of marketing a product or brand. Understanding the types and quantity of media consumed by the target customer allows effective placement of advertising messages to reach the desired audience (see Chapter 15). Data in this category includes:

- Types of media consumed (TV, radio, print, Web)
- Levels of media consumption
- Cannibalization of other media types by Web use
- Programming watched, read, or listened to

Clearly, profiling your market is a broad undertaking with applications that are as varied as the metrics collected. Because this area of inquiry is so vast, you should concentrate on obtaining only the information that is critical to your business objectives. As we discussed in Chapter 7, there are many things that would be "nice to know" about your customer, but that aren't essential. Staying focused on your objectives will help you avoid research that sprawls out of control.

For example, if you are building an online business that has no plans to establish a local presence or execute regional advertising, there is little reason to know whether your potential market lives in Boise, Boston, or Brooklyn. You would, however, be concerned with issues like Web experience levels, home versus work usage, Internet connection speeds, and other Web-specific characteristics. On the other hand, convenience delivery firms like Kozmo.com, which need to open distribution and delivery networks to operate on a local basis, would be very concerned with collecting geographic data to determine areas with the highest concentrations of their target customers (even as far as identifying specific neighborhoods within a city).

In addition to describing your market, a primary application of profiling is to allow the market to be *segmented* into meaningful subgroups that benefit from being treated differently in terms of strategy, and promotion. Segmentation is discussed in Chapter 9.

How to Get This Information

The resources used to profile the market depend upon your level of measurement. Recall that there are three basic levels:

1.   your current customer base;
2.   the online target market; and
3.   the overall target market.

Current Customers

When studying your current customers, primary research is certainly the best option. You are unlikely to find detailed information in a syndicated research report or other secondary source about something as specific as your own customer base. No one has the opportunity to understand your customer as well as you, and we urge you to leverage this opportunity to its maximum. Web site owners who wish to study their own visitors can easily survey a representative sample by randomly sampling users as they access the site. The process is simple and inexpensive. Companies that have non-Web-based products can also profile their customers via a Web survey, but they will need to contact customers via a customer list, preferably one that includes email addresses. Off-line companies that choose this route over traditional mail or phone surveys should be aware of the bias introduced by excluding customers who do not use the Web. Internet penetration is projected to top 60% of U.S. households by 2003 (and will become near ubiquitous among many target demographics), so this bias will diminish. But for now, most off-line products stick to traditional methods (such as product warranty registration cards) of profiling their customers.

Online Target Market

Beyond your immediate customer base is the universe of consumers you haven't yet reached. For online ventures, the most pressing concern is understanding the online target market. In our chapter on sampling (Chapter 5), we discussed how obtaining a private representative sample of your online target market can easily break the bank. The RDD (random digit dial) methodology is the best way of obtaining a representative sample of the general population. Unfortunately, it can be very expensive when you need to talk to consumers with specific characteristics (e.g., online users who repair their own cars and spend more than $400 a year on the necessary parts).

For ventures attempting to understand their online marketplace, there are really only two viable methods:

1. consumer panels, and
2. syndicated research.

Consumer Panels

Panels, introduced in Chapter 5, were created because of the massive expense associated with studying anything but the most mainstream of markets. Panels exist for any of a variety of specialties, such as technology, executive decision makers, medical and health fields, and of course, online users.

To profile a target market via an online consumer panel, you must first define the key characteristics that make a consumer a likely candidate for your product or service. For example:

- female,
- age 25 to 44,
- spend more than $50 a month on fashion products,
- exercise more than twice a week, and
- ski at least six times a year.

Panel members complete an initial background survey that gathers metrics (primarily demographics and some broad consumer behavior measurements) commonly used to define target markets. To the extent this background survey permits, your targeting criteria will be used to field your survey to panelists who meet the requirements. Having background information on panelists saves you the effort and expense of soliciting, surveying, and screening out large numbers of respondents who fall outside of the target market. If your target market definition is very specific, it is unlikely that a panelist's background survey will include all the metrics needed. In the example, a panel's background survey might gather age, gender, and sporting activities, but nothing about the frequency of participation in those sporting activities.

In this case, the survey will be fielded to the closest possible sample of panelists, with the remaining screening questions included in the survey itself. Panelists who take the profiling survey but fail to meet the target criteria will be eliminated from the final sample. You will usually still be charged for every panelist you interview, so this results in additional sample costs. Overall, however, the process is still more efficient than attempting to contact consumers via RDD and going through the extensive screening process that methodology would require.

A word of caution on using panels to profile your target market: Most online panels are developed or statistically manipulated via weighting techniques to reflect the national population. As you drill down into more specific subgroups, any bias that exists in the panel (e.g., over- or underrepresenting some types of consumers) may be disproportionately magnified within the specific group you are studying. For this reason, panels that employ strict random solicitation techniques (preferably RDD) are recommended for this application. In theory, these panels should be less vulnerable to self-selection bias or other distortions caused by an incomplete sample frame.

Syndicated Research

If it is available for your market, *syndicated research* is generally a more cost-effective profiling option than panel work. The savings in cost comes at the expense of being able to specify a customized set of metrics that have meaning to your particular business objectives; but quality syndicated products typically contain most of the profiling information outlined earlier in the chapter. Most of these studies have the added advantage of having been fielded against random samples (yielding reliable data), and all, of course, are ready to use immediately, with no work required on your part.

Syndicated profiles are widely available for off-line markets, and recently for online markets as well. As we mentioned in Chapter 2, syndicated studies are only done for markets with a well-established information demand. You can expect to find good coverage in established or fast-growing markets like personal wireless products, online investing, food and beverages, or information technology. Good places to begin your search include online market research directories like Marketresearch.com (www.marketresearch.com), MarketSearch (www.marketsearch-dir.com), Profound (www.profound.com), or Publications Resource Group (www.prgguide.com). Online ventures that wish to obtain comprehensive profiling and analysis of major online sectors can turn to Jupiter's or Forrester's expensive (but well-written) industry analyses.

Those wishing to profile a niche or emerging market, however, will find slim pickings.

If you find yourself unable to locate a study that profiles your market explicitly, USADATA (www.usadata.com) may offer a solution. USADATA takes the data obtained via respected national studies conducted by firms like Scarborough (www.scarborough.com) and Mediamark (www.mediamark.com) and resells customized "slices" as Data-To-Go™ reports. You can obtain demographic profiles, media consumption habits, cross-category utilization, and a host of other information about a target that can be defined very precisely. USADATA specifically targets smaller businesses with its services, and has kept prices down to very reasonable levels. For less than $1,000 you should be able to obtain a reasonably projectable, reasonably comprehensive profile of your target market. That is certainly more than can be said for other approaches you might try.

Market Trends

Given the astonishing pace of change in today's business environment, looking to the future of your market is no longer a competitive advantage. It is a prerequisite.

Customers are becoming increasingly fickle; they switch brands quickly when the competition anticipates their next unmet needs. Knowing where the market is headed will enable you to catch it as it turns the next corner, breaking new ground instead of being a follower.

Online markets will be particularly impacted by market shifts as the Web population moves toward the mainstream. New Web users bring new attitudes, needs, and demographics. Globalization of the Internet presents new opportunities and challenges to reach and capture markets in different cultures and different languages. The competitive landscape is constantly shifting as well. New companies emerge each day, with new technologies and solutions to problems that didn't exist a few short years ago.

Trends can take many forms. Some trends are attitudinal, while others are behavioral. Understanding attitudinal shifts is critical, because many behavior patterns are actually manifestations of underlying attitudes and values.

How to Get This Information

A first step toward predicting the future is to understand the present. Read the general press and specialty publications that chronicle your industry. Always be on the lookout for signals that a new trend is emerging.

Numerous firms dedicate a great deal of time and effort to helping their clients anticipate impending shifts in the playing field. Strategy consultants like Forrester (www.forrester.com), Jupiter (www.jup.com), and The Yankee Group (www.yankeegroup.com) publish advisories and analyst reports that address the impact of emerging technology and market trends on e-business strategy. Highly respected SRI International's Business Intelligence Center (future.sri.com) specializes in predicting a wide range of future consumer trends, and has long been known for identifying important shifts in the way consumers spend their money as a result of technology and societal changes. USADATA (www.usadata. com), beyond offering slice-and-dice-data, is also a reseller of analyst reports on a comprehensive range of industries, many of which discuss the trends that will shape these industries in the future.

For those looking to curl up with a good book, Faith Popcorn's *Clicking: 17 Trends That Drive Your Business—and Your Life* (1998) and its best-selling predecessor, *The Popcorn Report: Faith Popcorn on the Future of Your Company, Your World, Your Life* (1992) discuss broad changes in societal behavior that ultimately boil down to implications for business. Check out her site (www.brainreserve.com) while you're waiting for the book to arrive in the mail. In this spirit, another entertaining and potentially useful read is *The Future Ain't What It Used to Be: The 40 Cultural Trends Transforming Your Job, Your Life, Your World* (Mary Meehan et al., 1999).

CHAPTER 9

Segmentation: Developing Target Markets

The days of mass markets are numbered. Customers across the country are becoming increasingly differentiated from each other. These fragmented consumers are no longer interested in one-size-fits-all products; they demand that marketers design and create offerings customized to their specific needs. The trend is even more apparent online. With the cost of production greatly reduced, businesses find it profitable to target more and more specialized subgroups of consumers through niche offerings. The process of identifying and understanding these special populations is known as *segmentation.*

WHAT IS SEGMENTATION?

The concept of market segmentation is based on the idea that large markets are comprised of a number of subgroups. Each subgroup, or segment, has different characteristics, such as demographics, lifestyles, product requirements, or consumption habits, that could benefit from different product features or marketing approaches. Ultimately, these differences suggest that the greatest profitability may be achieved by developing multiple strategies to address the unique characteristics of each segment.

Online, decreased development costs combined with technology that allows for greater customization drives many ventures to focus on narrowly defined targets—often many at the same time. Each target has very specific needs that can be addressed in a product. In many cases, a product focused on the needs of a specific segment can be brought to market cheaper and faster than one designed to have broad-based appeal. As such, one of the primary objectives of segmentation is to identify subgroups that may be more profitably targeted than the mass market. Segmentation can also be used as part of a multiple segmentation or multistage strategy. In a multiple segmentation strategy, a few key segments are identified and their independent needs developed for simultaneously. In a multistage strategy, a primary segment is targeted for early adoption, with other groups slated for later efforts after the brand has developed a core following and a solid customer base.

Choosing a Segmentation Scheme

There is no one right way to conduct market segmentation, and the many possible approaches vary in complexity. In some respects, segmentation is an art as much as a science. Ultimately, the goal is to develop segments that are *actionable and have strategic meaning to your business.*

Segmentation seeks to place consumers into groups that adhere to the following principles:

1. Individuals in the same segment are similar to one another on key attributes.
2. Individuals in different segments are different from one another on key attributes.

The attributes considered key are those that are most likely to predict other, strategically important characteristics such as the likelihood of switching brands in the next year, spending more than a certain amount in a product category, or trying a new product concept.

There are two basic approaches to segmenting your user base:

A priori. A priori segmentation uses a hypothesis about the marketplace to divide it into segments. This hypothesis is then tested by conducting firsthand data analysis to determine if the segmentation predicts differences in response to the marketing or product mix. A priori segmentation is often based on personal intuition or organizational experience, and frequently breaks up markets along demographic, geographic, or behavioral lines. The initial hypothesis may be informed by findings from previous qualitative or quantitative studies.

Post hoc. This approach allows the data to drive the discovery of consumer characteristics predictive of response to the product or marketing mix. Advanced analytical processes are applied to the dataset to determine factors that predict key metrics of strategic interest (e.g., likelihood of spending over \$1,000 on a personal computer or openness to trying a new brand). Once key predictors have been identified, respondents are assigned to groups based on a set of rules. The process typically involves statistical wizardry through a combination of factor analysis (www.statsoft.com/textbook/stfacan.html), correspondence analysis (www.statsoft.com/textbook/stcoran.html), k-means clustering (www.statsoft.com/textbook/tcluan.html#k), or classification-tree analysis, such as CHAID or CART (www.statsoft.com/textbook/stclatre.html). The primary research you may have conducted in order to profile your market or customer base can, in fact, be leveraged again to segment the market.

It is beyond the scope of this text to go into the details of the techniques. Advanced market segmentation techniques are typically conducted with the aid of professional consultation, but numerous

resources are available in print and online for those who choose to
tackle the problem firsthand. Introductory discussions of segmentation can be found on DSS Research's site (www.dssresearch.com/-
library/Segment/understanding.asp) and at the site of an Australian
university professor (www.buseco.monash.edu.au/Subjects/MKT/-
MTPonline/segment.html).

Whatever the approach, the ultimate objective of developing
a segmentation strategy is to arrive at a succinct set of predictor
metrics (and hence, survey questions) that can quickly tell you if a
consumer belongs in one segment or another. These questions can
then be leveraged in subsequent research or ongoing performance
tracking (see Chapter 16) to provide critical context for the information you obtain going forward.

If you have a few evenings to spend cozying up to the topic
of segmentation, we recommend checking out The Clustered
World, by Michael J. Weiss. Though not a textbook, it provides an
entertaining sociological look at segmentation, focusing mostly on
the PRIZM geodemographic approach. For a more rigorous treatment of the subject, pick up Art Weinstein's *Market Segmentation:
Using Demographics, Psychographics and Other Niche Marketing
Techniques to Predict and Model Customer Behavior.*

Once a market has been segmented according to differences
in the key predictor variables, segments can be described with all
the other variables you collected. Profiling each segment provides
a rich insight into the similarities and differences among the subgroups in the market.

Most segmentation definitions are on based on a combination
of variables from four categories: geographic, demographic or
socioeconomic, psychographic, and behavioral.

Geographic Segmentation

Segmenting markets by location typically occurs when a business anticipates regional differences in needs, wants, or distribution
strategies. A brewery may market heavier, darker beers to colder
northern states and lighter beers in warmer climates, for example.

Localized online city guides such as Citysearch.com also practice geographic segmentation, developing products and marketing programs for highly populated (and profitable) regions and specific urban areas.

Geographic segmentation variables include:

- Country
- Region (e.g., Northeast, West, Southeast)
- State
- Metropolitan area
- City
- Zip Code

Demographic or Socioeconomic Segmentation

These variables distinguish segments using demographic or socioeconomic variables such as age, gender, income, or family size. It is a very popular approach, especially in many packaged goods applications, since product needs often follow demographic lines (parents of young children buy diapers; women buy lipstick). Online, demographic segmentation strategy is evidenced by ventures like ChickClick.com, which operates a network of properties targeted at granular submarkets of young women—teenage females, 20-something women, and single mothers.

Demographic or socioeconomic segmentation variables include:

- Age
- Education
- Gender
- Home ownership
- Household or family size
- Income
- Marital Status
- Occupation
- Parental status

- Race, nationality, or ethnicity
- Religion
- Social class

Psychographic (Attitudinal) Segmentation

Attitudinal segmentation variables allow identification of differences in consumers' lifestyles, beliefs, or personalities. They can be utilized when consumers with similar demographic characteristics prefer different brands, have different product requirements, and follow different spending habits. They are particularly valuable, however, for supplementing more concrete demographic or behavioral segmentation variables. For example, psychographic segmentation is often used to refine a brand's personality and marketing message to appeal most strongly to the targeted audience. SRI International popularized the use of attitudinal segmentation with the development of its VALS (Values and Lifestyles) classification scheme (future.sri.com/VALS/VALSindex.shtml) in the late 1970s.

Psychographic segmentation variables include:

- Lifestyle characteristics ("Eat out regularly," "Homebody")
- Agreement with personality self-descriptors ("I hate surprises," "I like to dress fashionably")
- Attitudes on social issues ("There is too much violence on TV," "Prayer should be allowed in schools")

Behavioral Segmentation

Grouping consumers based on their behavior is one of the most powerful and effective approaches to segmentation. Previous behavior is often the best predictor of future activities, so the majority of segmentation strategies contain at least some behavioral component. A sporting equipment Web site might segment customers by the number or type of sports they participate in regularly. An investment Web site might segment customers by their trading frequency, and can focus specifically on the active day trader or the less-involved retirement investor. As we'll see in Chapter 11 on sitecentric research, a behavioral segmentation scheme can be as simple as dividing your customer base into heavy versus casual users.

A particularly useful variant, called *benefits segmentation,* groups consumers according to their reasons for using a product. Email users, for example, might be grouped into those who primarily use the technology to keep in touch with family and friends, and those who consider it integral to business communications.

Yet another variant widely employed in determining the primary and secondary targets for new product rollout is grouping consumers based on their reaction or stated likelihood to adopt a tested product concept. Those who exhibited the greatest response are targeted with marketing for early versions to develop a core user franchise before more widespread investment is made.

Variables driving behavioral segmentation include:

- Amount of product or category use
- Benefits sought from usage
- Brand loyalty and switching behavior
- Brand or category awareness
- Reaction to a product concept
- Satisfaction level
- Substitute products
- Type of use
- Unmet needs
- Usage scenarios

OBTAINING SEGMENTATION DATA

Because segmentation requires the examination of the interrelationships among multiple variables, syndicated reports and other secondary resources are unsuitable for the job. Data should be gathered in a way that allows customized analysis. Some providers of secondary research data, like Simmons (www.smrb.com), Scarborough (www.scarborough.com), and Mediamark (www.mediamark.com), may be able to provide customized access to their databases of consumer research studies. An additional secondary research option is USADATA. Its LifeStyle Connect product links consumer behavior and demographics to the PRIZM geodemographic clustering system developed by Claritas (www.claritasexpress.com/med/med.htm#prizm).

Most frequently, market segmentation requires primary research. Panels are one option, and are especially relevant when segmenting narrow online markets. While gathering data to segment the market for office supplies might be cost-effectively accomplished via nationally representative phone research, doing the same for Web users who purchase laptop computer peripherals would be far more expensive.

A more affordable approach is to perform a segmentation of your existing sitecentric user base, if you already have a site and an audience. Even if you eventually hope to segment the larger marketplace, the easy access to a sample population and the ability to execute flexible survey designs make sitecentric approaches excellent for experimenting with your segmentation strategy before turning to costlier approaches.

USING SEGMENTATION DATA

Selection of a Marketing Approach

Having segmented a market, a business must decide how to deal with it. Should it take on the whole market, or concentrate on a small part of it? A business traditionally chooses to attack a segmented market in one of three ways:

1. If differences between groups are not significant, or the payoff of a specialized treatment of each segment is not high enough, an *undifferentiated approach* many be

pursued. Here the same product and marketing mix are provided to all segments.

2. If segments are highly differentiated and independently pursuing each is considered more profitable, a business may take a *differentiated approach.* Here, multiple segments are pursued simultaneously, with a product and marketing combination tailored specifically to each segment.

3. Finally, in the *focused approach* (aka niche marketing), a business decides that some segments have more potential than others, and chooses to concentrate its efforts on serving a subset of the total market. This approach may be extended as part of a multistage approach, whereby an initial seed market is pursued and maximized before opening up the focus to broader targets.

Marketing Strategy

Whether you elect to take on all segments or a small target, a marketing strategy must be developed. How will you reach the intended consumers? How will you speak to them once you've gotten their attention?

Different market segments may require different marketing strategies. Because a marketing effort is half message and half medium, a business must understand what information to convey to each segment, and how each segment can best be reached with advertising. Knowledge of the demographics and psychographics of target segments can set the tone of advertising efforts to speak to each group in the language they understand best. Many segmentation studies also examine the media consumption habits—favored television shows, Web sites, radio programming, magazines, and newspapers—of each segment. This data enables media planners to place the advertising in the locations most likely to reach the intended consumers with the appropriate message.

Product Development and Positioning

Different segments may seek different benefits from product usage. Indeed, this is a primary means of segmentation to begin with. In addressing each segment, developers can identify differences between groups as to their expectations from the product. If differences are significant and each group is sufficiently valuable, variations in the product may be developed to best satisfy each group. Often it is impossible to economically develop variations of a product for each segment. Instead, marketing efforts can be used to emphasize different features or advantages of the same product to different segments. This powerful approach, known as *product positioning,* is seen everywhere in modern marketing practice; it is one of the fundamental applications of segmentation strategy.

Distribution

It may be discovered that, while a market has a universal need for a product or service, different subgroups obtain it in different ways. A business may need to develop distribution strategies that reach each target segment with the product or service through different channels. For example, Adam.com develops and publishes content for online users who desire detailed health and medical information. Originally operating as a health destination, it has segmented its market and developed a distribution strategy to repackage its core content and distribute it through multiple outlets. The company now reaches its market through distribution via general consumer sites, health organizations, academic channels, and other organizations that have a need for detailed health content but don't have the budget to create it on their own.

SEGMENTATION PROCESS EXAMPLE

All of the discussion thus far may have seemed very abstract. To close out this chapter, we present a hypothetical example that illustrates the basic process and principles.

A business in the process of building an online sporting goods store realizes that there are more specific target markets out there than simply "sports enthusiasts." Realizing that they have only a limited amount of funding and time available to prove their concept, they hope to narrow their focus to a few particularly lucrative segments and, once successful, broaden their strategy accordingly.

Having only marginal information on the sporting goods consumption habits of online users, they decide to undertake their own segmentation research. They enlist the help of a professional consultation firm (ours, of course!) to assist with the study. Since a nationally representative sample of Web-using sporting goods consumers is too expensive to obtain via RDD phone sampling (the preferred method), we suggest turning to an online consumer panel.

Because we are interested in understanding only consumers of sporting goods, we contract with the panel provider to execute a survey of 1,000 panelists who indicated that they engaged in a sports-related activity in the past six months. We are not especially concerned with whether the panel is nationally representative, because we plan to use the research only to understand relevant differences between segments we identify. All we care about is whether the panel is diverse enough to represent the full spectrum of consumers in the overall online sports market.

Given the stated strategy, our client wants to identify subgroups who will be the most attractive early adopters of their service. Three issues are of key interest:

1. spending level in the sporting goods category;
2. previous online purchase behavior; and
3. willingness to purchase sporting goods online.

Our preliminary objective will be to identify other factors that are most likely to influence these metrics. Later, we will seek to understand all the supplementary characteristics that define each segment.

We conduct an extensive survey of the panel sample, gathering a variety of data including demographics, webographics, attitudinal data, media consumption habits, and of course, the three key metrics, along with consumer behavior metrics relating to sporting goods.

Performing data reduction techniques and correlation analysis, we discover that two of the key metrics, prior online purchase behavior and willingness to purchase sporting goods online, are intrinsically linked. In other words, if a consumer has purchased online in the past, they'd certainly be willing to buy a soccer ball on the Web too. Since two of the metrics are basically one and the same, we continue with the analysis now focusing on spending levels and previous online purchase behavior.

A large part of segmentation is to develop a marketing strategy, so we need to understand what factors are most related to a consumer's propensity to purchase sporting goods online, and to spend a lot of money when they do!

Further statistical processing reveals that a few key factors are clearly predictive of our desired attributes:

- age,
- income,
- occupation, and
- Web experience level.

In other words, the age, income, occupation, and Web experience level of a consumer highly correlates to his or her likelihood of being a big online sporting goods spender. (In reality, things don't necessarily work out so cleanly, but that's the point of a hypothetical example.) Let's assume that we discover that consumers fitting the following profile comprise the most attractive segment:

- males
- aged 25 to 34
- employed as software engineers
- earning $75,000 to $100,000 annually
- expert Web users

We term this group our *primary target segment,* because they will be the first consumers we hope to market to, satisfy, and develop into core customers.

Another group, while still attractive, doesn't spend quite so much on sporting goods, but will still be likely to make some online purchases in the category. This *secondary target segment* has the following characteristics:

- males
- aged 35 to 49
- employed in professional services (doctors, lawyers, accountants)
- earning $150,000 + annually
- intermediate Web users

Our segmentation data can then be used to profile each of these segments to understand some basic characteristics, such as:

- their purchasing behavior (to identify the products they want);
- their attitudes (to suggest the marketing language that best appeals to their sensibilities); and
- their media consumption habits (to determine where they can best be reached with advertising).

Beyond these fundamentals, the understanding you can obtain is limited only by the data you gathered in the segmentation research. One of the dividends that the research will yield is the identification of the key metrics that predict segment membership. These metrics, and the survey questions used to gather them, can be used again and again in future research to provide context for each subsequent finding. We reference these key segmentation metrics throughout the remainder of the book.

Having identified segments within the overall market and profiled their characteristics, we must now select a marketing approach. If we can appeal to both segments with the same product offerings, marketing strategy, and site design, there is no need to pursue the segmentation strategy any further; we can take an undifferentiated approach to serving both segments. We discover, however, that our primary target segment, while spending big money, purchases only in a few select product categories. Golf, ski, and rock climbing comprise 75% of their anticipated purchases in the next year. The secondary target segment, on the other hand, desires products across the entire spectrum—from bathing suits to soccer balls. Additionally, our primary target segment tends to read, watch, and surf easily identified media outlets. Our secondary segment is, again, all over the board. As a result, a one-size-fits-all approach to serving both segments cannot work. We advise our clients to pursue the primary target segment, and save plans for broadening their focus until after the initial group has taken hold.

FIGURE 9.1 Post hoc segmentation process

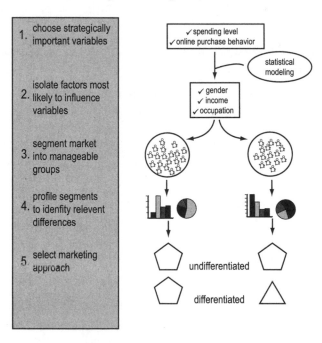

CHAPTER 10

Competition: Assessment and Positioning

Almost any business—but especially an online business—faces competition that vies for the same customers. As much as we hope it might, an isolationist strategy doesn't make them go away. A business that acknowledges and plans for the competitive environment stands a far greater chance of achieving success than one that develops strategy in a vacuum. Marketing research can enhance the prospects for success by assessing immediate and secondary competition in current markets; and can point out positioning opportunities by evaluating your business's competitive strengths and weaknesses vis-á-vis the competition. In some cases, research can even discover new, untapped markets largely ignored by competitors.

ASSESSING THE COMPETITIVE ENVIRONMENT

Within your chosen target market or market segments, any number of competing firms are courting the same customers. Some basic questions to answer about the competition include:

- Who are they?
- How much market share have they captured (and which customers are still 'in play')?
- Where are they focusing their strategy?
- What are their strengths or vulnerabilities?

Large corporations often maintain dedicated in-house *competitive intelligence* teams or contract out the work to specialists (see the Society of Competitive Intelligence Professionals' Web site at www.scip.org), but basic answers to most of these questions should be answerable within your organization. You can augment this knowledge through a program of competitive environmental scanning.

We've already discussed the ramifications of how you choose to define your market and how this impacts who you consider to be your competition. We won't begin another philosophical rant on this topic; instead we focus on competitors you consider most immediate.

If the major players in your space are unknown to you, start by consulting directories of businesses in your industry. Hoover's (www.hoovers.com) performs admirably in this respect, though a subscription (currently running $110 annually) is required to access in-depth information. Hoover's profiles publicly traded and numerous privately held companies, organized by industry, in an easy-to-use format. You can also get started using a site like Yahoo!, which also breaks out its 500,000-plus links to leading companies by major industry classification.

Industry associations may also make lists of their membership available, which is a useful avenue for identifying smaller fish on the rise to becoming bigger challenges. Start your online search at Association Central (www.associationcentral.com) or the American Society of Association Executives (www.asaenet.org/Gateway/OnlineAssocSlist.html). Attending conferences in your field is never a bad idea, either. They provide the opportunity to speak with representatives of your competition and see exactly where your strategies and product lines overlap. You can keep abreast of this year's conference circuit at ExpoGuide (www.expoguide.com).

Having identified the businesses that pose your direct competition, take some time to visit their Web sites. You'll find a wealth of firsthand information about their product offerings, gain insight into their future strategies, and get a good idea of who their target customers are. If the firm is publicly traded, sales and usage figures will be available in the investor relations section, which enables you to estimate the share of the market they've captured by comparing this data to your computation of the total value of the marketplace. If the competitor generates revenue from selling advertising space, it will have a media kit available for prospective advertisers. Requesting one will yield data on the types of consumers the company has succeeded in attracting. User tracking services like @Plan (www.webplan.net) and MediaMetrix (www.mediametrix.com) can provide you with a profile of the visitors who access the site, provided the traffic levels are high enough to be captured by their tracking systems.

Keeping up to date on the goings on of your primary competitors can quickly overwhelm you with information, but sometimes it's a necessary evil. Scanning the major industry news periodicals and Web sites can keep you tuned in to their latest moves. A comprehensive list of published magazines can be found online at in the National Directory of Magazines (www.mediafinder.com/-mag_home.cfm). Also be sure to check into PR news sites like Business Wire (www.businesswire.com) and PRNewswire (www.prnewswire.com), to be alerted when competitors make major announcements of product launches, management changes, and important business development deals. To have news on competitors sent directly to your inbox, sign up for DeepCanyon's (www.deepcanyon.com) Competitor Alert service. This useful tool continually scans online versions of all major U.S. newspapers for articles on your designated target, and emails you an alert whenever something turns up.

SPECIFIC COMPETITIVE ANALYSIS

A general competitive assessment can only suggest general actions. Your product development and marketing strategy can be significantly enhanced by conducting primary custom research that focuses on the specific strengths and weaknesses of your competitors—from the consumer's point of view. The remainder of this chapter concentrates on this process.

In conducting a competitive analysis study, you (and your respondents) will quickly become overwhelmed if you attempt to gather data on a large set of competitors. To make the process efficient and attainable, narrow your focus to include only four or five primary competitors. Select the ones that offer exactly or nearly the same type of product or services as you do, or ones that you hope to draw customers away from. Understanding their specific performance strengths and vulnerabilities lets you focus your efforts in later product development and marketing to have the maximum impact on building customer trial and loyalty.

Elements of the Analysis

A competitive analysis study employs a survey consisting of five main components:

1. customer profile;
2. awareness, trial, or usage of competing brands;
3. attribute importance assessment;
4. brand image; and
5. product performance ratings.

Customer Profile

As in most surveys, the first information you must obtain is background data on the respondents. Ideally, this data will be captured in such a way as to enable segmentation of the sample according to a scheme developed after reading Chapter 9. Analyzing each competitor's performance within the context of the segmentation allows you to zero in on the specific types of customers that each competitor has satisfied, and more important, those who are most likely to consider switching.

Awareness, Trial, or Usage of Competing Brands

Conducting primary research into the awareness, trial, or usage of your competitors' products is the most reliable method of determining market penetration and market share. Each metric provides a different comprehension of the competition's size and success.

Awareness measures the success of marketing efforts to build recognition.

Trial measures the success of marketing efforts to create a need and drive customers to try the product.

Usage measures the success of the product itself at meeting the needs of users and keeping them coming back.

When collected from a representative sample, these metrics establish which competitors are leaders in the market. Additionally, they provide a measure of each company's bottom-line success by evaluating the ability to convert consumers from awareness, to trial, to regular brand usage. Some competitors may have spent great amounts on advertising to generate high levels of awareness, but perhaps poor messaging failed to drive trial. Similarly, companies with high rates of trial may experience high rates of attrition, resulting in few regular users. Alternatively, brands with relatively small market share may have uniform awareness, trial, and usage rates. This could indicate that they have effectively targeted, marketed, and serviced a particular segment(s) of the marketplace. It could also mean that they simply have a well-performing but undermarketed product poised to take the industry by storm.

These simple metrics can be incredibly telling, but there is a catch. For this information to be reliable, it must be gathered via a nationally representative sample, or one that is representative of your market. Anything else can lead to a distorted perspective, since the sample might overrepresent some types of consumers and underrepresent others. Barring a nationally representative sample, collecting awareness, trial, and usage data is still critical to conducting competitive research. In order to learn anything about the performance of your competitors, you need to find users who have tried them. Further, you may analyze the types of consumers who have become regular users of the tested competitors to create a profile of their core user franchise.

Attribute Importance Assessment

Not all attributes are equally important in a consumer's decision-making process. Gathering this information has two main advantages. First, it allows you to identify the key performance factors driving brand choice among different market segments. Second, it enables identification of areas where the competition exceeds or underperforms customer expectations.

Brand Image

Another powerful type of data gathered in a competitive assessment study is the *brand image,* or *brand personality,* of your competitors. Much consumer behavior is more than simply choosing the brand with the best set of features and performance. Indeed, marketing plays a major role in positioning a brand in the minds of consumers, especially when the playing field is basically level in terms of real product performance.

Product Performance Ratings

The heart of the matter! Ratings can be gathered on very discrete elements of competitive performance, identifying specific areas where your brand must demonstrate proficiency simply as a cost of entry, and others where you have an opportunity to outshine the competition.

Conducting the Study

Ideally, a competitive analysis study is conducted against a nationally representative Web sample—presumably one that has been obtained from a Web panel. In reality, that's not always practical. Using a convenience or sitecentric sample, important issues can still be evaluated by focusing on the ratings of performance and the *types of customers* who provide these ratings. If we were to forgo gathering customer profile data, the projectability of the sample would become far more important. However, we will interpret the findings within the context of who is providing them. As we'll see in Chapter 14, you can conduct a similar study with users of your own site, include your own product in the ratings, and end up with a product-centric version of the classic SWOT (Strengths, Weaknesses, Opportunities, Threats) analysis.

Though projectability may not be critical, you need to obtain your sample from a source likely to have a high concentration of users involved in the category. Remember that respondents will have to have at least tried the tested brands to provide usable feedback. Ideally, you will obtain a sample that has a variety of usage styles and involvement levels. Light users and heavy users of the category are the minimum segments you should obtain.

Profile the Respondent and Screen, if Necessary

It is not necessary to profile your respondents to the extent that you might in a full-scale market profile study. Save the respondents' energy for the more critical focus of the study. The vital information to obtain is any data necessary to classify respondents into the market segments you defined in your segmentation scheme. If you haven't defined a segmentation scheme, the most critical data to gather is that which enables you to understand the respondents' relationship to the product category, for example:

- level of category usage,
- category experience level, and
- benefits sought from category usage.

In profiling the respondent, you also have the opportunity to confirm that he or she is sufficiently involved in the category to provide meaningful feedback. Respondents who do not use the types of products you are studying should be thanked for their participation and excused from the remainder of the study.

Gather Awareness, Trial, and Primary Usage of Tested Brands

The next step in the study serves two functions. First, it allows understanding of which brands have succeeded (or failed) in driving awareness, trial, and usage among different types of consumers. As we've mentioned, representative samples allow a particularly telling analysis: understanding the share of users a brand has succeeded in moving through a deepening relationship with the brand.

Second, the answers to these questions enable you to qualify users to answer more in-depth questions about their perceptions of the tested brands.

A quick way to gather this type of data is by means of a grid question like the one in Figure 10.1.

FIGURE 10.1: Brand trial and usage grid

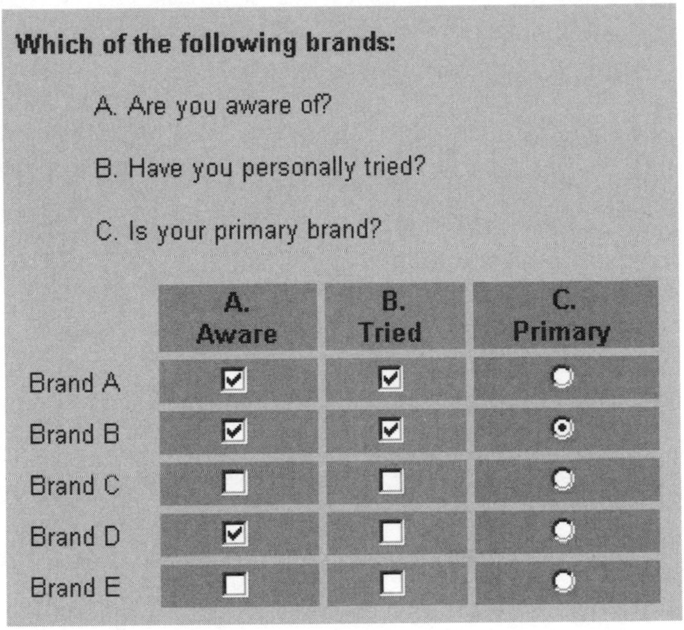

Which of the following brands:

    A. Are you aware of?

    B. Have you personally tried?

    C. Is your primary brand?

	A. Aware	B. Tried	C. Primary
Brand A	☑	☑	○
Brand B	☑	☑	◉
Brand C	☐	☐	○
Brand D	☑	☐	○
Brand E	☐	☐	○

Attribute Importance Assessment

Having obtained salient information about the respondent, and data on brand usage, the next step is to present a list of key product attributes that are then rated in terms of their importance to the respondent. The list of attributes should be as clear and concise as possible, since respondents have a limited attention span and may not discern subtle differences between similar attributes. Your organization should put significant thought into developing and refining the list of attributes tested in the study. Too many, and the quality of the data will suffer. Too few, and you risk missing a key driver of brand choice. An ideal place to develop the initial list is through qualitative research (either online or off-line) in which participants are asked to provide input on the issues impacting their decision to use one brand or another. This list should then be refined by members of your development and marketing teams to maximize clarity in the final survey. You need not restrict your list to include only specific product features. Issues like cost, customer service, and brand-related intangibles such as reputation, reliability, and prestige can also be included, for example:

Email updates on order status.

Live customer support.

No-questions-asked return policy.

Multimedia content.

Recognized brand name.

Is the one my friends use.

Detailed product information.

Lowest available prices.

Wide product selection.

Free shipping.

Online download of products.

Personalized recommendation.

Third-party product reviews.

There are many ways to measure the importance of product attributes, and unfortunately, no one right solution. When asking respondents to rate the importance of various aspects of product performance or the desirability of specific features, a common problem is that many respondents rank all factors as being highly important. They tend to hedge themselves, hesitant to say that anything is irrelevant to their decision.

This is understandable, but it is problematic from a research perspective. It results in an inability to identify issues truly motivating brand choice, and subsequently, an inability to identify specific areas of strength and weakness within the competition. One way of dealing with the issue is to use a larger number of ratings points in the scale. Rather than 5 or 7 points, 10 might be used in order to provide a greater opportunity for variation. Another approach is to use a scale that is intentionally biased to account for respondents' propensity to answer toward the high end of the scale. A question using such as scale appears in Figure 7.13.

This technique, while clearly biasing, has the intended effect of drawing out the range of responses and forcing respondents to discriminate between choices, rather than lumping every issue into the same category. Additional techniques, such as rank ordering and conjoint analysis, are discussed in Chapter 14.

The remaining stages of the survey will necessarily involve some degree of advanced survey functionality. As mentioned earlier, respondents can only be queried about brands they are familiar with. The section of the survey that gathers information on trial and regular usage will provide the required data to execute survey branching.

Theoretically, data could be gathered from any respondent who has had at least a trial experience with the tested brand. In practice, however, the complicated back-end custom programming necessary to meet the survey requirement leads us to suggest that you stick to obtaining performance metrics based on the respondent's primary brand. Though it's done mostly for logistical reasons, this approach has another important rationale: In a competitive situation, at least some market share will be gained at the expense of other competitors. To accomplish this goal, it makes the most sense to understand the toughest challenge you will face— breaking a customer's bond with a primary brand.

Brand Image

Preliminaries out of the way, you can now turn to sizing up the competition. One useful component is to gather the associations consumers have with each brand in your competitive set—the *brand image*. These associations are not necessarily driven by actual product performance, and are often more a result of the marketing function. Brand perceptions can be analyzed by a statistical modeling process known as *perceptual mapping*, whereby the brand image of each competitor is plotted in graphical form. The technique is useful for determining which brands are perceived as

FIGURE 10.2: Routing survey based on respondent's indicated primary brand

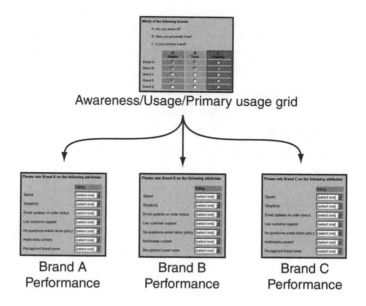

Awareness/Usage/Primary usage grid

Brand A
Performance

Brand B
Performance

Brand C
Performance

being similar (perhaps interchangable) and which ones have successfully developed a distinct identity for themselves. Perceptual mapping, like advanced segmentation approaches, is typically done with the aid of professional consultation. It's beyond the scope of this book to include an in-depth discussion of this tool, but a useful primer can be found online at Dr. Marshall Rice's site (www.yorku.ca/faculty/academic/mrice/index/docs/brandmap.htm).

Valuable data can be obtained without perceptual mapping, however, by simply comparing brand attribute scores from one competitor to another. First, develop a list of personality descriptors, or descriptive phrases that might be used to describe brands in the category. Again, this list can be developed via internal brainstorming sessions, or even better, guided by consumer feedback obtained in qualitative research. The list should contain a relatively equal number of positively-loaded and negatively-loaded items. All attributes are then placed in the survey, asking respondents to select the phrases that they feel best describe the tested brands.

FIGURE 10.3: Simple brand image assessment

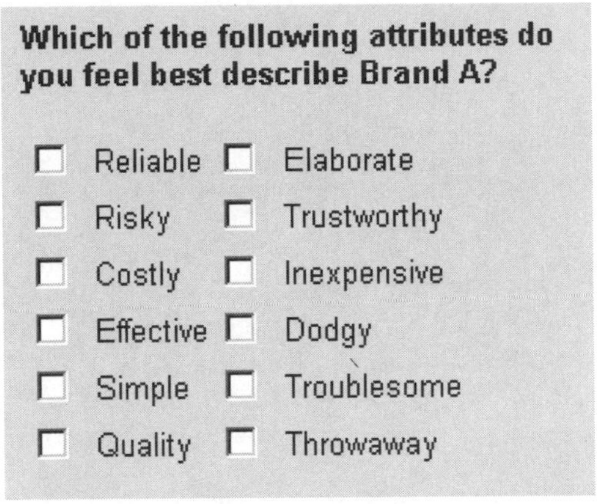

Which of the following attributes do you feel best describe Brand A?

☐ Reliable   ☐ Elaborate
☐ Risky   ☐ Trustworthy
☐ Costly   ☐ Inexpensive
☐ Effective ☐ Dodgy
☐ Simple   ☐ Troublesome
☐ Quality   ☐ Throwaway

A basic analysis consists of comparing the percentages of users who checked each descriptor for each tested brand. Often, clear differences in brand personality can be identified using simple cross-tabs. More sophisticated analyses, like perceptual mapping, are best enabled by a data type that allows for more variability in the results, in order to develop the statistical model. Rather than using a simple Boolean variable, a ratings scale is employed whereby respondents are asked to rate how well each attribute describes the brand, as in the example in Figure 10.4.

Unless you intend to conduct statistical modeling, however, we recommend the use of checkboxes for this type of data. Using checkboxes, a large number of attributes can be rated quickly, saving respondents' energy for later questions.

Competitive Performance

Assessing competitive performance consists of rating the identical list of dimensions gathered at the attribute importance assessment stage. In the subsequent analysis, product performance ratings are overlaid with the stated importance of these factors in choosing the brand. The result is a powerful tool for measuring the competition's areas of strength and vulnerability.

FIGURE 10.4: Detailed brand assessment

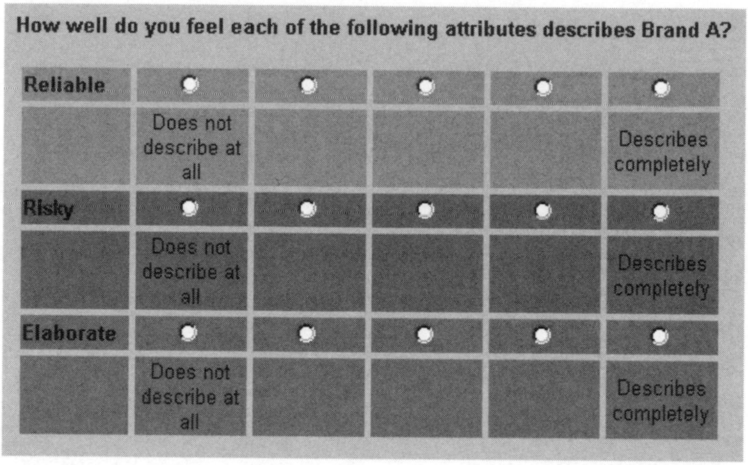

There are several approaches to getting performance ratings. One is to phrase the question in terms of users' *satisfaction* with each attribute.

This method is quick and easy for consumers to answer, but it suffers from the fact that the idea of satisfaction is actually comprised of two measures. First, it captures the importance a consumer assigns to that area; second, it captures perceptions of performance. For example, if you discover that consumers are "very satisfied" with a peripheral service like a brand's offer to include a free box of chocolates with every purchase, you still know nothing about the overall importance of this service relative to other product attributes, or whether it drives the decision-making process. Satisfaction data is less granular than other information, but because of its accessibility and ease of implementation, it is relevant when you know that the attribute being measured is a key driver of brand choice. It is therefore a useful tool for conducting short, ongoing studies among your current audience to track your own product's ability to meet expectations (see Chapter 16, Tracking).

Instead of gathering simple satisfaction ratings, studies work better when respondents are asked to think about the attributes and then rate brand performance *within a competitive context.* In our

FIGURE 10.5: Satisfaction scale

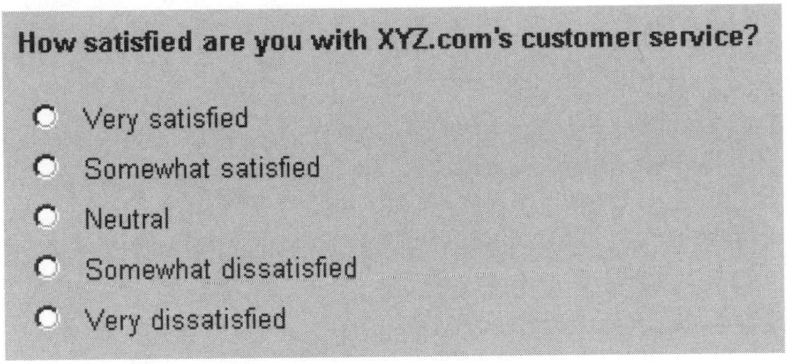

How satisfied are you with XYZ.com's customer service?

○ Very satisfied
○ Somewhat satisfied
○ Neutral
○ Somewhat dissatisfied
○ Very dissatisfied

experience, the problem with using standard ratings scales (e.g., 10 = Very good and 1 = Very bad) is that users tend to rate these scales rather generously, again showing little variation in their responses from attribute to attribute. As a result, it is very difficult to identify the items comprising a competitor's key competency or weakness. Better results can be obtained using scales that are modified like the question in Figure 10.6.

Similar to the approach utilized to determine the importance of attributes, a scale like this tends to draw out the range of responses, with key performance strengths or weaknesses becoming evident.

Switching Behavior

A final metric to obtain in a competitive performance assessment is consumers' stated willingness to try a new brand in the category. Simply put, a competitor with a large base of very loyal customers is more of a threat than one that has a base who are looking for other options. This information can be obtained by asking a question like this:

> How likely would you be to consider trying a new brand of [product category]?
>> Definitely
>> Very likely
>> Somewhat likely
>> Might or might not

FIGURE 10.6: Performance rating scale

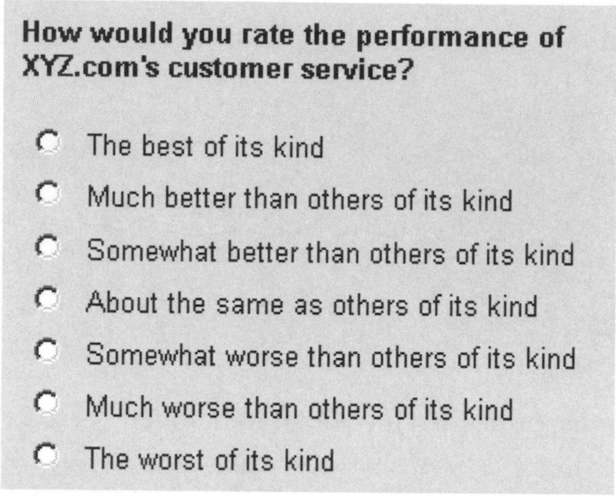

How would you rate the performance of XYZ.com's customer service?

○ The best of its kind

○ Much better than others of its kind

○ Somewhat better than others of its kind

○ About the same as others of its kind

○ Somewhat worse than others of its kind

○ Much worse than others of its kind

○ The worst of its kind

Somewhat unlikely

Not very likely

Definitely would not

Analyzing the Data

There are many levels of complexity to pursue in an analysis of a competitive performance study, each providing a deepening understanding of how to develop and position a product to best succeed in the competitive space.

Not all useful data has to come from a complicated analytic approach, however. In fact, we argue that much of the power of high-end analytics is lost due to organizational misunderstanding or mistrust of the results. In an operational setting, we find that simpler concepts are easier to convey and easier to act upon. As such, in the remainder of this chapter we provide examples of simple analysis you can conduct yourself, without professional consultation.

A first step is to analyze data on competitor trial and usage. If you are confident that you have obtained a representative sample, you may even obtain estimates of market penetration simply by looking at the share of respondents who have tried and become primary users of the tested brands. However, if your sample is not nationally representative, or at least market representative, it is dangerous to estimate such data simply by looking at rankings or rate of trial and usage among the overall market. Why? Because the sample may be overrepresentative of some types of users and underrepresentative of others.

If you consider that the primary goal of a competitive performance study is to develop a strategy to best compete against these brands, you'll realize that this isn't a major stumbling block. Instead, analyze this information by the customer segments you have developed. Identify which brands are most and least likely to have captured a share of specific types of customers. In the search engine market, for example, we might discover that Yahoo! has captured a significant share of the casual searcher market, while Google and Altavista are the primary competition among serious searchers. If you are developing a specialized, advanced search product, you'll quickly realize that Yahoo! isn't really your competition at all. You'll need to pay much closer attention to the activities of Google and Altavista.

TABLE 10.1: Trial of search service

Brand	Heavy Searcher (10 + searches per day)	Moderate Searcher (5 – 9 searches per day)	Light Searcher (Under 5 searches per day)
Yahoo!	98%	98%	98%
Altavista	95%	70%	40%
Google	90%	50%	20%

TABLE 10.2: Search service primarily used

Brand	Heavy Searcher (10 + searches per day)	Moderate Searcher (5 – 9 searches per day)	Light Searcher (Under 5 searches per day)
Yahoo!	20%	50%	80%
Altavista	40%	30%	15%
Google	40%	20%	5%

Next comes an analysis of the performance priority assessment. The first level of analysis you can perform is to look at the weight consumers place on various attributes of product performance. Later, you should also compare this data to specific competitor performance to identify areas of strength and weakness.

Again, if you are not developing a product targeted at the general marketplace, it is preferable to analyze the data within the context of the customer segments you've developed. As mentioned earlier, a common issue these studies face is that consumers tend to rate all attributes as being quite important. Using a scale similar to the one we suggested should help to alleviate this problem somewhat, but additional analytic techniques will still generally be required to tell the true story.

One useful and simple technique is to look at, and rank scores in the top 2 box[1] for each attribute. An attribute that is reported as being Absolutely critical or Extremely important to the brand choice of a respondent is likely a high-priority issue, regardless of the tendency to overstate. You can sort these scores and plot them in an easily readable bar chart. What frequently occurs is a natural distribution of these scores, with items grouping together in high, medium, and low ranges. Special attention should be paid to understanding the performance of competitors among the top grouping of attributes. Later, in your development efforts, the same emphasis should be placed on achieving high performance in these critical areas.

While brand image data is frequently analyzed with complex modeling techniques, simple approaches can still provide valuable positioning intelligence. Assuming you have used a checkbox-style question, a quick way to summarize each brand's image is to generate a chart that compares the level of each attribute from competitor to competitor, as in the example in Figure 10.8.

---

[1]Researchers frequently refer to the percentage of respondents who answered with the top 2 or bottom 2 points in a scale, and have dubbed these aggregations the "top 2 box" and "bottom 2 box."

FIGURE 10.7: Attribute importance—top 2 box scores

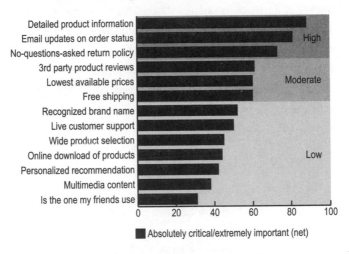

FIGURE 10.8: Brand image summary

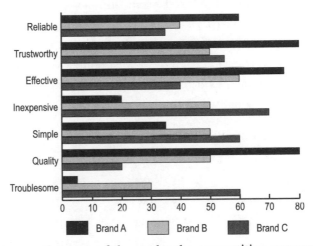

Last comes the crux of the study: the competitive assessment of key areas of product performance. As in other parts of this type of study, there are complicated approaches and simple ones. We focus on a technique that has proven very effective at summarizing key competitive strengths and vulnerabilities, and equally important is easily conveyed to the decision makers who will act upon this information.

Each tested brand has a group of respondents who rated its performance on a defined list of attributes, and also rated the level of importance each attribute holds in the purchase decision process. What is needed is a way of combining the two groups of data and summarizing the results to quickly convey areas where the competitor is exceeding expectations, meeting them, or underperforming.

In order to allow an intuitive comparison, it is necessary to place the importance and performance metrics on identical scales. Calculating an *indexed mean* is a popular technique for accomplishing this goal. It allows you to evaluate the ratings using a scale of 0 to 100. Much like test scores, you can then grade all the elements on a curve. Indexed means are particularly useful if you are attempting to compare metrics that were gathered with scales of unequal size (e.g., comparing a 10-point importance scale against a 7-point performance scale).

Calculating an indexed mean from a 7-point scale is done as follows (see Table 10.3):

Divide 100 by the number of points on the scale, minus one $(100/(7-1) = 16.67)$. Assign the lowest point a value of zero. Assign the highest point a value of 100. Each remaining point on the scale is distributed equally according to the calculated value. Calculating

TABLE 10.3: Calculation of a indexed mean

Scale Choice	Index Value		Distribution		Product
Absolutely critical	100	×	20%	=	20
Extremely important	83.34	×	25%	=	20.84
Very important	66.67	×	15%	=	10
Important	50	×	10%	=	5
Somewhat important	33.34	×	10%	=	3.34
Not very important relative to other considerations	16.67	×	15%	=	2.5
Not at all important relative to other considerations	0	×	5%	=	0
			Indexed mean	=	**61.68**

an indexed value requires that you multiply the percentage of respondents selecting each choice by the indexing value. These new values are summed, yielding an indexed mean.

The same procedure is then applied to each brand's performance ratings. This is not a statistical procedure per se; but it's a simple way of allowing easy interpretation of the data in a form that most end-users are familiar with, no matter how many points are on the scales you are comparing.

Two important caveats apply:

1. This process assumes that the scale provides interval data. In other words, each point on the scale represents an equal increase in the attribute being measured (e.g., importance or performance). The performance rating scale introduced earlier in the chapter may arguably be stretching this assumption slightly, since it's unclear how much "better" a brand must be to jump from being "Much better than others of its kind" to being "The best of its kind." We typically account for this by examining the top 2 box scores on this type of question as well as the indexed mean.

2. Any type of averaging process is only a measure of central location. It is possible that a given metric may have a large group of users rating at the high end of the scale, and another at the low end. The mean will not give any indication that there are two diametrically opposed groups of users, which in itself may be a strategically important finding. The two extremes will simply cancel each other out, leaving the impression that opinions on the issue are middle-of-the-road. As a result, we recommend conducting at least a cursory examination of the distribution of data, as well as averages, to avoid missing something critical. You may do this simply by examining the frequency distribution of the question, or by using a summary statistic like the *variance* or the *standard deviation* to see how closely the range of values clusters around the mean. A

FIGURE 10.9: Performance/importance gap analysis

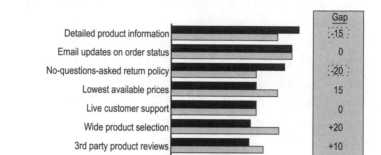

large standard deviation may indicate that subgroups within the population have distinctly different views on the issue.

Having converted ratings to indexed means, it is now a simple matter to compare importance and performance ratings.

Sort the data to place attributes that are rated most important first in the list. Note the gap between users' expectations and the competitor's performance. A positive gap suggests that the brand is exceeding its users' expectations. A negative gap indicates a vulnerability.

Factors that are rated as being highly important to consumers and on which the brand is performing well should be considered cost-of-entry items. In other words, *your product must attain equal levels of performance in these areas if you hope to compete in the market.* The ability of your product to achieve this goal can and should be tested as well. That process is discussed in Chapter 14.

Areas of high importance but low satisfaction should be viewed as strategic opportunities to position your product against competitors' perceived weaknesses. A strong showing here can help you carve out a niche for your brand, even in a highly competitive marketplace.

Strategic implications can be enhanced by examining the types of consumers who have large importance–performance gaps among their current brands. The exercise can yield valuable information about targeting users who are dissatisfied with the current offering and might easily be swayed by an alternative product (namely, yours) that outperforms the competition.

Finally, examine consumers' stated likelihood to try a new brand. A customer's willingness to try a new brand is not always a factor of unsatisfied needs. Online, where the cost of trial is extremely low, some types of users (especially experienced ones) are always looking for the next big thing. Analysis of the types of users of each brand who are most willing to try a new offering can suggest ideal candidates for your early product testing and launch period (see Chapter 14).

CHAPTER 11

Existing Online Products: Audience Composition and Performance Testing

In previous chapters we've discussed many measurement spheres—the off-line marketplace, the entire Internet, the online marketplace, specific competitors, and your current customer base (sitecentric measurement). The remaining chapters focus on the latter, which we consider the most accessible and arguably the most powerful application of online research techniques. We first discuss how to use this research to greatly expand your understanding of your current online product and its relationship to your user base. This, of course, assumes that you already have a Web presence. Subsequent chapters address the process of developing sites using a data-driven approach, covering sitecentric methodologies for:

- testing new online product concepts,
- building online products,

- testing online products,
- marketing online products, and
- tracking the success of online products.

Sitecentric evaluation is one of the most powerful applications of Web-based research, due in large part to the availability of large, inexpensive, and extremely representative samples. In Chapter 5 on sampling, we discussed the ease of obtaining sitecentric samples by implementing a JavaScript sampling algorithm on the front page of your site and provided you with the necessary JavaScript code. Armed with this information, you can conduct as many studies of your users as you desire (or they'll tolerate) without incurring the incremental costs that apply to other samples, like off-line telephone methods or online Web panels.

Because of this affordability, data can be gathered to answer very specific questions. As we'll see in this and the following chapters, nearly every decision related to the development, marketing, and improvement of your online product can be informed by research. Further adding to the attractiveness of sitecentric methodologies is the great speed at which online studies can be executed. Even unforeseen topics that inevitably arise during the development of online products can be quickly evaluated, understood, and acted upon intelligently.

We don't mean to imply that simply researching an issue magically provides answers to difficult questions about how to effectively develop, market, and maintain your site. We do, however, argue that you're not leveraging all the Web's power to develop your online product if you do so without incorporating research into each aspect of the process. It would be difficult for anyone to contend that a greater understanding of the elements surrounding a decision would not improve the likelihood of choosing the best course of action. It makes sense to obtain as much relevant information as possible to drive the decision-making process, so long as doing that does not create an undue burden of cost or delay the process.

Allowing a data-driven approach to developing Web strategy and products is, in our opinion, one of the fundamental benefits the Web provides. It allows businesses to focus in great detail on building relationships with customers. Retaining and maximizing the share of mind (or wallet) of your current customer base is a far cheaper proposition and than luring new customers. This is illustrated vividly by the astronomical valuations of audience aggregation sites such as portals. Once customers look to you for one service, they are easy marketing targets for other services or products. Determining additional cross-sell opportunities requires an in-depth knowledge of customers and their needs. Enter sitecentric research.

Currently, there is quite a bit of waste in the online industry. A majority of sites conducting initial research discover that 40% or more of their traffic is comprised of first-time users. It's safe to say, however, that none of these sites have traffic levels that are growing by anything close to the same rate. This is an indication that marketing efforts are driving new users to the sites, but many are not finding what they expected, or are otherwise dissatisfied with the offering. Sites should strive to minimize customer attrition, because the costly process of driving trial is wasted when individuals leave because they cannot achieve their objectives. Additionally, dissatisfied customers are probably lost forever; no amount of marketing hype is likely to overcome a negative first experience. A bad first experience is particularly dangerous because much of the awareness and trial of Web sites is driven by word of mouth. Customers who have negative opinions of a site share those opinions with others. Any way you look at it, customer attrition is *bad*. Sitecentric research has the potential to uncover the reasons for this attrition and drive the process of redesign to address the needs of customers and *keep them coming back*.

PROJECTABILITY OF SITECENTRIC RESEARCH

Despite all the benefits of sitecentric research, it has one major drawback: The information collected via random sitecentric samples is only projectable to the site from which the sample was drawn. Hence, a sitecentric sample from an investment site like E-Trade could not reliably be leveraged to understand the nature of another investment site's audience or the characteristics of online investors as a whole. To find out those things, we would need to conduct nationally representative research, typically via a nationally representative Web panel. Unfortunately, as we've already discussed, Web panels are expensive and, in some cases, unreliable.

The officially "correct" use of sitecentric research is primarily to gain an in-depth understanding of a site's current users. But given the accessibility and inexpensive nature of sitecentric research, wouldn't it be helpful if it could be used to research issues outside the site, like the competition or the response to new product ideas among the entire online marketplace?

It's true that you can never be certain sitecentric research is representative of the entire marketplace or of a competitor's audience. But with a little common sense and an understanding of the risk involved, sitecentric research can be used to inform just about any part of the marketing process. Certainly, one would never collect a sample from a site comprised entirely of teenagers, then attempt to project it to the entire online marketplace, because the sample lacks a very large component of the population—namely, people over 19. However, using this sitecentric sample to understand the attitudes and behaviors of young women who use the Internet would result in far less error.

There is no perfect approach to collecting sample research data, only a continuum of more or less risky techniques. As with all things, you are required to use your brain and question the validity of research results. But it is also important not to be frozen or incapacitated by fear of obtaining any but the purest research results.

Concentrating solely on collecting highly projectable samples of the entire marketplace will put many useful testing and product development methodologies out of reach of your budget or time table and leave you grasping at straws. Focusing too intently on what's lacking in sitecentric samples will keep you from identifying valuable information that can shape your business into a successful venture. Take, for example, qualitative research: It is highly unrepresentative of the marketplace and quite unreliable, but thousands of companies rely on it—successfully—to create business strategy and profitable products. Know the limitations of your data, but don't be afraid of those limitations. Push, prod, and poke them a bit to see what happens. Don't spend a billion dollars based on dubious data; but don't discount every piece of information that isn't based on census data. Keep in mind that we're building products for profit, not writing papers for science journals. Use what works.

Chances are good that the users of your site share many of the same views as the users of the competition's site, and of consumers in general. What is not certain is how prevalent these views are outside your site. If you already have a site, a safe option is to use sitecentric research as an investigative tool to identify the traits, needs, and trends that may exist in the entire marketplace. Once you have a list of hot issues, you can then, if necessary for a critical business decision, test the existence of your most relevant findings in the general population through nationally representative research.

Another method of furthering your understanding is to use *data weighting* techniques to mold your sitecentric sample into the image of the another known population. Many secondary sources can provide accurate information about the characteristics of the general Internet population or those of a specific consumer category, like online software purchasers or online investors. By applying different weights to each respondent in your sitecentric sample, you can increase the consideration of underrepresented populations at your site and decrease the impact of those who exist in proportions greater than the population you want the data to mimic.

Let's assume, for example, that an e-commerce Web site specializing in the sale of books, videos, and CDs wants to gauge response to a number of new product concepts among online purchasers of these products. Not having the time, fiscal resources, or inclination to use a nationally representative Web panel, they choose to use a sitecentric sample and weight the data to match nationally representative data (obtained from secondary sources) on the purchase of books, videos, and CDs.

When weighting, the trick is to identify the key factors in an audience's composition that are most likely to impact the primary issues you are studying. Theorizing that the major driver in response to the new concepts will be the level of purchase activity of a consumer, the company includes in its survey a question that is designed to determine online purchase levels. The question is intentionally worded exactly the same way it was in the nationally representative study that will be used as the benchmark:

> *In a typical month, how many books, videos, and CDs do you purchase online?*
> *None*
> *1–2*
> *3–4*
> *5–6*
> *7 or more*

TABLE 11.1: Weighting Step 1: Collect comparison data

Books, Videos, and CDs Purchased Monthly	Nationally Representative Sample	Sitecentric Sample
None	10%	5%
1–2	30%	10%
3–4	35%	25%
5–6	15%	40%
7 or more	10%	20%
Median	**3.6**	**5.5**

Using identical questions in each survey allows the company to accurately compare the purchase activity of their customers to that of the entire marketplace.

As we might have expected, the sitecentric sample of the online retailer is comprised of far heavier purchasers of books, videos, and CDs online (a median of 3.6 versus 5.5). Given this finding, it would not be reasonable to attempt to project the desirability of new online services among the overall online marketplace based on the *unweighted* opinions of the sitecentric sample. However, by increasing the weight given to the opinions of lighter purchasers and decreasing the consideration of heavier purchasers' answers, we can get a more accurate understanding of how desirable our product concepts might be among all online purchasers of books, videos, and CDs.

TABLE 11.2: Weighting Step 2: Calculate and apply weights

Books, Videos, and CDs Purchased Monthly	Nationally Representative Sample	Sitecentric Sample	Weight
None	10%	5%	2
1–2	25%	10%	2.5
3–4	30%	25%	1.2
5–6	25%	40%	.625
7 or more	10%	20%	.5
Median	3.6	5.5	

To obtain our target weights, we divide the incidence of a metric in the nationally representative population by the observation in the sitecentric sample.

Target population value / Sitecentric value = Weight

Once weights are established, they are applied using an analysis package like Excel or SPSS to weight the responses to other questions in our sitecentric sample. In data processing, applying a weight means that a respondent who answered "None" to the question (and was given a weight of 2) will be counted as if he or she were 2 respondents. A respondent who answered "7 or more," and was given a weight of .5 will be counted as if he or she were half a respondent. The net result is that the sample is transformed to more closely reflect the target national population. Now the data about the desirability of the new product concepts mirrors the overall marketplace better than it would have before weighting occurred.

Data weighting, while helpful, does not alleviate all the problems of attempting to project sitecentric data out to other areas. It is still fundamentally sitecentric data, and there is no guarantee that the metrics you choose to balance through weighting are the ones that drive underlying differences between your site's audience and the overall marketplace. In the example, we weighted for purchase frequency; but there could be a number of other metrics that affect a person's desire for the new product concepts tested. Weighting based on personal characteristics (age, income, gender), behaviors (type of books, videos, and CDs purchased), or other measures could have very significant effects on the findings. Before you attempt to use weighted data, take some time to familiarize yourself with the process. Some resources for doing so can be found at:

darkwing.uoregon.edu/~osrl/miscpapers/weighting.htm

www-cta.ornl.gov/npts/1995/courseware/toc.html

www2.cdc.gov/nccdphp/brfss2/training_gu/method.asp

EVALUATING YOUR CURRENT SITE AND CUSTOMER RELATIONSHIP

Now that we've discussed some of the fundamental considerations of sitecentric research, let's turn our attention to applying it to evaluate your current Web site. Many of you are reading this book with an eye toward using research to develop new products or enhance your existing offerings, and you may be eager to jump ahead.

Before you do, consider this. In our experience, developers seldom use research to drive the development of their first release. Financial pressures, personnel scarcity, and a host of other political and administrative issues often put the cart before the horse, for better or worse.

By the time online businesses look to marketing research, they've nearly always put up a first version of their site. Companies typically take a reactive approach to research. They look to it because their sites are not performing as they anticipated, and they hope to leverage the information obtained from site evaluation to redesign the product. When companies do build successful sites without the aid of research, they (quite reasonably) put research on a back burner until their investors or sales teams pressure them for customer information for business development purposes. Whatever the reasons for the introspective focus, a wealth of knowledge and financial opportunity comes from a comprehensive understanding of your customer base and its relationship with your current offering. We highly recommend that you leverage this powerful and accessible tool as a regular part of your research program.

EXPANDING YOUR USER PROFILE

We have discussed the types of metrics you should obtain and understand about your marketplace and customer. Secondary sources of data may already have given you an idea of who your customers are (or should be), but chances are that the limited data left you with some outstanding questions. Here is your opportunity to discover every little thing you ever wanted to know about the consumers using your site. You may be surprised at how they differ from your original vision.

In Chapter 8 we discussed in detail all the measures of your customer's characteristics, behaviors, and attitudes you might seek to understand. Here we briefly list some of the common profile attributes that most marketers and developers rely upon in their daily business. If you don't have reliable data on most of these metrics, we recommend that you first conduct a detailed sitecentric user profile study. Doing so will put you ahead of the curve. Surprisingly few companies have credible, detailed profiles of their user bases. Having this data will undoubtedly improve your decision-making abilities, greatly increasing the likelihood that your site will succeed.

Demographics

- Age
- Gender
- Geography or region
- Household or family size
- Marital status
- Parental status
- Race, nationality, or ethnicity
- Religion

Socioeconomics

- Education
- Employment status
- Income
- Home ownership

Webographics

- Access locations
- Browser or computer platform
- Connection speeds
- Internet service provider
- Popular online activities
- Web experience level
- Installed browser add-ons (multimedia players, plug-ins)
- Web usage level

Corpographics

- Employer size
- Industry
- Occupation
- Organizational role

Attitudes, values, and lifestyle (psychographics)

- Personality self-descriptors
- Opinions on social issues
- Participation in social activities
- Recreation, hobbies, and interests
- Political party affiliation

Consumer behavior

- Products shopped for or purchased
- Sales channels used
- Consumption patterns and spending levels

Brand relationship

- Usage or consumption of your brand
- Ratings of satisfaction or performance with key aspects of your offering
- Attitudes toward the overall category you represent

Competitive environment

- Competing brand awareness
- Competing brand trial
- Competing brand usage
- Competing brand perceptions
- Switching habits
- Brand preferences

Media consumption

- Types of media consumed (TV, radio, print, Web)

- Levels of media consumption
- Cannibalization of other media types by Web use
- Programming watched, read, or listened to

Seem like a lot of information to collect about your users? There's even more! Beyond profiling and market-related data, you should collect a number of site-specific metrics about how your audience relates to your site.

USER–SITE RELATIONSHIP

Besides segmentation techniques that are based on customer characteristics and behaviors, understanding the levels of usage that exist at your site can uncover distinct user populations that often have very different characteristics. Each group may benefit from a site experience that is tailored to best speak to their particular needs. These segments fall into two major groups: first-time users and repeat users.

Segmentation on this basis is a simple process, and is accomplished by asking a question similar to this one:

How often do you typically visit Site X?
> Every day
> 4–6 times per week
> 2–3 times per week
> Once a week
> 2–3 times a month
> Once a month
> Less than once a month
> This my first visit to the site

First-Time Users

First-time users represent a new opportunity for you to grow your customer base. Some marketers mistakenly believe that the struggle ends once the user has been convinced to try out the site. That's not remotely true. In fact, motivating a consumer to trial is a very risky proposition. No matter what messages are conveyed by the marketing campaign, the ability to deliver the goods remains the bottom line. No amount of advertising can undo a first-hand experience, as many companies who have tried to reinvent their brand image have discovered.

It is important to recapture the cost of inducing consumers to try your site by identifying the unique needs of this population and ensuring your ability to satisfy those needs. Beyond simply having the capabilities, your site must be able to communicate its virtues to the newcomer—quickly. Web users are fickle. If first-time customers do not find what they need immediately, there is little motivation to exert themselves further. The competition is only a click away.

First-time users have one important attribute that can go a long way toward helping you understand the effectiveness of your promotional activities: They have no previous site experience. When they first enter the site, perceptions of your brand and product held by these customers have been created almost entirely by marketing. Presumably, the promotional messages are still fresh in these users' minds. By asking where they first heard about your site, you can determine which promotional vehicle (TV, print, online, trade shows) is working hardest to drive traffic. Beyond this, you can question users about their perceptions of the brand to evaluate how well the advertising achieves key branding objectives and sets expectations. We discuss these strategies further in Chapter 15, which focuses on using research to market your online product effectively.

Repeat Users

Repeat users are a notable group because they have found some value in your site and returned for more. The frequency with which users return and how much they use your site are key indicators of your site's success. When measuring usage levels, you may find that a relatively small percentage of your audience accounts for the vast majority of traffic. Alternatively, your site may have a great number of casual users who only access it sporadically. Regardless of the usage patterns on your site, repeat users represent your core profit center (or at least, the best chance at making a profit!). They also represent the most immediate opportunity to grow this profit. It is often cheaper to maximize the value of your existing customer base than to seek new visitors through advertising. Understanding the characteristics and needs of your group of repeat visitors can help you develop products to maximize the percentage of time spent or purchases made at your site. The flamboyant promotional expenditures in the recent scramble for market share among e-ventures leads us to believe that this principle is going unheeded! It is our opinion that online ventures tend to take current customers for granted and focus on the acquisition of new ones. While expanding your user base is certainly an important goal, it is critical to keep the needs of core users in mind as you develop aspects of the site that are designed to attract and retain new users. Alienating them could prove quite costly.

In most cases, it is useful to further subdivide repeat users into heavy, moderate, and light user segments. It is not surprising that a customer's level of involvement with a product is closely correlated with their behaviors and attitudes related to the category. Heavy users of a technology information site, for instance, are likely to purchase more computer products, be employed in high-tech jobs, and have a number of other characteristics that define them as desirable customers. For this reason, an excellent and simple segmentation strategy is to investigate the differences in customer characteristics and behaviors at different levels of site usage.

In addition to knowing how frequently repeat customers access your site, it is also relevant to obtain information about their relationship to the types of content and services you offer. Which areas of your site are customers aware of? Of those, which have they tried? Finally, which content and services are used regularly? Detailed information about this value chain can help you understand a variety of issues about the performance of different sections of your site. Overall, usage of a section is obviously a good baseline measure of success; indeed, it is common to track utilization of content via a host of available traffic analysis tools like Accrue or Web Trends. But what about areas that are apparently unpopular, because they don't have high traffic levels? After gathering information in a survey, further probing can take place to determine whether the lack of utilization is due to a lack of awareness, poor performance, or a host of other reasons. A further benefit of gathering content utilization and awareness metrics is the ability to identify the *types* of users who use (or don't use) each type of content. This knowledge has ramifications for developers, marketers, and even advertisers who might purchase space on your site to reach specific types of consumers.

Content utilization metrics can be combined with access frequency metrics to shed further light on the visitor–site relationship. By cross-tabulating these measures, you may find that heavier users access very different types of content and services than moderate and light users. Simply understanding the features that are driving core visitors to return can prevent costly mistakes, like a

FIGURE 11.1: Awareness, trial, and usage conversion

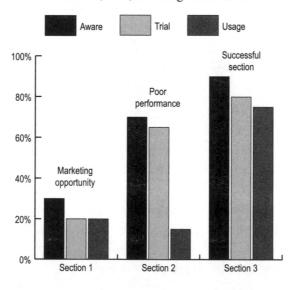

redesign process that inadvertently destroys the precise reason why you have a base of loyal users. Further, it will suggest content that has demonstrated appeal and power to pull visitors back again. Developing site messaging and navigation to induce trial of this content among casual users can help convert more of them into core customers.

Elements critical to the value chain depend on the type of site. E-commerce sites, for instance, may be primarily interested in determining the share of visitors who achieve each of four steps in the process:

1. Visit the site.
2. Visit product information pages.
3. Add products to the online shopping cart.
4. Make a purchase.

At each step in the value chain, there will undoubtedly be some attrition. Often the level of attrition is dramatic. Researching this process can help you identify the areas that have been successful at driving users through to the next stage and those that cause users to drop like flies.

Evaluating the attributes of customers who fall out at each stage is the first step toward identifying the reasons behind the attrition rate. When problem areas are identified, asking follow-up questions that specifically gauge perceptions of performance among those who've fallen out is the best method for pinpointing the root of the issue.

PERFORMANCE RATINGS

You can gain a host of powerful insights simply by analyzing the composition of your audience; but the key to improving your relationship with them is to understand how your site measures up to their expectations. Whether in preparation for a full redesign or simply to enhance the day-to-day tweaks that all sites undergo, gathering performance data can yield a high return on your investment by informing and prioritizing development efforts. This data can also be leveraged in marketing and positioning efforts, addressed in Chapter 15.

In measuring your site's performance, a good first step is to have your users rate their overall satisfaction with general content or service areas. Similar to the utilization data discussed in the previous section, these general ratings help you determine which sections of your site resonate most with customers.

Though one might expect to find high ratings for heavily trafficked sections and poor ratings for areas with lower utilization, our experience has been that this does not always hold true. We frequently find that heavily trafficked areas contain the most pertinent information or service to the customer (the factor driving usage), but customers have poor opinions of them. Perhaps familiarity breeds contempt. On the other hand, some sparsely populated areas rate favorably among the small group of customers who do use them regularly. Sometimes these users represent a previously unidentified "fringe segment" of customers; more typically, it's an indication that increased visibility and promotion of these areas will drive utilization of the hidden gems and enhance the overall experience of visitors.

When overall ratings of major areas of the site have been gathered and considered, the next step is to drill down into each section, obtaining ratings of key performance attributes to determine the drivers of the overall ratings or utilization levels of the section. We've discussed how rating scales are used to determine the overall desirability of attributes key to online products. We also reviewed the process of obtaining performance ratings of your competition, and showed you how to compare the two to determine areas of competitive advantage and vulnerability. Now it's time to perform this same test on your site, to determine which attributes exceed or fall short of customer expectations.

FIGURE 11.2: Including your product in the competitive analysis

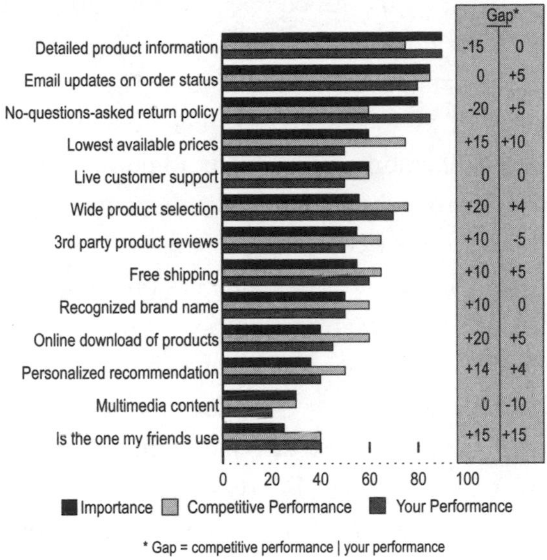

* Gap = competitive performance | your performance

In Chapter 10 we demonstrated the importance of sizing up the competitive landscape. But in addition to using nationally representative samples, panels, or syndicated research, you can gain powerful insight from your own customer base. This exercise should not be viewed as a replacement for the techniques presented in Chapter 10 that obtain an objective assessment of the competitive environment. Instead, it provides a means of understanding the relationships your current customers have with the others who are vying for their business. Perceptions of strong performance by the competition among your visitors can be an early warning sign of a competitive disadvantage, especially among the heaviest users, who are likely to have a predisposition toward your brand.

In a sitecentric study, you can gather this data by asking respondents to rate the competitive performance of your primary competitors, then compare those scores against the ratings for your own site. This analysis provides an in-depth understanding of the performance attributes for which your product outpaces various competitors. By suggesting marketing efforts that emphasize your strong performance versus the competition on critical attributes, this knowledge can guide a strategy for winning new customers who are currently using an alternative brand. The comparison also reveals attributes of your site that lag behind your competitors. Identifying these vulnerabilities is equally important, as it provides you the opportunity to address them and reduce the number of customers who switch to your competitors' sites.

When conducting competitive analysis on a sitecentric basis, it is important to keep in mind that users of your site are likely to be biased toward your brand. That said, when performance ratings reveal a major weakness of a competitor, it is likely that similar customers at that site have the same complaint and are open to trying an alternative product. Likewise, if you find that your users feel your performance in a specific area is worse than a competitor's, this should be interpreted as a serious warning sign: Those users may be actively looking to switch to another product.

OTHER METHODOLOGIES

The accessibility, speed, and flexibility of sitecentric research allows limitless creativity in survey design to be applied to the smallest of research problems. The online researcher can use a vast array of methodologies in evaluating an audience and their relationship with the site. In this section we present a few techniques we've used extensively that illustrate the potential of sitecentric online research.

Point-of-Sale Studies for E-commerce Sites

A fundamental research objective for many e-commerce sites is to evaluate customer satisfaction with the purchase process and subsequent fulfillment. Customer service is also a key component of the buying experience, so this is a typical area of inquiry as well. The primary challenge this research objective creates is twofold.

First, respondents cannot be sampled from the front page, because they have yet to browse the site, select products to purchase, or go through the checkout process. Experiencing the checkout process is an obvious prerequisite to providing informed opinions on it. One of the convenient aspects of JavaScript sampling is that the sampling script can be placed on any page or set of pages within a site. This enables sampling to occur after a customer completes a certain task or views specific content. In our point-of-sale study, we can strategically sample respondents by placing a sampling script on the order confirmation page of the purchase process.

With the checkout process fresh in respondents' minds, we can collect opinions of critical components such as:

- ease of ordering,
- perceptions of secure ordering,
- product information,
- product selection,
- product pricing, and
- satisfaction with privacy policies.

While the above metrics are critical, we still don't know anything about the customer's satisfaction with the subsequent delivery and customer service aspects of purchasing from the site. Because these components of the customer experience occur after the sale, we need to allow sufficient time for these experiences to take place before seeking feedback. This is typically done by way of an email follow-up study. A week after the order is placed (or other appropriate time frame), respondents are sent an email solicitation asking them to participate in a follow-up survey. The email solicitation contains a URL linking to the survey; respondents can either click on the URL directly or cut and paste it into their browser's address window.

Respondents have presumably received the products they ordered, so they can provide feedback on:

- timeliness of delivery,

FIGURE 11.3: Point-of-purchase study design

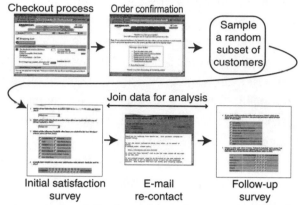

* usage and satisfaction with order status and package tracking services,

* satisfaction with product,

* satisfaction of return process and customer service among respondents who utilized these services,

* overall satisfaction with the purchase process, and

* likelihood of purchasing again.

Point-of-purchase studies are not the only application of email recontact research. A number of methodologies require collecting data from the same respondents over two or more separate occasions (known in research lingo as *waves*). Conducting multiple waves of research requires that data for all waves provided by a given respondent be joined into a single data set. To accomplish this, a unique identifier must be assigned to each respondent and maintained from one wave to the next. The identifier will act as a key in a database or other joining process, and allow each set of information to be matched to each other. Some examples of identifiers are:

* a combination of a respondent's first and last names;

* an email address; or

* a unique number you generate.

The advantage of using names or email addresses is that respondents can fill in this information themselves at each wave, saving you the difficulty of designing a system to automatically generate and pass a unique code. If you are working with minimal technical resources, this is one option. However, respondents can be hesitant to provide their full names, and many people have multiple or constantly changing email addresses, so the rate of success achieved in matching data on this basis can be rather low. We've found that the most reliable method is to dynamically create and assign our own unique number to identify respondents.

In using numbers to identify respondents, the question next faced is how to pass this number reliably from one study to the next. Two options are available. If you have the ability to serve and read cookies in your survey package, you can write the number into the respondent's cookie file during the first wave of surveying and retrieve it again from subsequent waves. Alternatively, you can dynamically generate email invitations that include a respondent's number in the query string[2] of the subsequent survey's URL. For redundancy purposes, we use both methods, and are typically able to match about 99% of respondent data. Fortunately, many of the surveying packages available on the market have the ability to gather numeric identification strings and pass them into the data set. Some (including Inquisite) also have the ability to generate a recontact email with the string automatically inserted into the body of the message.

Another option for conducting point-of-sale studies is provided by BizRate (www.bizrate.com). The company provides e-commerce ventures with a free survey that interviews customers after they purchase a product. It also has an email recontact element and collects many of the same metrics mentioned. There is a catch, however: BizRate publishes the results of these surveys at a site that helps customers determine the sites with the best levels of customer satisfaction. For sites that perform well on BizRate's

---

[2]See Chapter 6 on data collection for definitions of cookies and query strings.

tested metrics, then, conducting research also acts as a promotional vehicle. But what if you perform poorly? A smart move would be to first conduct your own internal study to measure your site's performance. Then you can address any problem areas before sharing your customers' opinions with the world.

Consumer Behavior Studies for Advertising-Supported Sites

Advertising-supported sites often conduct detailed consumer behavior studies to help sell advertising space. These studies are really just an extension of audience profiling techniques, but focus in great detail on audience purchase behavior and perceptions in a variety of product categories (traditionally those with the largest advertising budgets). These studies therefore often include sections on automotive, clothing, finance (credit cards), telecommunications (long-distance), travel, consumer electronics, computing (hardware and software), and any other category for which the site is interested in pursuing sponsor relationships.

The goal of these studies is to gather information about the audience that can be used to help prove to media buyers that the audience is well-suited to their promotional objectives. One media buyer may be looking for large quantities of college students who are in the market for new cars. Another might seek Web users who have switched their long-distance provider in the past six months. Whatever the objective, an ad sales team can pitch media buyers and provide credible data on the share of the audience that fits the target profile.

Ad profiling data can also suggest opportunities to develop relationships with sponsors who had not previously been considered. A site might discover that 80% of its audience is planning to buy a new computer in the next three months. Armed with this information, any salesperson could refocus a sales approach toward technology marketers and sell out the advertising inventory in a few hours! Few studies, of course, result in such monumental findings; but most contain a handful of gems that more than pay for the cost of the study through increased ad revenues.

A couple of problems related to collecting consumer behavior data at the level of detail necessary to make it truly valuable are:

1. It takes a long time to complete the surveys.
2. The surveys are very boring.

As a result, you face a formidable challenge in getting respondents to answer 30 minutes of question about shoes, computers, and fast food. If you attempt to overload the respondents, nonresponse bias will be high, because nearly everyone will quit the survey out of frustration. Even worse, they'll leave with a negative perception of your brand. While your customers may be willing help you out by answering a *few* questions about their consumer behavior, they'll certainly feel exploited by the time they've answered 50 questions.

The flexibility and affordability of online research addresses this dilemma by allowing you to rotate subsections of the total survey to randomly selected groups of the respondent population. Because the assignment of questions to respondents is done entirely at random, the data provided by a subset of the sample can be projected to the entire sample, and to the total population. Thus, each respondent answers only a small fraction of the total survey, but the net result is a detailed, comprehensive set of data.

FIGURE 11.4: Randomly rotating question sets for consumer behavior studies

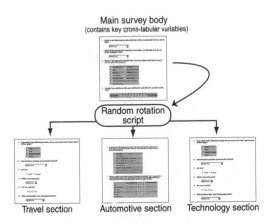

To obtain projectable data using this technique, it is necessary to increase the study's sample size so that each randomly rotated subsection is answered by a sufficiently large group of respondents. Because advertising data of this nature is not used to make critical business decisions, the amount of sampling error that is tolerated is typically higher. The incremental cost of collecting additional respondents is low, so we still recommend that you seek to collect between 250 and 500 respondents per randomly rotated subsection. This number will yield statistically stable base sizes for top-line results, while still allowing for some room to drill down into the data for more detailed analysis.

Fielding a survey using random rotation is a powerful technique. But the technique can limit the flexibility of your intended analysis if you do not take the time to create an analysis plan at the time you write the questionnaire. Because the nature of the approach causes different respondents to answer each randomly rotated section, metrics collected in one rotated section cannot be cross-tabulated with those in another section. For example, if you want to analyze the beverage buying habits of heavy television watchers, you will be out of luck if the two metrics were gathered in different rotated sections. No respondents provided data for both questions; hence, no cross-tabular analysis is possible.

For this reason, it is critical that important variables (such as demographics) that may be used as banners in cross-tabulation analysis are answered by the entire sample. Conveniently, data collected for advertising purposes does not often need to be cross-tabulated by consumption data in other product categories. While you'll certainly have to be able to tell media planners how many men between the ages of 20 and 30 are planning to purchase cell phones in the next six months, few will be interested to learn that those shopping for a new SUV own an average of six pairs of sneakers. Having an analysis plan can help you ensure that whatever analysis is required, no matter how esoteric, it can be performed from a survey utilizing randomly rotated subsections.

Site Impact Studies

The two methodologies we've covered thus far are most appropriate for commercial sites attempting to generate revenue by selling either products or advertising, but either methodology could easily be adapted to help sites of any type. The random rotation approach is well-suited to any application for which the survey is longer than can be completed in a comfortable amount of time. The point-of-sale methodology, with its email recontact component, is an ideal means of gathering data both before and after an experience has taken place. Another very useful application of the email recontact approach is the site impact study.

As the name implies, a site impact study is used to quantify the effect your site has on those who visit it. Many sites have branding, rather than direct sales, as their primary objective. They seek to provide visitors with product information in a compelling manner that positively changes perceptions of the featured brand. Ironically, in a medium that churns out gigabytes of data as a byproduct of its existence, a primary difficulty faced by branding sites is how to effectively quantify their success.

Unlike e-commerce sites that measure success in completed transactions or quality leads, branding sites achieve success when a visitor leaves feeling better about the brand. It might be tempting, therefore, to measure the success of marketing sites by the number of users they attract and have the opportunity to impact. While the sheer number of visitors is certainly a component, marketing sites are not analogous to advertising-supported content sites, whose profitability is directly tied to page views. It's quite possible (and often the case) to find branding sites that achieve large traffic volume, but fail to improve the product knowledge or brand perceptions of visitors. Poorly executed sites may even negatively affect perceptions and, in turn, purchase probability. In such cases, heavy traffic patterns can actually be an undesirable attribute.

Rather than traffic analysis, the key objective in evaluating a branding site is to measure its ability to achieve the intended branding goals of its developer. These goals typically include attracting a certain type of user, conveying useful product information, increasing perceptions that the product or brand is better than alternatives, and in the end, improving the likelihood that visitors will purchase the product or service. The challenge to the researcher is to isolate the effects of the Web experience from all the external factors that might influence a consumer's attitudes.

Advertising, word of mouth, and personal experience are just a few of the powerful external factors that shape perceptions of your brand. When users first visit your branding site, opinions of your brand are already set in a particular way. With any luck, users will learn something about your brand and be more inclined to select it by the time they leave. But such an effect is not represented by page views or ad banner click-through. How can you measure this change?

Separating the effects of the world from your site is accomplished by conducting something called a quasi-experimental study. The unfortunate fact that the methodology is dubbed "quasi" does not undermine its ability to provide you with a powerful picture of how your site is shaping customers' perceptions of your brand. The "quasi" label simply designates that this methodology is not truly experimental. As we'll see, the control and test populations are not treated identically, which is the fundamental premise of a true experimental study.

The study begins by randomly sampling visitors as they enter the Web site. These respondents are asked an initial set of questions to determine their segmentation membership (if segments have been established) and to gather other characteristic or behavioral variables. Gathering these metrics satisfies the first of the two research objectives: to determine whether the site is attracting the desired audience—qualified consumers who are, for instance, heavy users of the product or service category that the site is marketing.

After the initial questions, the sample is randomly divided into two equal subsamples—a control and a test sample. To obtain

FIGURE 11.5: Quasiexperimental design to evaluate branding effectiveness

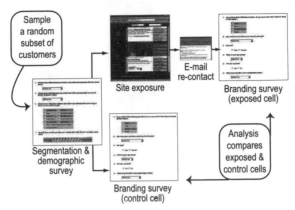

a baseline measurement, the control sample is immediately asked a series of questions about their knowledge, perceptions, and purchase probability of your product or service. Because these users have not yet had any exposure to the site, any perceptions they have are due to external factors.

The test group is thanked for their participation in the initial survey and returned to surf the site, unaware that they are still part of the research. It is critical that test respondents believe that the study is over; test subjects who are aware of their role in a study tend to be artificially sensitized. As the test users surf the site, their product knowledge, brand perceptions, and purchase probability are all impacted in a natural way. To determine how the site affects these metrics, we can now solicit these users via an email recontact to complete a short follow-up survey. This survey contains the identical questions that were answered by the control group at the time they were sampled.

Because the surveys completed by both groups are identical, we can evaluate the effects of the site by comparing the responses of the control and test samples. The analysis process is discussed further in subsequent chapters.

12

New Product Concepts

REASONS FOR TESTING PRODUCT CONCEPTS

In previous chapters, we discussed methods of evaluating customers and learned how to measure their satisfaction with existing sites. The expanded understanding of your customers you gain will soon lead to ideas for new products and services to meet their needs. To assist in your evaluation of new ideas, this chapter focuses on concept testing techniques for new online products. The types of concepts you can test range from entirely new products to specific features you're adding to an existing product. Most often, concept testing is applied to the latter—testing reception of new features or sections for your existing site.

Why should you take the time to do concept testing before beginning development? We hope the answer is obvious! *Testing product concepts maximizes the value of limited development resources by ruling out poorly received ideas.*

The Web is a quickly changing environment; new trends, tools, and technologies emerge seemingly every day. Each change brings the opportunity to implement new functionality on your site. Features run the gamut from functional to frivolous: free Web-based email, personal homepages, customizable start pages, streaming media, email updates, animations, chat rooms, live customer support, stock tickers, and skiing conditions are just a few things that can be added to the user experience. Deciding which, if any, of these newfangled attractions to incorporate into your site can be mind-boggling. Choosing is even more challenging when limited resources force you to choose between several new ideas that appear to be closely related to your business model.

It's common for new features to be developed and released without first determining their need or desirability. Often, rapid development is a reactionary measure. Your competitors begin offering free email to their users, so you spend a great deal of effort and money to replicate the service on your site. Then, the worst happens: Nobody uses it. Your million-dollar investment becomes just another feature on the site, distracting users, and your organization, from the brand's core focus. Without a structured approach to evaluating whether the competition should be copied or ignored, you could keep playing catch-up without ever satisfying or retaining your customers.

Beyond the many industry innovations that sites must decide to implement or forgo, are ideas that are born within your own company. In the course of everyday business, new ideas are constantly conceived of and considered. Executing every idea that floats across a conference table would be impossible, as well as confusing to your customers. After preliminary investigation, many ideas turn out to be duds; but inevitably you end up with more apparently good ideas than you have resources to implement. Concept testing helps you to separate the wheat from the chaff by going directly to the source: your customers.

Most importantly, concept testing helps ensure that, once implemented, ideas will be well and profitably received. A company can only afford to pursue a limited number of poorly conceived ideas before the laws of economics force it out of business. Online's hyper-paced environment means that ventures don't get three strikes; they only get one. Given the stakes, it certainly makes sense to spend some time evaluating the market's need and desire for new products or features before dedicating costly resources toward development.

Still, many companies skip concept testing altogether and begin development immediately. They dedicate months to writing code, building infrastructure, and designing interfaces, often turning away other opportunities because they're consumed with the project at hand. Only after a working prototype is completed do they consider utilizing customer research. Primarily, it's a last-minute test of the product's usability. These companies assume that the underlying concept of the product is sound, and that a significant need and desire for free Web-based email or some other feature exists within their market. But what if that isn't the case? What if, in the course of usability research, it is discovered that no one wants it? No amount of interface tweaking or fancy code will make an inherently undesirable product widely utilized. Unfortunately, by this point it's too late, and few decision makers are likely to consider research that refutes the idea they've already committed to. These late findings will almost certainly be received with great resistance, and ultimately cast aside as the company moves forward, throwing good money after bad.

Concept testing can be executed against a general sample, like one from a panel or a convenience source, or it can be done using respondents from your current site. Forgoing concept tests of online products is virtually inexcusable, especially considering the simplicity and affordability of a sitecentric approach. As in all of our sitecentric methodologies, respondents who provide feedback on concepts are randomly sampled from the site. Therefore, the only cost associated with conducting the research are incentives paid to respondents. While incentives are always recommended, they may not even be necessary for many types of concept testing, because the surveys are short and easy for respondents to complete. Equally important, the subject of new features and added functionality engages respondents. The combination tends to result in higher response rates than are typical of other online research topics.

The trade-off in conducting sitecentric research is that it gathers the opinions of only your current users. Admittedly, major product launches with high strategic importance should be reviewed by members of the general marketplace; but in many situations, sitecentric approaches are the only ones that can provide critical feedback quickly and cheaply enough to have any impact on the decision. A skilled in-house researcher can guide the development of a questionnaire, field it online, and have results in just a few days. The majority of that time is dedicated to the creation of concept statements: concise descriptions of the new ideas being considered for development. As we'll see later in this chapter, the process of generating concept statements is moderated by the researcher, but the statements themselves are developed in group sessions by key decision makers.

The process of developing statements is itself a core benefit of conducting concept testing, because it helps organizations to focus their ideas and think about them from the consumer's perspective. Often, individuals in an organization have divergent ideas about the scope or specifics of a new feature. Developing statements will help identify and correct disparities before they become full-blown problems. As we have discussed, a common pitfall is beginning implementation of new functionality without first considering how customers would use it or what the key benefits are. Developing concept statements forces you to clearly convey the benefits of the new idea to the customer. Frequently, the inability to develop clear, concise, and agreed-upon statements is enough to rule out weaker ideas.

A final benefit of concept testing is that it provides the ability to evaluate the desirability of concepts among different segments of your customer base. Concepts that are highly desired by one segment of your audience may be considered nonessential or fluff to another segment. In many cases, new features are implemented to improve the perceptions of site performance for a specific customer segment. Advanced searching features, for instance, could be implemented to increase customer satisfaction among the profitable heavy-searcher segment. To assist in determining which advanced capabilities to include, you could isolate the opinions of heavy searchers and measure their reaction to concepts, independent of the reactions of lighter searchers. Equally important is monitoring the reactions of moderate and light searching segments to ensure that implementation of advanced searching features does not negatively impact their perception or intended usage of the brand. As we'll see, implementing concept testing early in the process will guide your development to ensure that all segments are satisfied.

METHODS OF TESTING PRODUCT CONCEPTS

Concepts can be tested either qualitatively, through focus groups, or quantitatively, through sitecentric or other online methods. We'd recommend the latter. In spite of our opinions, the use of qualitative methods to understand the desirability of concepts is a common practice, and one that warrants a few words of praise and criticism.

We'll start with the praise. Because concept testing is primarily an investigative type of research, it makes sense that qualitative research would be an appropriate approach. In fact, focus groups provide an excellent means of understanding customers' reactions to concepts. They are especially effective when concepts are not fully formulated or difficult to convey in only a few short sentences. Since most sessions are conducted in person, results are rich and visceral. This provides your development team with a thorough understanding of the issues underlying customers' reactions. Additionally, sessions encourage tangential thoughts that can bring to light unconsidered issues or entirely new concepts which themselves may warrant further investigation.

Now the criticism: Traditional focus groups are time-consuming and expensive. The cost and commitment required to conduct qualitative research may be justified if you're considering launching an entirely new product from scratch. But in the case of implementing new Web-site features or sections, allocating a month to determine the desirability of a concept is unlikely to fit within the development schedule. The bill for recruiting participants, renting facilities, hiring a moderator, and covering all the other expenses of qualitative research will add up quickly. The combination of these factors will likely make traditional focus groups an unrealistic approach to testing most concepts.

Online focus groups provide one possible solution. The cost is certainly cheaper, and obtaining participants is likely to be a simpler proposition as well; but even if you could afford focus groups and complete them in time, would you still want to pursue them? We argue not. The primary advantage of conducting quantitative research is the ability not only to identify customer opinions, but also to measure the degree to which those opinions exist. Because of the small sample of participants, focus groups can never be truly representative of your customer base. As such, they run the risk of providing biased and misleading results. Additionally, qualitative research cannot accurately differentiate interest in concepts between relevant segments of users. This will make it extremely difficult to strategically develop products designed to meet the needs of specific segments (e.g., heavier searchers).

The major problem we have with opting to use focus groups in lieu of sitecentric methodologies is that it seems an ill-suited solution. Focus groups were developed for use in traditional industries that have limited access to customers and lack the dynamic tools for communicating with them. For traditional off-line companies, focus groups were (and possibly still are) the best solution for conveying and testing concepts, prototypes, and final products. In many cases, these companies need people to handle and react to physical items or be shown pictures and diagrams. Before the Web, the only efficient means of doing this was to gather people together in a room and conduct a focus group. Unfortunately, when online companies first looked to research to aid product development, they adopted the tradition of conducting focus groups instead of striving to leverage the full power of the interactive space to inform development quantitatively.

One argument for using qualitative methods is that they help businesses that are unclear about all the issues surrounding a research topic to gain contextual understanding. But this same objective can be achieved by including open-ended text fields in your survey. These fields allow respondents to provide qualitative feedback in addition to answering structured question sets. Incorporating this qualitative element into your survey provides similarly rich and visceral data. And, like focus group data, it can reveal previously unconsidered concepts. Unlike focus group data, it can also be coded, processed, and treated as reliable quantitative data, since the sample is representative and significantly large.

SITECENTRIC CONCEPT TESTING

Now that we've stated our views on why quantitative, sitecentric methods are the preferred means of testing product concepts, let's review the details of developing concept statements and conducting these studies.

DEVELOPING A REPRESENTATION OF YOUR PRODUCT CONCEPT

The most critical and difficult step in testing product concepts is developing good representations of the concepts. These representations are in turn provided to respondents so they can react to and provide feedback on your ideas. By definition, no product yet exists, so you'll generally need to rely on written concept statements to convey your ideas to respondents. Creating these statements is a challenging but rewarding exercise that will help focus your perception of the product and the customer.

Be certain to dedicate adequate time and energy to developing quality concept statements. The "garbage in, garbage out" principle is in full effect when conducting this type of research. Statements that are convoluted or do not adequately convey key benefits to the customer will be poorly received, even though they may represent intrinsically good ideas. Conversely, statements that are too general may rate well, but they might not provide you with a clear consensus on what specific factors drove the ratings. Do yourself a favor and convey the importance of concept testing to decision makers involved in the project; then, solicit their help in developing statements.

A concept statement can range from one line to a paragraph of text. Strive to make statements as succinct as possible while still conveying all relevant information. As with all survey questions, respondents may not be entirely focused on reading things all the way through, instead scanning the text to quickly absorb the gist of its meaning before giving an answer. Long concept statements may actually be attempts to convey more than one idea. Whenever possible, long statements should be divided into their component parts and tested individually to obtain a better read on the customer's opinions.

It is helpful of think of concept statements as mini-advertisements or positioning statements. They should convey both a synopsis of the concept and what its key benefits are. If you move forward with development, eventually you'll need to market the product to existing or new users. In doing so, you'll have limited space to capture their attention, describe the product, and entice them to try it. The ability to do these things is key to the success of any product, so it should be a factor in deciding which concepts to pursue and which to pass up. Try to avoid being too "persuasive" when describing the benefits of your idea to respondents. Save terms like "the most advanced," "the best," and "the first" for the actual marketing campaign. What you're testing here is the merit of the idea itself; focus on actual benefits to the customer.

Be honest and realistic about what you can deliver. Don't bother to test statements beyond the scope of what you intend to provide. Anyone can create product concepts that resonate favorably with nearly everyone. Unfortunately, companies need to implement both profitable and desirable services if they hope to stay in business. Testing overly ambitious concepts is a waste of time and negatively impacts respondents' perceptions of more realistic concepts that are tested at the same time.

The process of developing concept statements should involve the entire product and marketing team. Make sure that each member of the team provides input and that consensus is reached as to whether statements accurately describe the product concept. Ideas, by their very nature, are open to interpretation. One team member may think a statement precisely reflects the concept, while another believes otherwise. Unless there is agreement about the accuracy of statements among the entire team, the results from the study are likely to be disputed.

The first step is to decide on a tentative list of concepts to be tested. Circulate this list among the product team, and ask every person to anonymously write concept statements for each idea. If there are too many concepts for each individual to write about, divide ideas up into subsets and assign them to different members of the team. Be certain to distribute concepts among departments; you don't want all the engineers working on one idea and all the marketing folks considering another.

Schedule a group meeting and read the statements for each concept aloud. In our experience, these meetings can be quite entertaining; the statements often vary wildly, and sometimes comically. Edit all versions for a given concept into one refined statement. Be certain to resolve any disputes or misgivings within the group, so everyone will be confident in the subsequent results. If agreement on a particular issue cannot be reached, consider dividing the statement into two concepts or possibly scrapping the idea altogether.

Throughout this process, the researcher's role should be that of a moderator. Avoid leading the development of statements.

Instead, focus your efforts on pointing out when multiple concepts are being tested in one statement, or when statements are overtly persuasive. Too often, researchers take the lead in developing statements. This allows product teams to avoid focusing on the topic; then, while they may initially agree with the statements, they are more likely to find fault with them later and question the research findings. Getting the product team to participate may require some prodding and elicit some grumbling at first; but your efforts will be rewarded when they have a clear and unified understanding of what customers desire and why.

Here are three examples of concept statements:

- *Free Web-based email:* This service would provide members with free email accounts. The accounts could be accessed 24 hours a day from any computer with an Internet connection and a Web browser. Members could read and send email (and file attachments) to friends, family, and colleagues, all through a simple-to-use Web interface.

- *Portfolio tracking:* This feature would provide the ability to create, manage, and track the performance of stock portfolios. Members could input their current portfolio to supervise its performance, and indicate stocks they were interested in monitoring. Price trends could be illustrated using charts and graphs, and industry news would be available to assist interpretation.

- *Chat rooms:* Real-time interaction between members would be made available via Web-based chat rooms. Users could log on to chat rooms of specific interest to them (like "knitting" or "heavy metal") and conduct typewritten conversations with other participants who are interested in the same topic. Participants would also have the ability to create rooms for new topics or create private rooms for chatting with friends, family, or colleagues.

CONDUCTING CONCEPT TESTS

Armed with a set of agreed-upon concept statements, it's time to conduct the study itself. The first step is to develop a questionnaire. The questionnaire can be simple as having respondents read and rate concept statements using a desirability scale. This spartan study design is not recommended, as it does not provide customer characteristics or behaviors that may drive the ratings. A given concept may be highly desired by men, but not at all desirable to women. Without asking about gender, all we know is that part of the population loved the idea and another part hated it. Include additional metrics to illuminate who the respondents are and why they react to the concepts.

Metrics to Include

Segmentation: Hopefully, by this point you should have developed segments to represent distinct groups of your customer base. If you've done so, you've also developed a succinct set of questions to place customers into these segments. These are critical questions to include in the study, as they enable analysis by segment of the respondents' reactions to concepts. This is an important capability, because many concepts may be targeted toward particular segments—heavy users, for instance. Equally important, it will allow you to evaluate reactions to these concepts by other segments, to ensure that they do not react negatively. Balancing the needs of different segments can be tricky; it should be a key consideration throughout the development process.

If you haven't created a detailed segmentation of your market, collect relevant background information to help you interpret reactions to the concepts. Perhaps earlier sitecentric research (or common sense) revealed some metrics that are especially relevant to how customers relate to your site. Examples might include site relationship (heavy, moderate, or light users), characteristics (gender, age), or behavioral metrics (heavy online shoppers). Include the most pertinent of these in the study, but be wary of burdening respondents by asking too many background questions. One appealing aspect of concept studies, from a respondent's perspective, is that they are short and interesting. If you ask too many background questions, respondents will become fatigued before they have an opportunity to carefully read and respond to concept statements.

Behavioral: If it is not already part of your segmentation scheme, relevant behavioral data should also be collected. For instance, if you are testing the concept of offering free Web-based email from your site, it might be relevant to collect data on the number of personal and work email accounts respondents already have. Later analysis may show that the concept of free Web-based email is especially desirable among users who have work, but not personal, accounts. Or, perhaps the number of different computers respondents use for checking email is the key determinant in their interest in a Web-based service. Whenever possible, attempt to include a few relevant behavioral questions, but don't get carried away. Remember your key objective.

After gathering background data, it's time to present the concept statements to respondents. After respondents read the statements, a few metrics are used to quantify their reactions.

Overall desirability: First and foremost, measure the overall desirability of the product concept.

Purchase or usage likelihood: In addition to overall desirability, purchase or usage probability is a standard metric to collect. It makes the concept less abstract by encouraging respondents to consider if and how they would integrate the product into their lives. While many concepts are desirable, fewer are deemed purchasable or usable. Current ownership or usage of similar products, for instance, is a factor that could affect purchase probability but not desirability.

FIGURE 12.1: Measuring reaction to the concept

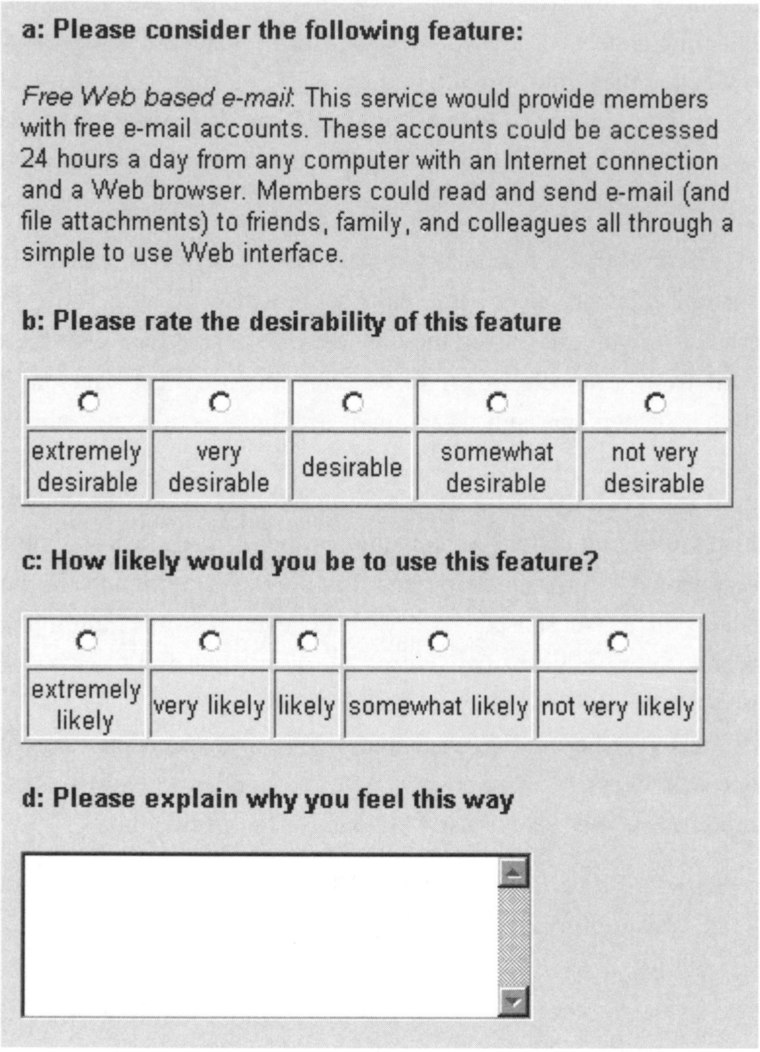

a: Please consider the following feature:

Free Web based e-mail. This service would provide members
with free e-mail accounts. These accounts could be accessed
24 hours a day from any computer with an Internet connection
and a Web browser. Members could read and send e-mail (and
file attachments) to friends, family, and colleagues all through a
simple to use Web interface.

b: Please rate the desirability of this feature

○	○	○	○	○
extremely desirable	very desirable	desirable	somewhat desirable	not very desirable

c: How likely would you be to use this feature?

○	○	○	○	○
extremely likely	very likely	likely	somewhat likely	not very likely

d: Please explain why you feel this way

Open-ended question for additional feedback: Concept testing is primarily an investigative research format, so it is
helpful to include an outlet for respondents to provide rich
and unstructured responses. This is best done by including
an open-ended response field.

One method is including one open-ended question for each concept you test. Chances are, however, you'll be testing a number of concepts at once. Asking respondents to write a brief essay on each concept will quickly burn them out. You may get considered answers for the first and second concepts, but little usable feedback on the remaining ones. There are two ways to deal with this problem. The first, and simplest, is to include only a single open-ended response for all the concepts. This field will allow you to gather respondents' free-form opinions after they've considered and rated everything. The difficulty with this method is that, in analysis, it becomes difficult to determine what concept(s) respondents are referring to in their commentary.

The second option is to increase the sample size and randomly distribute a smaller number of concepts (no more than three) to each respondent, similar to the way random rotation is used to allow collection of comprehensive consumer data. (Refer to Figure 11.4.) It's preferable to collect open-ended comments on each concept, since the rich nature of such data can be critical in helping you understand some of the issues driving customers' reactions. Verbatim comments from those who responded well can be separated from the comments from those who reacted negatively. Reading through and comparing each set can help you determine which concepts to move forward with.

RANDOMLY ROTATING CONCEPTS

There are a number of good reasons to consider randomly rotating concept statements. We've mentioned that random rotation provides the ability to collect open-ended data on every concept. Even if collecting open-ended responses on each concept were not a concern, it is still possible that the overall number of concepts to be tested will be too many for a respondent to give a sufficient degree of consideration to. Typically, respondents are able consider and rate approximately five to ten concepts. The actual number depends primarily on the length of the statement. Reading long paragraphs can exhaust respondents' attention quickly. A general rule of thumb is that it shouldn't take much more than 10 minutes to complete the entire questionnaire, including background questions. If more than 15 minutes are needed to complete the questionnaire, consider rotating concepts through subsets of respondents.

Beyond rotating concepts to reduce questionnaire length for any one respondent, it will also be necessary to randomize the order of concepts on the page. Concept testing is especially prone to order bias, for two reasons:

1. You are measuring customers' attitudes. Attitudes toward later concepts are affected by consideration of previous ideas. A respondent who particularly likes an earlier concept may rate subsequent ideas more negatively than if those concepts had preceded the highly desirable concept.
2. Concepts appearing later in the survey receive less consideration than those that appear earlier.

To eliminate order bias, you need to randomize. When randomizing concepts, make certain that any related questions rotate as sets along with the concept statements. It will be confusing to respondents unless the behavioral and open-ended questions specific to the concept are asked alongside the statements and their corresponding desirability and purchase probability ratings.

Unfortunately, randomly rotating question sets either on the page or to subsets of respondents is not a trivial task. Few survey packages provide the ability even to randomize answer choices, much less answer sets. Unless you're fielding studies using custom-built scripts, you'll probably need to enact an inelegant but effective work-around by developing independent surveys and using JavaScript to randomly assign respondents to each survey. In the end, you combine the data from each survey into a single dataset for analysis. To assist you with this process, we provide at our Web site JavaScript to randomly sample users from a page, then

FIGURE 12.2: Randomly rotate the order of concepts to respondents

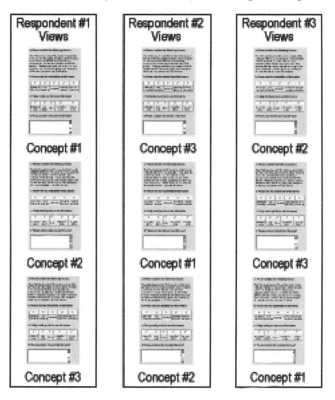

randomly display one of four survey locations. This script and the other JavaScripts mentioned in this book are available at www.site-centric.com/handbook/javascript/.

CHAPTER 13

Development

In Chapter 12 we discussed how to use concept testing to determine which product ideas warrant further investigation and investment. While testing concepts is a great method of whittling down a number of general ideas into a few promising prospects, it provides little specific information about how to build the concepts into products that customers will find appealing and will use. Strategic development requires that you have information about how customers relate to the category and their need for specific product features and functionality. Online products are as much functions of their interfaces as their feature sets, so it is also helpful to have a quantitative method of evaluating the merits of different prototypes and design ideas. In this chapter, we present a data-driven process for developing promising concepts into successful products.

Conducting research before and during the development process greatly increases the probability that a launch will be successful. Still, many companies take great risks by developing online products without understanding customer behavior or soliciting feedback on the types of features the site should include. Such companies assume they know the customers' needs better than the customers do. Developers occasionally create innovative features that customers could not foresee as useful or desirable; more frequently, a lack of detailed information on customer habits and preferences results in products that contain superfluous features or lack critical functionality.

Development research falls into two distinct categories:

1. identifying the features and functionality customers want from the product under development;
2. testing and refining different interface treatments and prototypes to best appeal to target customer groups.

In determining what customers are looking for in a product, the first step is to develop a thorough understanding of the characteristics that might affect how they relate to or use the product. Previous chapters have dealt with the collection and application of this type of information, and we won't repeat ourselves. If the concept you're developing is simply an extension of your core business model, you should already have information about how customers relate to the category. Perhaps that very information spawned the new idea you are now developing. On the other hand, if your concept is unrelated to your core business, return to Chapter 8 to review how to develop a detailed profile on your new target market.

Understanding the characteristics of your customers has obvious benefits that we've discussed throughout this book. During the product development process, as in evaluating the competition (see Chapter 10), there is a more specific application: It enables interpretation of consumer feedback within the context of who is providing it. You won't always be able to satisfy everyone, but having this data will let you make an informed decision as to whose opinions matter and whose should take a back seat.

IMPORTANCE RATINGS OF PRODUCT FEATURES

The central challenge in any product development effort is determining the ideal feature mix. The possibilities always outnumber the choices that can affordably be developed. Research can provide a systematic method for deciding which features to include and which to leave out.

Some parts of the feature mix are not at your discretion. Some core functionality must always be included, at a bare minimum for the concept to have any hope of success. These cost-of-entry features are often based on standards set by the competition. For instance, if you're developing a site to market automobiles to consumers, many of the features you'll include on the site will be determined by what similar sites are already offering. Suppose that every competitive site allows customers to view interactive 3D models, price out car models with different luxury features, and read third-party product reviews. Chances are good that when you test the importance of these features, consumers will rate them as essential and you'll decide to include them in your site as well.

Aside from cost-of-entry attributes, a brand should seek to identify other highly desirable features that can differentiate the product from the competition. If every product provided only the bare minimum, it would be impossible to select the "best product" to use—they would all be the same.

The process of determining the set of features to include in your product is very similar to that used to identify strengths and weaknesses of specific competitors. Begin by developing an extensive list of potential features. Like concept statements, this list is best developed with the help of the entire development team. Features differ from concepts in two major ways:

1. Features are far more granular. A product concept is the sum of many individual features.

2. Feature testing involves descriptions that are, by necessity, quite brief. Features tend to be described in a few words, rather than a few sentences.

While concept testing lends itself well to the rotation of sub-sets of concepts through the sample (reducing the workload on any individual respondent), feature testing does not. Because a primary goal of this research is to identify priorities for development, it is essential that respondents consider and rate all the possibilities. Thus, feature testing necessitates the use of concise descriptions that can be read and answered quickly by study participants.

Here is an example of a feature list for an automotive market-ing site:

- Interactive 3D models of automobiles
- Links to independent third-party product reviews
- Detailed information of model specifications
- Interactive pricing tool
- Car reviews from current owners
- Scheduled maintenance reminders
- Ability to request a test drive
- Search function to find nearest dealer
- Ability to purchase cars from the Web site
- Financing information
- Online owner's manual
- Warranty information
- Calculation of trade-in value of used automobile

An actual feature list would likely be much longer, but this will give you the idea. After an extensive list of potential features has been developed, it is time to incorporate them into a survey to determine their importance. The sample used to conduct the study will depend upon whether the product you're developing is new, an addition to an existing site, or a redesign of an old site. Products tar-geted toward users of existing sites can leverage the current user base through a sitecentric study. (See the discussion of JavaScript sampling in Chapter 5.) Entirely new sites, or those targeted toward a new audience, require research data from respondents who match the target market definition. (Refer to the discussion in Chapter 5 on sampling.)

Similar to concept testing and all development research, the study begins by gathering background behavioral and classification data. By this stage in development, you should have taken time to conduct a segmentation analysis of your customer base and developed a succinct set of questions to assign respondents into market segments. This study, like the others detailed thus far, should lead with these questions. They will be critical for identifying some of the reasons that drive ratings of potential site features. In the previous example, one could easily see how a consumer's status as a new vehicle owner or an interested shopper would dramatically impact ratings of the features. Without first developing distinct segments of current owners and shoppers, subsequent analysis would be extremely limited.

After initial background data is collected, we move directly to the importance ratings of potential features. Such ratings can be gathered using an array of different scale types. Some researchers prefer scales with 5 points because they are smaller and require less space on the screen. Others favor larger scales (10 points) that provide the opportunity for more granular results. Some researchers insist on using an even number of points in their scales to force respondents to fall on the positive or negative side of an evenly distributed semantic scale. Our opinion is that the best scale for determining exactly how important features are to respondents is a 7-point scale. We've already touched on the reasons behind respondents' hesitancy to state that a feature is "Not at all important" or simply "Not important." Unless care is taken in the development of the scale, all features might end up rated as "Very important" or "Important" and you might end up scratching your head and wondering which to implement in your site.

To combat this, we typically use a seven-point scale that is skewed toward the positive. This gives respondents a more

granular set of responses to choose from, without greatly expanding the size of the scale.

> *Please rate the importance of the following elements in an auto
> manufacturer's site, using a scale where:*
>
> 7 = Absolutely critical
> 6 = Extremely important
> 5 = Very important
> 4 = Important
> 3 = Somewhat important
> 2 = Not very important relative to other considerations
> 1 = Not at all important relative to other considerations

Regardless of the scale you use, respondents will generally
tend to overstate the importance of features. If you are testing only
a few elements (no more than ten), you might opt to use ranking

FIGURE 13.1: Rating and ranking the importance of product attributes

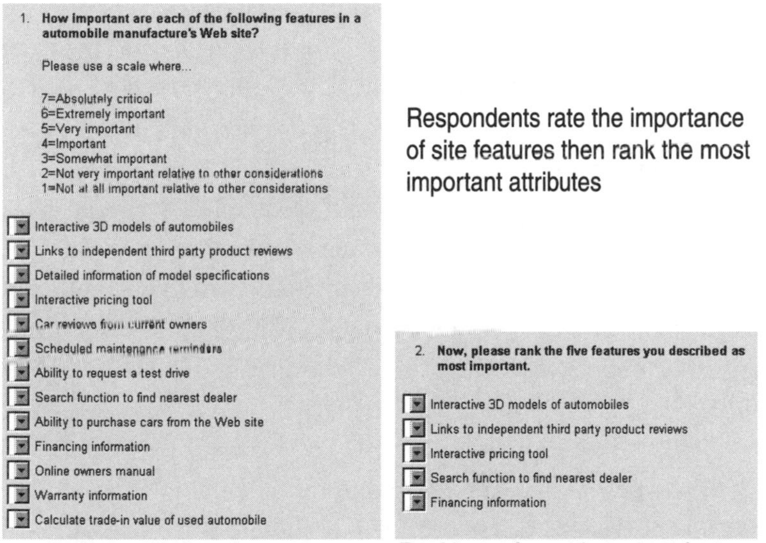

Respondents rate the importance
of site features then rank the most
important attributes

Ratings of feature importance   Rankings of most important features

rather than a rating scale, to force respondents to decide which elements are most important.

Though ranking is an excellent way to get a true reading of priority, most site development efforts deal with far more potential features than can be ranked in a simple manner. It is not uncommon for a site development team to test 20 or more potential features. When asking respondents to rate this many items, it is important to remember that this is attitudinal data in the fullest sense of the word. As we discussed in Chapter 12, the data is subject to order bias. If the list of features to be rated is not randomized, features at the top of the list are likely to receive more consideration than the rest. Additionally, attitudes toward subsequent features are affected by reactions to those preceding it. In any case, this bias can be eliminated by rotating the order of answer choices.

One possible though slightly advanced means of improving the discriminating power of the research is to use a hybrid technique that combines both rating and ranking methods. Respondents are first allowed to rate the importance of all the possible features. Once these ratings are submitted, the survey program asks respondents to rank the features that were rated as "Essential" and, in some cases, "Very important." This technique provides actionable data about the relative level of importance among highly desirable features, and serves as a tie-breaker among items that scored equally well.

Unfortunately, the commercially available survey packages we've seen are not equipped to handle the necessary logical structures to execute this technique. The technique will likely require the development of a custom questionnaire using Perl, Unix, or ASP. Using a combination of ratings and rankings also poses a few unique challenges on the analysis end.

Don't fret if combining ratings and rankings seems too difficult to pursue. In our experience, ratings alone almost always suffice. We discussed the power of using top 2 boxes and indexed mean scores to tease out meaningful findings from importance ratings (see Chapter 10), and these approaches also apply to importance ratings of features.

CONJOINT ANALYSIS

Many researchers become frustrated when attempting to determine the ideal feature set for a product using importance ratings alone. Combining rating and ranking information certainly improves this information a great deal, but it still leaves some researchers wanting a better understanding of the interplay between different elements. Rating and ranking the importance of various features is done independent of cost considerations. For instance, a customer might rate features of a product as essential, and subsequently rate their importance in order of desirability. However, the cost associated with each feature may not be equal.

Consider a truck, for instance. A respondent may rate and rank the features "4-wheel drive," "air conditioning," "6-cylinder engine," and "CD player" as being essential. However, the answer may change when asked if they'd rather purchase a $20,000 truck with a 6-cylinder engine or a $15,000 truck with a 4-cylinder engine.

To address this issue, clever researchers have devised a type of testing known as conjoint, or trade-off, analysis. This technique asks respondents to trade off different combinations of features and cost considerations to arrive at the most desirable set. The term conjoint relates to the measurement of relative values of things considered jointly. The appeal of conjoint analysis is that it more closely mirrors the decision process consumers go though when selecting a product to purchase. While all of us certainly want the best-performing product, that costs next to nothing, we must trade features off against each other and against the product's price to arrive at the product we're realistically willing or able to purchase.

By way of example, let's take our truck buyer and perform a simplified conjoint analysis on price along with two of the four most desirable attributes (4-cylinder versus 6-cylinder engine and 2-wheel drive versus 4-wheel drive). Assuming that high cost is an undesirable feature, and that a larger engine and 4-wheel drive are extremely desirable features to the respondent, simply asking for importance ratings does little to enhance our understanding of what type of truck to market to the respondent. The analysis will obviously recommend that we build a cheap truck with both features! If we went a step further and asked respondents to rank the importance of these features, perhaps the result would be:

$$1 = \text{Price}$$
$$2 = 4 \times 4$$
$$3 = \text{V6}$$

This certainly provides a much clearer picture of what is important to respondents, but still does not depict the distances between each rank order. Is price far and away the largest concern, such that the consumer would never pay more for a 4-wheel drive, or is price only slightly more important than 4-wheel drive capabilities? What about the relationship between 4-wheel drive and the larger engine, or the engine and price? To determine this, we need to present respondents with and have them rank all possible product combinations. In our simple example, we have two attributes with two levels and a third attribute (price) with three levels. Hence,

TABLE 13.1: Considering product attributes jointly

Product Combination	Rank
4×4 V6 $15,000	1
4×4 V6 $20,000	2
4×4 V4 $15,000	3
4×4 V4 $20,000	4
4×2 V6 $15,000	5
4×2 V4 $15,000	6
4×2 V6 $20,000	7
4×2 V4 $20,000	8
4×4 V6 $25,000	9
4×4 V4 $25,000	10
4×2 V6 $25,000	11
4×2 V4 $25,000	12

the total number of combinations is $2 \times 2 \times 3 = 12$. With so few attributes, a conjoint analysis could be performed simply by having respondents rank all the scenarios.

As we can see, while respondents stated that price was the number one concern, they are willing to pay more for their desired feature set. Furthermore, we see that while they are willing to pay more for a truck with 4-wheel drive but not for a V6 engine, they would not pay more for a truck with a V6 engine but not 4-wheel drive capabilities. When considered jointly, we obtain a more through understanding of the type of products we can develop and market successfully and profitably.

The chart in Table 13.1 shows the power of considering product features jointly, but it is not actually an example of conjoint analysis. In reality, few feature sets are as simple as that. Most contain many more attributes and more levels of depth. If we were to include air conditioning and the CD player in our analysis, and add two additional relevant price levels, the number of possible combinations would rise to $2 \times 2 \times 2 \times 2 \times 5 = 80$ product concepts. Obviously, this is too many for any one respondent to rank.

Computer-aided conjoint techniques are used to somewhat reduce the number of decisions respondents must make. While a description of the actual methods used is too lengthy for us to include here, Sawtooth Technologies (*http://www.sawtooth.com/*) has posted a number of introductory white papers on specific conjoint techniques. In addition, the company has developed a number of computer-aided conjoint administration and analysis tools that will be of value to those interested in pursuing such studies.

The downside of conjoint techniques is that respondents must answer a large number of ranking or rating questions. The number of questions required goes up exponentially with the number of attributes tested. As a result, conjoint techniques are often ill-suited to site development research, for which it is common to consider the development of 20 or more product features. Testing 20 attributes using even the most efficient conjoint techniques would require that a respondent answer enough questions to fry anyone's brain.

There is another, less-obvious, reason why conjoint techniques are not widely utilized online. Most Web products are either online shopping locations or content destinations. While most attempt to make a profit by getting users to visit more often or to purchase more goods, they seldom charge for site use. There are exceptions, of course, like online stock trading sites or highly specialized content sites. However, for the most part, using a Web site is free. Conjoint techniques work poorly in the absence of cost considerations, because respondents are not placed in a realistic purchase decision process.

Another problem with conducting conjoint analysis in online development is that conjoint analysis functions best when there is a large range of possible variability in the attributes tested. If we were doing a conjoint study for a digital camera, for instance, one attribute might be the number of pictures stored. This attribute might range from as low as 10 pictures to as high as 100 pictures. Web sites, however, tend to employ features that lack different levels of service. Our automotive Web site would either provide customers with the ability to view 3D models of cars or not. It isn't a question of determining "just the right amount" of 3D modeling needed to convince users to purchase a car. Even if it was, how would we measure it?

We offer one last dig on the otherwise appealing conjoint analysis: It's hard to conduct, difficult to analyze, and, like nearly all multivariate techniques, almost impossible to convey to the layperson. The net result is that all your hard work in this area will be for naught unless you are particularly adept at translating complicated statistics into simple English.

TESTING DIFFERENT INTERFACES AND PROTOTYPES

Having determined the ideal feature set, it's time to fire up Photoshop and begin developing your product. During the development phase, you'll inevitably face numerous questions on how best to arrange and present the features. Multiple design schemes will be sketched out and considered in the search for the best look and feel. A logo and other brand identity issues will need to be decided on. The many possibilities can quickly become overwhelming if you don't have the right criteria on which to base decisions.

What's needed is a method for evaluating different interfaces, design implementations, and product prototypes in terms of some metric that will predict bottom-line success. For many Web sites, this metric is the likelihood that customers will respond to and use the site. It's quite easy to become deeply involved in the process of creating a site, and to lose sight of the customers who will eventually use it. Therefore, it makes sense to involve the customers in the decision-making process to ensure that the site you're developing is in line with their expectations.

Involving customers in every decision is obviously excessive and would not result in a cohesive or innovative product. The development of online products should be left to designers, engineers, and project managers who have experience in developing usable and intriguing Web sites. In every project, however, there will be inevitable tension in the development group when divergent opinions arise over the best course of action. Some team members may think the design of the product should be outlandish and striking, while others think a subtle, understated design is better suited to the task at hand. Or, perhaps one camp insists that navigation features should rely solely on iconography with no underlying text, but others believe supporting text is necessary to immediately convey site value, functionality, and ease of use. If you've spent any time developing a Web site, we're certain you can easily recount your own examples of such conflicts.

ENTER INTERFACE TESTING

Interface testing is the process of developing and testing multiple interfaces to determine which is best received by potential customers of the site. It provides the best combination of soliciting customer feedback on development efforts and allowing developers the freedom to create engaging and creative products. But best of all, it is an outlet for resolving conflicts within the development group by giving the final say to the customer—and we all know the customer is always right. Right?

Interface testing can be pursued on a case-by-case basis or embedded systematically into the development process. Implemented case by case, interface testing is employed to understand a specific issue that may be tripping up the development process. For instance, which of three possible product logos best conveys the intended brand image of the product being developed? On a systematic basis, interface testing is formalized into the development process. From the beginning, developers conceptualize and create mockups of possible product designs and interfaces. These mockups are then tested to evaluate which best meets customer expectations, brand identity objectives, and business goals. Developers then proceed to implement the superior interface mockup or, if necessary, head back to the drawing board, to create something entirely new.

The process of testing different interfaces is based on powerful experimental design methodologies, similar to those used in medical research to measure the effectiveness of new drugs. We've briefly discussed experimental design research in other chapters; interface testing is where this technique proves most useful in online research.

Conceptually, an experimental design is quite simple. The idea is to take two or more identical populations of respondents, expose them to varying stimuli (e.g., different interface mockups), and then ask them identical questions afterward to determine the effects of the stimuli. Because the populations were identical to start with and the subsequent questionnaires are identical, any differences between each population's responses must be driven solely by differences in the stimuli each received.

By way of example, let's assume that we want to determine which of three possible product logos best conveys the brand personality of a new streaming audio product. Let's also assume that our audio product is targeted toward high school and college age students who listen to music more than 15 hours a week and purchase or download the equivalent of three or more CDs per month. Previous behavioral research has determined that this target audience listens primarily to alternative, electronic, and hip-hop music genres. Previous attitudinal research shows that they identify with traits such as *hip, counterculture, intelligent, underground,* and *real.*

Given the characteristics, behaviors, and attitudes of our target audience, how do we best determine which of the three logos to use?

The first step is to acquire a representative sample that is likely to fit the definition of the target market. As we discussed earlier, this sample can be randomly solicited from your existing site if some portion of those users share the characteristics, behaviors, and attitudes of the target customer. Otherwise, you'll need to look elsewhere for respondents.

The next step is to develop the initial questionnaire. It should collect relevant background information to screen for the target consumer. In our example, those variables would include:

- educational status,
- hours of music listened to weekly,
- number of CDs purchased monthly, and
- types of music listened to.

After asking the initial questions, we randomly assign respondents to one of three groups, known as *cells*. The cells are created randomly, so the composition of respondents in each cell should be statistically identical. This can be confirmed by comparing the background metrics of the respondents in each cell. If Cell 1 has 45% high school students, then Cells 2 and 3 should also have 45% high school students, give or take a few percent within the confidence interval. When conducting this type of research, it is important to check the similarity of the cells, because strange statistical aberrations can occur. If they do (which is seldom), weight your data to bring things back into line.

Each cell is assigned one of the tested logos, which in turn is presented to respondents in that cell to review. In our example, these logos would likely be in a final state. However, in many cases, developing multiple finished interfaces or prototypes of online products would prove overly taxing for the development team. Typically, when whole interfaces or design schemes are tested, it is more realistic to develop mockups rather than finished products to test. Mockups can vary from extremely rough sketches to nearly completed working prototypes. Typically, the level of detail devoted to mockups is somewhere in between. Obviously, more comprehensive mockups result in better quality data, because less is left to the respondent's imagination. The general rule of thumb is to develop the mockup sufficiently to give respondents a clear idea of the issues you're attempting to understand. A static Web page, free of links, can be sufficient to inform respondents of the functionality and design of a site. Another interesting approach is to build interactive demos using third-party plug-in technology, like Flash or ShockWave demos, to convey features to respondents.

FIGURE 13.2: Testing creative with an experimental study design

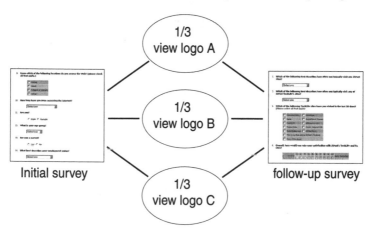

In our example, respondents would be asked to view the logo and answer a number of questions about how it made them feel about the brand. Given what we know about the audience's attitudinal traits, these questions would likely focus on how *hip, countercultural, intelligent, underground,* and *real* the logo and the company behind it seemed. These metrics are what we might consider the key drivers of the brand, and indicators of likelihood that our target audience will find the product appealing and choose to use it over others. The key drivers of brand choice vary for every product and also depend upon the features being tested.

For instance, if we decided to test interfaces in addition to logos for our streaming audio product, we would also investigate differences between interfaces on a number of other metrics beside those that were purely image-oriented. The impact of each interface on perceptions of product performance would undoubtedly be a main concern. We might measure which interface gave impressions of having the greatest range of musical selection, the largest database of songs, the most intuitive navigation, the most appealing design, or even the fastest loading time. These types of metrics drive the online product a consumer chooses to use on an ongoing basis, so it is crucial that the interface and design chosen immediately convey the brand's strength in the *key drivers of brand choice.*

Developing a set of key drivers of brand choice for your product may take some additional cerebral effort up front, but it pays off royally in the development process and later in marketing and site evaluation efforts. Similar to the set of questions developed to succinctly segment potential customers, identification of the key drivers of brand choice provides a means for evaluating the effectiveness of every development decision, marketing campaign, or other business activity with a standardized measuring tool. For each action you take, you can answer the most important business question: "What effect did the decision have on the customer's likelihood to use our product?" When combined with segmentation metrics, measurement of key drivers can help you develop and evaluate strategy to meet the needs of one group of customers without alienating others.

Some other metrics that are helpful for interpreting reactions to interfaces are:

- overall desirability ratings,
- probability of usage or purchase, and
- open-ended responses.

Analysis is one of the most enjoyable aspects of using experimental design research to drive the development process. Because all respondents answer the same questionnaire, there are no sticky issues involving measurement bias. Any bias that exists is equal in each tested cell, and hence, cancels itself out in the analysis. Therefore, we can confidently state that any differences in responses are the result of differences between interfaces. This is an excellent situation for the researcher, since the analysis simply consists of comparing the response from one interface to that from another. In general, the interface with the highest scores wins!

Statistical significance is an issue to be aware of when analyzing the results from an experimental design. This refers to the size that a difference between cells must achieve before it can be considered *significant,* or more accurately, not attributable to randomness. For instance, if 60% of Cell 1 rated the logo as hip versus 20% of Cell 2, we could confidently conclude that logo 1 is more hip than logo 2. But what if the difference was smaller, say 45% versus 50%? To answer the question, we'd need to perform some statistical testing on the data to determine whether the difference was real or simply attributable to randomness. There are many types of brain-crunching statistical tests used to determine the significance of research findings. Luckily, online researchers have access to robust samples and the ability to create rigorous study designs via random sampling and random cell assignment. This alleviates much of the confusion and statistical hocus-pocus that researchers in other fields must endure. For our purposes, we rely primarily on a few simple significance tests to determine the validity of our results.

The chi-squared test and the Z-test are the significance tests you'll likely find most useful for determining whether the observed differences between cells can be attributed to randomness or not. However, this handbook is not the place to wax on about statistics. That's what statisticians are paid to do, and they have done so extensively. Every college textbook on statistics in every library explains these tests in plain English and covers methods of calculation. In addition to book references, there are online sources for statistical wisdom:

> *HyperStat* (*http://davidmlane.com/hyperstat/*): This is one of the best introductory statistics books online. In addition to introducing concepts and calculation, the site also links to programs (in many cases Web-based) that actually calculate the statistics you're interested in.

> *StatSoft,* the makers of a data analysis package called Statistica, provide an electronic statistics textbook online (*http://www.statsoft.com/textbook/stathome.html*). The searchable and well-organized site covers everything from elementary statistical topics to specific advanced statistical procedures.

> *Intelliquest* (*www.intelliquest.com*): The home of a large online panel, this site also provides a number of useful calculators for determining the statistical significance of experimental designs and confidence levels for survey samples.

CHAPTER 14

Testing

A fter developing a product prototype or beta version, it's time to turn your research focus to product testing. Assuming you've taken the time to pretest the concept and conduct early product development research, testing should go smoothly. By testing concepts you've greatly reduced the risk that the underlying idea will prove undesirable. Additionally, research conducted on the feature set and interface design have ensured that the major aspects of the development process were in line with customer expectations.

What does that leave to test?

Primarily, the testing phase of research helps you fine-tune the product: catch the inevitable programming bugs, evaluate the usability of the product, and guide the forthcoming marketing push. The testing phase can also provide a real-world setting to evaluate how customers actually adopt and use the product you've developed.

At this stage, many managers (who haven't yet read this book) find themselves faced with a larger set of research concerns. As we've mentioned, in a rush to market, some companies skip initial concept and development research, and jump directly into building online products. Only when the product nears completion and they begin to think about testing do other research-related questions surface. In addition to evaluating the usability of the new online product, these companies widen their research scope in an attempt to determine the fundamentals: market size, market value, target customer, receptivity to the product concept, satisfaction with the feature set, and ratings of the interface design.

These additional metrics will certainly aid future product decisions, but they will have little effect on the current product. What's to be done, if, after developing a beta version, testing reveals weak reception to the feature set? Perhaps the development team could frantically implement additional functionality in the short time before the product launch. In a worst-case scenario, the product launch could be pushed back—assuming, of course, that media time has not been purchased to support the launch. But what if research suggests that the product concept is undesirable or the market is far smaller than originally anticipated? No amount of scrambling or all-night coding sessions can address either of these issues.

As a researcher, you'll be setting yourself up for failure if you allow fundamental product issues to be tested this late in the game. Since the course is basically set, for better or worse, any research findings contrary to the company's vision of the product will meet with heavy resistance. The backlash will cast doubt on the reliability of all research and will compromise the value of legitimate, actionable findings. If this is your situation, attempt to focus decision makers on testing elements of the product that can be fixed before the product launch. Reserve the fundamental issues until afterward. If intuition prevails and the product succeeds, then the research that was conducted will receive its due praise and encourage a more data-driven perspective toward future product development. If the product doesn't meet expectations, the company is more likely to be receptive to research that can shed light on actual market size or desirability for the product.

We hope this situation will not apply to you, because you've read this book and conducted initial research into the marketability and design of your product. Though the initial research you conducted should prevent major product catastrophes, the product testing phase can detect issues that still need to be addressed before the launch. This is the first stage in development at which consumers have the opportunity to use a working prototype of the product. The hands-on experience immerses customers in the product and is likely to elicit more detailed feedback than abstract interface, feature, or concept tests do. This is also the first large-scale test of the site. Having a number of different types of customers accessing the site will inevitably surface previously unforeseen issues with the interface design, feature set, and in some cases, back-end scaleability.

Because product testing can detect significant product flaws, it is important to build enough time into the release schedule to allow for a thorough evaluation as well as time for any major problems to be remedied before the official launch.

METHODS OF PRODUCT TESTING

There are both qualitative and quantitative approaches to testing the usability and acceptance of new online products. While we usually consider most qualitative techniques ill-suited for the development of online products, they can be invaluable at this stage. Sitting down, one on one, with consumers and watching them navigate a site is the best method of identifying any interface elements that are confusing or difficult to use. No survey or other quantitative method can detect the expression on the face of a respondent who is stumped trying to find the "help" section, or having difficulty navigating the purchase process. The only reliable method of identifying these usability issues is to hold in-depth, in-person sessions where a researcher watches a respondent navigate the site and probes into what causes any hold-ups that present themselves.

Methods of planning and conducting in-person usability tests were covered in Chapter 2. We recommend that you review that chapter and consider holding these sessions as the first step in testing your new online product.

While qualitative product testing can evaluate the usability of a product, the sessions will not evaluate how the product will be adopted in the real world. The qualitative environment is contrived. Respondents are paid handsomely to sit around eating pizza and focus on the site. In the real world, the merits of your product alone must be sufficient motivation for customers to log on and use it regularly. In reality, many who try the site will not find enough value in it to warrant a second or third visit. To refine your final product offering and minimize attrition rates, you must determine who your product resonates with, who it fails to satisfy, and the reasons for both. This is also crucial for developing marketing strategy. Knowing *who* the product appeals to identifies the target(s) for your media planning. Knowing *why* it appeals to them suggests messaging to include in the marketing to maximize its motivational power. Qualitative testing cannot offer this information with the statistical rigor required for a multimillion-dollar ad campaign.

Qualitative usability testing also fails to provide the rigorous large-scale test of the product needed to flush out programming bugs that are hidden away in dark corners; nor does it stress-test the servers and systems to evaluate their ability to scale smoothly to larger usage patterns. To address these issues, we execute a beta test of the product.

BETA TEST

For most ventures, standard beta testing technique involves emailing friends, family, and colleagues with the URL of a new site. These emails invite recipients to "Come check out the reason you haven't seen me for the past six months." They additionally request that visitors surf the site thoroughly, reporting bugs or making suggestions to site developers though an email feedback link. There are a number of problems with this beta testing strategy. While it is effective at identifying some bugs within the site, the beta testing

group is not representative of your target market and tells you little, if anything, about how the site meets the needs of and fosters
relationships with real customers.

A structured quantitative approach to beta testing, using carefully constructed beta groups, provides much more reliable and
robust information. Primarily, it enables the controlled test of the
product in a natural setting. A well-selected group of customers
who are representative of the product's target market(s) begin using
the product simultaneously. Over time, some customers will find
the site valuable and begin using it on a regular basis. Some may
visit a few times and drop out. Others will find no value in the site
and never return after the initial visit. Evaluating the characteristics, behaviors, and attitudes of those who achieve each level of
retention is a powerful way to determine under actual working conditions, who the site best engages and why—or who the site turns
off and how to fix it.

Selecting the Beta Testing Group

In an ideal world, the population of your beta group would be an
exact (albeit much smaller) reflection of the market into which the
product will be launched. Each segment identified in the initial
stages of research would exist in the same proportion it exists in the
overall marketplace, with the smallest segment large enough to provide statistically significant results. Using a random sample from a
nationally representative Web panel or gathered via RDD phone
solicitation is the most reliable method. In practice, however, executing such a rigorous beta test of your new online product would
likely prove prohibitively expensive and time-consuming.

A more viable and cost-effective method of developing a
qualified beta testing group is to leverage samples from previous
stages of research. Respondents from the marketplace, segmentation, competitive, and product development stages of research can
be invited back to participate in the beta program.

The major advantage of using an existing sample is that you
already have much, if not all, of the background metrics on

respondents required to conduct in-depth analysis. At earlier stages, you collected extensive information on respondents' characteristics, behaviors, and attitudes that informed later segmentation strategies. In later studies, you collected a succinct set of metrics that enabled you to quickly categorize respondents into segments. In most cases, you should have enough information on previous respondents to divide them into relevant segments. This will save you a great deal of effort in beta testing, because respondents won't be required to answer an initial screening and background survey before beginning the beta test.

Another advantage to using an existing sample is that, having already participated in one survey, these respondents tend to be more likely to participate in additional research—especially for a product based on their original feedback. In our experience, approximately 40 to 50% of those who complete marketplace analysis or product development research return to participate in the beta program. This high response rate can significantly reduce the cost of soliciting beta testers from opt-in lists or other pay-for-access sources.

Leveraging past samples presupposes that you collected a means of recontacting respondents from these earlier studies. In all likelihood, you offered some incentive to respondents and needed some means of contacting them for fulfillment purposes. This contact information can now be used to invite individuals to participate in the beta program.

A word of caution is in order: Before recontacting respondents, be certain to review any privacy statements that may have been present when the contact information was initially collected. Frequently, the collection of this information is accompanied by sweeping statements that define how personal information will or will not be used. Be certain that recontacting respondents is permissible before initializing the effort.

If you plan to use a given sample for multiple waves of research, there are some technical considerations. As we mentioned earlier, a multi-wave study requires the ability to join data for each respondent from wave to wave. To accomplish this, you'll need to collect a unique identifier from each respondent and pass it from one wave to the next. The simplest examples are a combination of respondents' first and last names, email addresses, or a number you generate yourself. It is advisable to use more than one unique identifier (e.g., email address and last name) for each respondent, to maximize the likelihood that you'll be able to join the data from different waves together.

If you are prohibited from recontacting your earlier samples, or the samples are too small to form a robust beta testing population, other sources such as Web panels, newsgroups, or opt-in email lists can be used to solicit or supplement the beta testing group. We discussed resources and procedures for collecting these types of samples in Chapter 5.

The downside to collecting a new sample is the need to conduct an initial study to collect relevant segmentation, competitive usage, and behavioral data. With any luck, this initial study can be very short. By this point in the research process, you should have narrowed the questions needed to segment users down to a few succinct metrics.

If you haven't yet developed at least a basic segmentation strategy, now is the time to do so. This controlled test of your site offers a rare opportunity to evaluate the accuracy of your segmentation design. Ideally, those you've defined as the primary market segment will also be those who find the most value in the site and become its heaviest users during the beta period. Secondary target markets should use specific sections of the site specially designed (based on previous research) to meet their needs. Depending on which segments have the highest retention levels or which areas of the site different segments find valuable, your initial segmentation strategy can be confirmed or modified.

Conducting the Beta Test

After conducting the initial background screening survey (when recruiting from a new source of participants) or selecting respondents from previous studies, respondents are invited to join the beta program. As encouragement, be certain to mention that potential participants are a select group of consumers chosen to be part of a limited "sneak preview" whereby their feedback can have a major impact on the final form of the product. It is also advisable to offer some financial or other incentive. Many companies choose incentives that tie into the site's basic business model as a way of getting the beta program off and running. E-commerce sites, for instance, might offer a significant discount or free purchase from the site as an incentive to participate. An online brokerage might offer a few free stock trades. Sites that are not transaction-oriented (such as an online magazine) might fare better by offering an opportunity to win something highly desirable to their target audience—like the latest gaming console for a video gaming site, or the newest PDA for a technology site.

Those who choose to participate in the group should receive a briefing on the scope of their involvement; be introduced to the site; and be asked to begin using it regularly. Similar to any other beta program, participants are asked to provide feedback or suggestions to site developers. Be certain to specify the types of feedback you want participants to contribute. Encourage not only bug reports, but feedback on the feature set, usability, comparisons to competitive products, and an array of other issues that might be of specific interest to you.

The mechanism for providing feedback should not be left to an obscure link at the bottom of the page. Instead, design every page on the site to include an obvious, consistently located graphical element that links through to a beta-tester's feedback area. If the site design does not lend itself to having this element in the same place on every page, consider building the entire site within a frame set, with one frame holding the site and the other holding the beta tester's link. This setup can easily be undone when the testing period is completed. In our experience, providing this constant reminder significantly increases the amount and quality of feedback obtained during the test. Another method is to solicit beta feedback through a separate pop-up window that appears each time the site is loaded.

Capturing Feedback

We advise that you depart from the tradition of collecting beta feedback via email by setting up Web-based mini-surveys to segment and qualify feedback. A beta test can generate a significant amount of feedback. Pages and pages of email can quickly become too much to read though and make sense of. You're conducting a test of a Web-based product; it only makes sense to leverage the medium's power and use a Web form to structure the collection of feedback.

The feedback form should contain:

- *Segmentation questions:* These can be collected either by asking the set of segmentation questions again or by encoding a segmentation identifier into a cookie earlier in the research process.[1]
- *Type of feedback:* Is it a bug report? Commentary on content or features? Design-oriented?
- *Open-ended Web form field* to collect user feedback.

The small investment of time and labor required to shift feedback from email-based to a Web form will be rewarded with an expanded ability to route customer responses for interpretation. Bug reports can easily be separated from other commentary and funneled directly to the responsible development or engineering team. Other comments can be set aside for later evaluation or automatically forwarded to designated team members for immediate consideration.

More important, the form allows you to evaluate the relevance of feedback. You can't please everyone all the time, and some testers are bound to react negatively to the product. Should

---

[1]Encoding and reading cookie data is an advanced research technique requiring the use of either Perl cgi or JavaScript. See Chapter 6 on data collection for resources on this topic.

FIGURE 14.1: Collect user feedback through a Web form

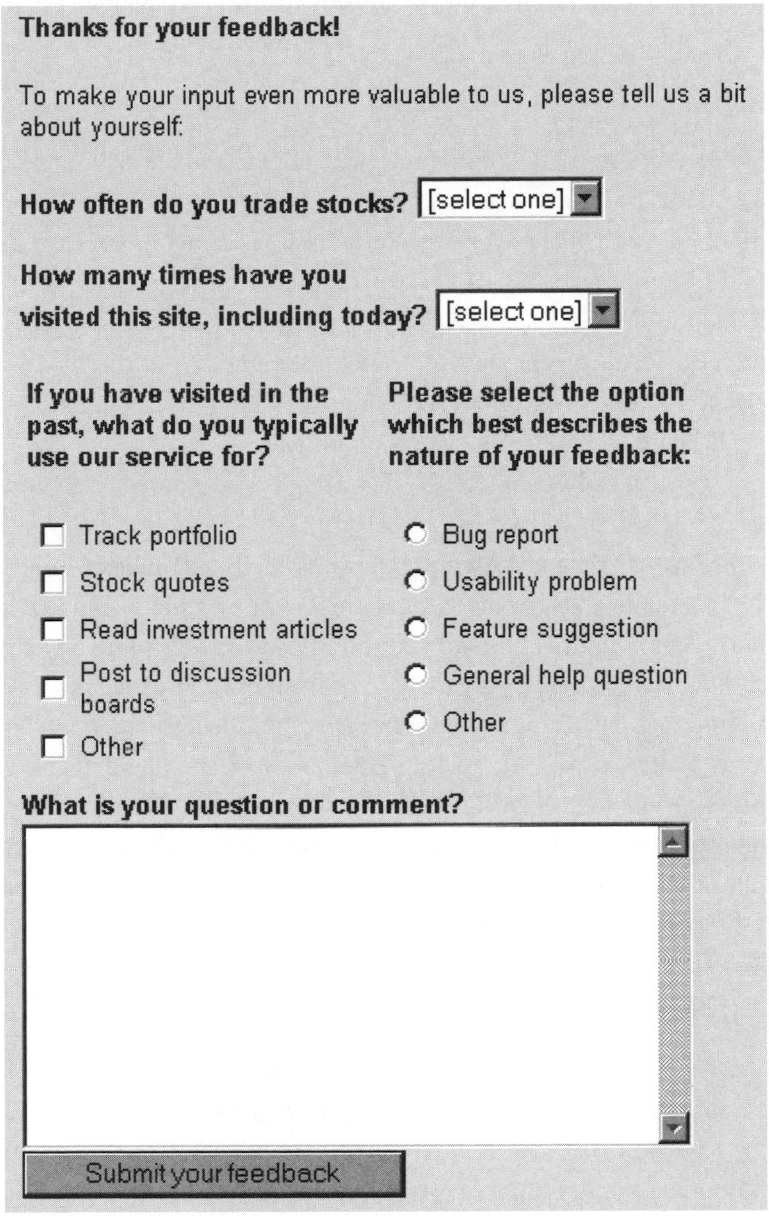

Thanks for your feedback!

To make your input even more valuable to us, please tell us a bit about yourself:

How often do you trade stocks? [select one] ▼

How many times have you
visited this site, including today? [select one] ▼

If you have visited in the past, what do you typically use our service for?

☐ Track portfolio
☐ Stock quotes
☐ Read investment articles
☐ Post to discussion boards
☐ Other

Please select the option which best describes the nature of your feedback:

○ Bug report
○ Usability problem
○ Feature suggestion
○ General help question
○ Other

What is your question or comment?

Submit your feedback

you be concerned? Assuming you are taking a focused business strategy, and not attempting to appeal to every consumer on the Web, some users' opinions should count more than others.

Traditional email approaches make this assessment difficult. Certainly, product issues that come up again and again can be considered more important than those that are mentioned only once or twice. But beyond frequency, without having some indication of who the participants are or why their opinions count, the researcher has little criteria to rate one participant's opinion over another's. Collecting feedback via a Web form alleviates this problem, as the customer feedback can be classified by segment. Your strategy will typically place more weight on some segments than on others, so you'll know which comments to act on first.

Though collecting feedback through a structured Web form instead of a free-form email greatly increases the quality of user responses, the data gathered is still qualitative and subject to bias. The most outspoken or involved members of the beta testing group are likely to dominate the information flow, while less-involved or subdued visitors quietly go about their business using the site. Keep in mind that the views of loudmouths are not necessarily representative of the entire beta testing population. Ever heard the term "Silent Majority"? During the beta testing phase, focus on fixing bug reports rather than spending time considering individual users' opinions. The qualitative issues will be quantified in the next phase of the beta testing program: the follow-up survey.

The Follow-Up Survey

Beta testers are given a period of time, ranging from a few weeks to a month, to use the site, provide bug reports, and offer qualitative feedback on features and functionality. Afterward, they are invited via another email to participate in a follow-up study. This study constitutes the core findings from the beta test. In contrast to the qualitative feedback received during the test, these study results are quantitative and provide actionable information about who the site worked for and why.

Usage Levels

As we mentioned earlier, one of the most powerful pieces of information gleaned from a beta test is an understanding of the types of customers who became regular, moderate, or light users of the site. Because this is the best real-world indicator of the level of value testers found in the product, it deserves special attention.

Evaluating the profile of testers who became regular, moderate, and light users should reveal groups closely matching your segmentation hypothesis: Your primary target segment became the heaviest users, the secondary segment became moderate users, and so forth. If the distribution of usage does not correspond to your initial segmentation hypothesis, it should be revisited to determine where the discrepancies lie. Perhaps something was lost in the translation from an idea into a real working product. Or perhaps this group of customers has other characteristics that make them more difficult to satisfy than originally anticipated. Whatever the reasons, you need to decide whether to pursue the original target or to modify your segmentation and marketing schemes to reach the consumers who became heavy users of the current product.

In addition to those who used the product to some degree after the initial introduction, there will be participants who failed to discover enough value in the site to return again. Evaluating the

FIGURE 14.2: Gathering usage level of tested

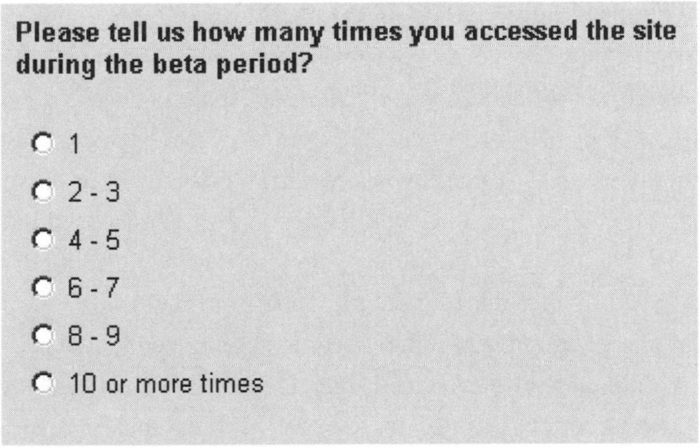

Please tell us how many times you accessed the site during the beta period?

- 1
- 2 - 3
- 4 - 5
- 6 - 7
- 8 - 9
- 10 or more times

reasons for the attrition so that you can take steps to combat it is another major aspect of the follow-up survey.

Beyond gathering data on the overall usage levels of the product, the follow-up study evaluates the utilization and appeal of individual features or sections of the site. This analysis uncovers aspects of the site considered most valuable to customers. Likewise, it uncovers problem areas that require attention by the development team before the product launch. It may be discovered that while overall usage levels are high, most of the usage is restricted to a small set of features. Of course, these metrics could be gathered from server logs, but logs do not provide the ability to evaluate the characteristics and behaviors of users to determine what's driving the success or failure of specific site features or sections.

Performance Ratings

The performance of individual sections or features can be understood by comparing usage and performance metrics. Usage levels provide the baseline measure of value to the consumer. To supplement usage measures, we recommend collecting performance ratings of individual sections or features. This provides another dimension for understanding the role each feature plays in the overall value of the site. The fact that a section is not heavily utilized does not always signify that it needs development attention. If performance ratings of the section prove high, the rate of trial was high, but repeat usage was low, then perhaps the need for the service is not as high as initially anticipated (or it is a type of feature that people use once and then don't need to use again). Another possibility is that few users tried the section, but those who did used it extensively and rated it quite highly. This could indicate the existence of a new customer segment that has a unique set of needs. More likely, the few people who stumbled upon it found it highly engaging. Perhaps the section should be displayed more prominently in the interface design. Finally, sections that receive poor performance ratings might still be extensively utilized, because the value of the service provided outweighs any flaws in the functionality or design. Make an effort to understand the shortcomings of a popular feature; you may be able to improve on an already promising concept.

We have discussed ways of identifying issues that are of critical importance to your target customers (importance ratings) and of measuring perceptions of your performance (performance ratings) in these areas. By measuring your product's performance against your customers' expectations, you can confirm that your product is ready for prime time.

You may already have one half of this data (importance ratings) if you are leveraging respondents from earlier stages of research that attempted to determine the importance of features. A competitive study (see Chapter 10) and a feature set desirability study (see Chapter 13) will both give you this information.

As we demonstrated in competitive assessment, using the follow-up study to collect performance ratings on the same attributes whose importance you've already determined allows a comparison of the two metrics. This comparison will reveal whether the current version of the site is on par with, exceeding, or falling short of user expectations.

To take this analysis a step further, you can also compare the performance of your beta product to competitive offerings. Again, the ratings of competitive products required to do this analysis may already exist in a previous stage of research. If they do not, gather this data in the manner described in Chapter 10. Because your product is not likely to be the only one of its kind, you need to consider how it stacks up against the competition. Areas where your product underperforms should be looked at closely. If they are areas that customers have placed high priority on (cost-of-entry items), you must improve their quality or risk a near-certain beating in the marketplace. If you discover areas where you outshine your competition, you have discovered competitive advantages that should be emphasized in your marketing program.

Validating Qualitative Feedback and Internal Ideas

The follow-up study is also the place to test the validity of unsolicited qualitative comments received during the beta testing period. Perhaps a number of participants in the beta group clicked on the feedback button to inform you that the speed of the site search feature was not up to par, or commented that the site should include more independent product reviews. The degree to which these opinions exist in the overall beta group can be quantified by including specific questions addressing these issues in the follow-up study.

In addition to quantifying the existence of similar customer opinions away the rest of the testing group, the follow-up study can be leveraged to address any last-minute internal development ideas that arise during the beta testing period. Frequently, the observed performance of the site during the beta period prompts new site functionality or design ideas. The customer's need and the level of appeal of these ideas should (as always) be tested before implementation.

FIGURE 14.3: Quantifying comments collected during the beta test

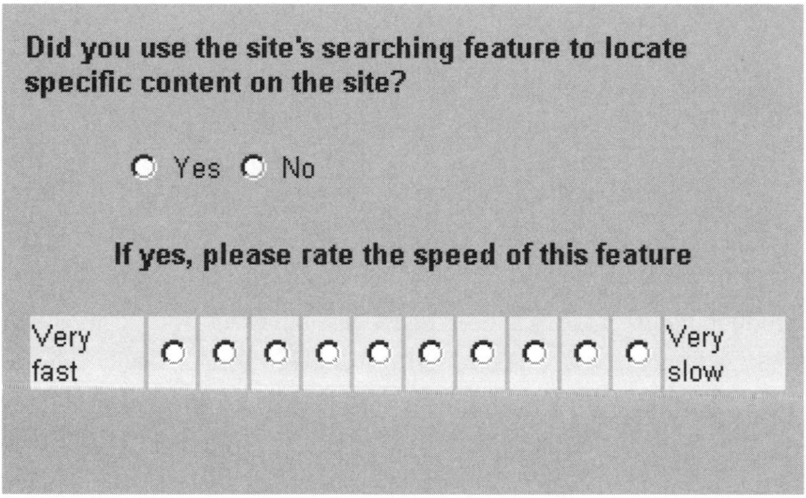

Open-Ended Questions

Collecting open-ended data provides necessary context to analyze the reasons behind different levels of usage and performance ratings. Reading though the comments of those who found value on your site versus those who didn't will help you focus the limited resources of the development team on fixing the most critical aspects of the site before the launch date. Unlike unsolicited comments from users during the beta testing period, this data can be coded so that it becomes quantitative in nature and can be relied upon to be representative of the entire sample.

AFTER THE BETA TEST

A controlled beta test and its associated research results will help you refine the final version of the site. Issues that are identified can be addressed early on, increasing the likelihood that the site will succeed when it is released into the general marketplace. The beta test provides a confident understanding of how the product will actually be adopted by real customers in a natural setting. If your product performed well in a beta test, it will likely enjoy widespread success when it is promoted by a strong marketing strategy. On the other hand, developers of products that experience high levels of attrition and low performance ratings in beta testing are well-advised to push back the launch schedule to allow enough time to address the problems and retest.

After a successful beta test, it's time to launch your product by aggressively marketing it to your target customers. Chapter 15 deals with marketing your product; the results from the beta testing process can be used to inform the initial marketing strategy.

The beta test provides a very good idea of the types of customers the site appealed to and why. This knowledge can be used strategically to tailor your promotional campaign to target the potential customers most likely to become regular users of your site. Common sense dictates that if one particular type of consumer readily found value in your site, other consumers with similar characteristics and behaviors are also likely to adopt the site.

Beyond aiding the targeted delivery of advertising, a controlled beta test can also assist in the creation of more compelling advertising messages. Evaluating the usage patterns and performance ratings of specific sections and site features can help you determine what drives acceptance of the site. It follows that general consumers will be driven to try a site by the same highly desirable and well-performing features that compelled the beta group to become regular users. By touting these features in your advertising, you increase the likelihood that consumers respond to your marketing efforts and try the site.

15

Marketing

I t goes without saying that effectively promoting your Web site is
a critical part of ensuring its success. Building a Web site is not
analogous to building a corner store; no existing population will
naturally pass by and consider whether your offering suits them.
The Web does, however, provide an infrastructure of search engines
and directory listings to help potential customers find your site—a
bit like the Yellow Pages. But just imagine if every business in the
world were listed in one giant phone book! Simply hoping that your
business listing stands out from those of thousands of competitors
is unlikely to generate sufficient quantities of customers. What's
required is a proactive strategy for locating potential customers and
convincing them to try your new site.

There are many avenues available for marketing online products. Anyone who has listened to the radio, watched TV, read a
newspaper, flipped though a magazine, or driven on a highway in
the past year can attest to this fact. Online companies have leveraged every imaginable outlet to promote their sites. Yahoo! has

even gone so far as to build a fleet of highly branded taxis that offer free Internet access to lucky riders. The vast number of online ventures scrambling to generate awareness and grab market share has dramatically impacted the advertising industry. Over the past few years, demand for advertising space has surpassed availability. A few extremely targeted sources, such as high-tech periodicals, have gone as far as implementing waiting lists for advertisers; and prices for mainstream media like radio and TV have increased substantially in urban markets, where Internet advertising is heavily concentrated.

Clearly, online brands spend a great deal of their budgets on marketing campaigns. What is not so clear, however, is how much research these brands conduct beforehand to ensure that these costly advertising campaigns will be effective.

It's puzzling when companies with very specific product markets buy extremely expensive mass media, like $2 million Superbowl television spots. Do these companies have detailed knowledge of their target customer profile? Did they research the media consumption patterns of these individuals and determine that the most cost-effective method of reaching them was to blow an entire year's marketing budget on a single ad? If so, were advertisements pretested to determine their ability to deliver the brand message? We can't help but wonder when 50 million of the general (slightly drunken) public are shown an ad directed to, and only decipherable by, a select few decision makers in IT departments.

Companies that have millions to spend on advertising are accountable to their investors, so questions naturally arise in attempting to evaluate the effectiveness of advertising campaigns. How much brand awareness and qualified trial did they get for their money? What media (TV, radio, print, or Web) proved most effective? Which creative best conveyed the desired brand image?

Online companies are not alone in asking these questions. Offline ventures must also quantify the return on their advertising investment. This need drives a large portion of the traditional marketing research industry, since some percentage of most advertising budgets is dedicated to advertising effectiveness research. With millions in potential revenue up for grabs, research firms have developed and refined an array of methodologies for evaluating advertising's effect on brand awareness, product perception, and sales.

The advent of online advertising and the rush to understand its effectiveness relative to other marketing vehicles has sparked a tremendous amount of development in the field of marketing research. Some companies, like Millward Brown Interactive (www.mbinteractive.com), have developed products and panels devoted entirely to understanding the branding effectiveness of Web-based advertising. Other companies (like ours, for instance) have developed studies to determine which advertising strategies are most effective at driving qualified traffic to your Web site. In this chapter, we outline the types of research you can conduct before, during, and after an advertising campaign to help ensure that your efforts have the desired effect.

DEVELOPING EFFECTIVE MARKETING STRATEGIES

The fundamentals of marketing an online product are no different from those that apply in any other industry. A compelling *message* must be developed to convey the product and achieve the core objectives of the marketing campaign (increased brand awareness, brand image, trial, etc.). This creative content is then placed in areas with the highest likelihood of reaching the intended consumer in a process known as *targeting*. Online or off, your marketing success depends upon well-executed creative development and targeting.

Good creative can have a tremendous impact on consumers' ability to remember and associate desirable attributes with your brand. If it's really good, advertising can create a desire for a product in consumers with no preexisting need. Take SUVs as an example. Individuals with no functional need for all-terrain vehicles purchase them by the lot-full because the creative offers a rugged, masculine, outdoor image many suburban and city-bound individuals find appealing. Compelling creative also positions a brand and builds preference when often, in fact, no discernible difference in product performance exists. Advertising for packaged goods brands like cola, vodka, toothpaste, and cleaning products are excellent examples.

Targeting is the other side of good advertising. Well-targeted campaigns are those reaching the greatest number of the target market with a minimum of overspray. It would be nice if you could place your advertisement in front of all consumers, letting those outside the target market simply ignore it if it didn't apply to them. Unfortunately, obtaining an advertising reach of 100% is nearly impossible, and definitely beyond your budget. Targeting advertisements to those most likely to be in the market for your product or service increases the return on investment for your advertising dollars.

From an advertising perspective, one of the most exciting aspects of the Web is that it enables the delivery of extremely targeted advertising. The delivery mechanism of television, radio, and print requires that every person receive the same advertisement. Use of these *mass media* is known as *one-to-many* advertising. As a result, such advertisements tend to appeal to the lowest common denominator, and are rarely relevant to consumers in the market for a specific product.

Web pages are requested by the browser, rather than broadcast to the browser, so every individual can be presented with a different advertisement each time a Web page is viewed. The Web can therefore be considered a *one-to-one* marketing vehicle with the potential for highly customized and relevant advertising. Most Web advertisements are delivered by a handful of third-party ad serving networks who, along with the advertisement, also serve a cookie to uniquely identify each consumer. Using the cookie, they track the types of sites and the content consumers access within their vast network of advertising sites. The resulting data allows these companies to learn something about a consumer's interests and then predict the advertising that would be most relevant to that person.

Imagine, for example, a daily user of a surfing site (the waves not the Web), who recently also visited sites in the advertising network that focused on home mortgages and local real estate. Based on this behavior, the advertising network might infer that this individual is in the market for a new home. This knowledge greatly enhances the network's ability to leverage the content of the surfing site. Instead of monotonous attempts to market surfboards and wetsuits (which the individual may have plenty of already), the site can market low interest rate mortgages or newly available real estate in the users' geographic area. Taking it a step further, the ad network might combine the need for real estate with the affinity for surfing and display advertising for real estate near the beach or with an ocean view.

Most people react negatively when they first learn of the behind-the-scenes activity of the ad networks, because they believe their privacy is being violated. We believe that this process will come to be accepted as the infant stage of a technology that will actually deliver real value to consumers. Consider what the consumer gets from hypertargeting:

1. *Advertising that actually means something:* One benefit of the targeting systems is the increased relevance of advertising. Significant portions of our lives are spent being consumers, searching out the best deals on products and services we desire. Hypertargeted advertising reduces the time required to find a suitable product, leaving more time for other pursuits. In this sense, it is more of a service than a necessary evil. If a friend tipped you off on a great home loan deal for your dream house, you'd be pleased. Friends can provide this type of valuable information because they know a lot about you. Companies (often for good reasons) are not typically entrusted with your personal information. Instead of being helpful, most companies end up deluging you with information you don't need.

2. *High-quality content for niche audiences:* There is a less obvious, but equally significant, benefit to hypertargeted advertising. Each of us is a tremendous consumer, spend-

ing nearly all of our income on one thing or another. Thus, an appealing advertisement with the proper targeting will have a high likelihood of success. Anyone with the ability to offer advertising space with a high probability of success can demand a handsome fee.

Where is the benefit to the consumer? Again, consider the surfing site. Without hypertargeting, its obvious advertising client base is limited to surfboard shapers, wetsuit suppliers, and other providers of surf-related products, few of whom have large marketing budgets. By partnering with an ad network that enables hypertargeting, the surfing site can expand its client base to broader, more lucrative markets. Together, the two companies can charge a premium, because each advertisement served has a greater likelihood of achieving its objective. The net result is more revenue for the niche content provider. The upside for the consumer is that the smaller content site, customized to the consumer's individual needs and interests, can support and grow its operations solely from advertising revenue. Instead of the surf site providing daily wave reports for large regions, it can afford to provide multiple daily reports for specific areas, or even a live video feed of your favorite surf spot. Perhaps, if you're lucky, it could even send you on a surf safari to write more revenue-generating content for the site.

Unfortunately, hypertargeting technology is still experiencing teething pains (many of them involving privacy issues), and has yet to reach its full potential. Some companies, like DoubleClick (www.doubleclick.com) and AdForce (www.adforce.com), are aggressively pursuing hypertargeting, but currently their media planning products allow marketers to select from only a limited scope of targeting variables. The ability to hypertarget will become increasingly important to the online advertising industry as understanding of consumer behavior online becomes more and more clear. Currently, an estimated eight in ten users have a particular product in mind when they head online to shop. Being able to predict what the product is and present users with an attractive offer will be an invaluable capability.

Though useful, the currently available hypertargeting tools are insufficient to guide your entire marketing campaign on their own. Besides having limited targeting ability, they guide only placement of online advertising, but nothing to inform media planning in off-line areas like television, print, or radio.

MEDIA CONSUMPTION STUDIES

Knowing the types of media your target customer uses on a regular basis can greatly increase your ability to plan an effective campaign. When conducting an advertising program, one of the most important decisions you'll make is where to purchase advertising space. Qualified and unqualified eyeballs cost the same, so the primary objective when purchasing media is to maximize the former and minimize the latter. This is accomplished though targeting and efficiency measurement. A targeted media purchase is one that has the highest concentration of your target market and the fewest out-of-market individuals. A cost-efficient media purchase is one that has the lowest cost per qualified consumer reached.

Often, a targeted and cost-efficient media buy are one and the same, but not always. Suppose an advertisement in a high-tech magazine reaches 100,000 readers, of which 80,000 (80%) are in the market for the product. Running this magazine ad costs $25,000. The cost-efficiency of purchasing this targeted advertisement is $25,000/80,000 users, or 31 cents per set of in-market eyeballs. On the other hand, suppose a prominent television advertisement reaches 20,000,000 viewers, of which 800,000 (4%) are in-market. If running the ad cost $200,000, the advertising efficiency is $200,000/800,000, or 25 cents. The advertisement in the high-tech magazine is more targeted, but it is less cost-efficient.

Strategic purchasing of advertising requires three key metrics. Combining these metrics as we did in our example, we can determine the advertising cost-efficiency of each media purchase:

1. The number of people the advertisement will reach, ingeniously dubbed *advertising reach.*

2. The cost of the advertisement. Overall cost is often combined with *advertising reach* into a metric called *cost per mille* or *CPM.* (*Mille* is French for *thousand.*) This metric provides a means of standardizing costs across different media properties with varying levels of reach. Television advertisements may seem to be more expensive, but the CPM can actually be quite low due to the enormous reach.

3. The proportion of the advertising reach that is comprised of target consumers.

The first two metrics (reach and cost) can be acquired simply by picking up the phone and calling a sales representative. The third metric, however, can be significantly more difficult to obtain. Most sales representatives have some information about the demographics of their audience. This may be sufficient if your primary market definition is simple, such as males aged 18 to 24. In all probability, the segmentation strategy used to create your primary market definition is more complicated, involving some behavioral and possibly some attitudinal metrics.

Some advertising properties conduct detailed consumer behavior studies about their audiences. Thus, sales representatives can answer intelligently when media planners ask, "What percentage of your audience are males between the ages of 18 and 24, and in-market for a new CD player?" Answers, however, are not always perfect. The sales representative may only have data on the percentage of 18 to 24-year-old males who currently own CD players, or the average annual spending on consumer electronics of these respondents. It may be necessary to work with incomplete data or tweak numbers to estimate the percentage of the audience that is in-market.

Half the battle of marketing your online product is locating targeted and cost-efficient advertising opportunities. With thousands of magazines, newspapers, radio stations, and television shows, how do you narrow down your list of potential candidates? The answer, of course, is to conduct primary research. An in-depth study on the TV, radio, magazine, and Web usage habits of your target audience will provide remarkable direction for your media planning efforts. Why? By understanding the media consumption patterns of your existing valuable customers, you'll know where to go to find others like them.

Media consumption research identifies the magazines, television shows, and radio formats your target customers are particularly fond of. If desired, such research may also determine specific hours when respondents consume time-sensitive media like television. Perhaps they watch TV only on weekends or after 10 p.m. on weekdays. You might discover that target customers listen to the radio during their morning commute, but not at work or during leisure time. All this information can help drive strategies for reaching target consumers and getting the word out about your site as cheaply and quickly as possible.

Metrics collected in media consumption research include:

- types of media consumed (TV, magazines, radio, Web);
- Frequency of consumption (hours watched, listened, surfed; number of magazines or newspapers read);
- time of consumption (for time-sensitive media like television or radio);
- specific content consumed (types of magazines, radio formats, TV shows, genre of Web sites).

Obviously, the more detailed the data is, the more useful it will be for selecting appropriate media to purchase. Unfortunately, asking respondents to select from extensive lists of specific magazines and TV shows may prove exceedingly tedious. Restricting choices to simply address genres of magazines or shows is the best way to get considered responses. Keep in mind that once you know where to begin looking, the advertising properties themselves can help determine whether their specific property is best suited to your needs. If you prefer to do it yourself and have room in your budget, there are a number of syndicated media research companies like Arbitron (www.arbitron.com), Scarborough (www.scarborough.com), Mediamark (www.mediamark.com), and Simmons (www.smrb.com) that can sell you granular media consumption profiles of target markets you define. Online media planning tools have taken off as well, with @Plan (www.webplan.net) taking the lead in profiling the sites most likely to be used by the consumers you need to reach.

Beyond assisting in the purchase of advertising, obtaining media consumption data on your current audience can guide your business development and PR activities. Properly executed, these comparatively low-cost marketing opportunities can actually deliver more bottom-line traffic than outbound advertising does. From a business development perspective, media consumption research is a valuable tool in selling other sites on establishing affiliate deals because a synergy exists between your audiences. It is common for smaller sites to acquire the majority of their audience from links or integration with select business partners. These deals are typically inked because one site has an extensive user base but lacks specific functionality. In joining forces, both sides win. You get a ready source of customers, while they keep users from switching to a competitor who offers a similar service. Media consumption research identifies these opportunities by discovering a cross-over between two sites. Once identified, further investigation can evaluate the nature of the relationship and how the sites can work together to their mutual benefit.

Media consumption research can also be used to drive PR activity and motivate editors at a magazine or TV show to write a story about or do a segment on your site. If a large proportion of your audience reads a particular magazine or watches particular programming, then perhaps other members of that audience would also be interested in the subject matter of your site. Your PR efforts, of course, must convey the newsworthiness of your site to representatives of these media outlets. At the very least, media consumption data can help you target your public relations efforts toward publications and programming that reach the highest concentrations of your target market.

DEVELOPING THE CREATIVE MESSAGE

Effective targeting, though critical, is not the only part of a successful marketing campaign. The other half if the equation is a good message and a good way of conveying it. We'd be scorned by our friends in the ad biz if we were to imply that research was responsible for the catchy taglines and intriguing imagery of successful advertisements. But it certainly can be employed to advise the product advantages such advertisements should convey and, to some degree, suggest the tone of your creative. The main power of research in the creative development process, however, is in testing multiple approaches to identify those that best meet the business' primary marketing objectives: building awareness, conveying positive brand attributes, and ultimately, driving site trial.

An initial step in the development of good creative is to determine a short list of features or attributes to put forth as the defining elements of the product. Is it the fastest? The most complete? Cutting-edge? The easiest to use? The least expensive? While it's tempting to try to convey all these factors simultaneously, you'll find that the limited space available in ad formats and the limited attention spans of those viewing them necessitate a strict focus on a few core product attributes. The question then becomes, which ones?

There are many schools of thought on the types of messages that best stick in the mind of the consumer, and which have the intended effect. In general, you want to focus on the attributes that are critically important to your target customer, have motivated users to try your site, and have differentiated it from the competition. Luckily, all of these attributes have been identified in previous stages of research on the marketplace and in the development of the product. Critical features were identified via importance ratings before you built the product. Elements of your performance that actually drove trial customers to become regular users of the site were identified during the beta test or site evaluation research. Finally, areas where you beat out the competition were identified by your competitive analysis. All that's left to do is evaluate this existing data (or conduct a competitive analysis) and decide which features to push.

Research can also guide the tone that your creative should take. A detailed profile of your customers' personal characteristics, behaviors, and psychographics has directed the editorial focus and tone of your site development. These metrics should again be leveraged when developing your advertising. If your demographic profile shows that your target customer is mature, and the psychographic profile shows that they have traditional values, the tone of your creative should reflect that. Using an MTV-style campaign will leave your customers scratching their heads, wondering what just happened! This is an obvious point, but often customer knowledge possessed by the development staff isn't leveraged when creating advertising messages. Frequently, third-party agencies that have little understanding of the product or the customer it serves are entirely responsible for developing creative ads. Agencies are experts at what they do and the best resource for engaging advertising content, but they're one step removed from the product. They need your input. Be certain to remove this limitation by providing them with all the relevant data you have on your customers.

TESTING THE CREATIVE

Research is a powerful tool in the testing phase of advertising creation. It can evaluate a number of possible creative approaches as to their ability to meet the business' objectives of building awareness, conveying positive brand attributes, and ultimately, driving trial. The stakes are high when selecting the creative content of advertising. Not only does it waste a lot of money (astonishingly quickly, we might add), but the wrong content creates negative brand perceptions that may never be undone. It's therefore very advisable to devote resources toward understanding how an ad communicates to customers before deploying it in a campaign.

Methods used to test creative vary with the medium. Due to the subjective nature of advertising, qualitative focus groups or viewing sessions are a popular means of testing. Such studies, also known as *copytesting,* are effective at providing visceral data. Researchers acquire firsthand reactions, and can then probe deeply into participants' reasons for liking or disliking an advertisement. Unfortunately, in-person tests are expensive to conduct. They are also highly subject to laboratory bias, a term used to describe impacts on users' response due to the fact that they know they are being observed or measured. As with most small-sample research, findings are not statistically rigorous,[1] an important issue when deciding how to spend a few million dollars on an advertising campaign. Often, qualitative copytesting is a service offered by the advertising agency you contract with. Though they have their acknowledged limitations, these tests may still prove useful, since

---

[1] There are numerous approaches to quantifying responses to advertising in copytesting scenarios. One approach in television ad pretesting is the use of meters controlled by participants that allow them to dial in how much they like or dislike an advertisement as it plays. These readings are then averaged and embedded in the prototyped commercial, providing an interesting feedback mechanism for the sponsors to review as they are refining bits and pieces of the final creative. Another approach is to have participants complete standardized exit surveys that gauge their reactions to various creative executions. However, the small nature of the sample and questionable methods of recruitment still leave some doubt as to whether we'd consider this data quantitative.

the agency has incorporated the testing into the development process and has experience in successfully interpreting and acting upon the results.

Off-line testing of advertising creative is especially relevant when part of the target audience does not exist online. Some television advertising campaigns for online products are partially intended to build status among non-Internet users, who will hopefully turn to this brand when they finally dial up. Attempting to sample and survey this population online is impossible. Luckily, few readers will face this problem; only brands with very deep pockets can afford promotional strategies that spend large amounts to build awareness among consumers who are not, and may never be, in-market. The rest of us are more concerned with how our promotional strategy affects users of the Web who can actually provide some near-term return on our investment. Considering this, conducting online quantitative research into the effectiveness of advertising creative is far superior, less expensive, and speedier than off-line methods.

The Web is a dynamic multimedia environment that permits quantitative testing of every advertising type. TV commercials can be displayed to respondents as real-media clips (*www.real.com*), a streaming video product that allows users with slow bandwidth speeds to view video without waiting for the entire clip to download. The audio capabilities of the same technology allow the testing of radio commercials. Print advertisements can be displayed as large static images; and Web banners can appear just as they would online.

Samples for online advertising research can be gathered in a number of ways. The population the advertising is attempting to affect is typically nationwide, so the most projectable sampling method is a nationally representative panel of Web users.[2] Of

---

[2]Many advertising campaigns are directed at specific cities or metropolitan areas know as *advertising markets*. Sampling methods for evaluating pre- and postadvertising effectiveness may change depending on the scope of the advertising campaign. For the purposes of this book we simply discuss nationwide advertising.

course, rigorous panels are not always available or timely, so it is common to utilize sitecentric samples for this research. The assumption made when leveraging sitecentric samples is that opinions of target customers currently using your site are similar to opinions of customers targeted for advertising. There are a few problems with this assumption. Primarily, sitecentric respondents have preexisting experience with the product, and this experience, not the advertising, shapes their brand perceptions. This limits the scope of questioning that can be pursued. While sitecentric respondents can evaluate the overall likability of advertisements, they cannot provide brand affinity or purchase probability metrics. For this reason, strive to develop samples that mirror your target market but have no previous experience of your site. Convenience samples gathered from opt-in lists or cheaper, lower-quality panels can be an excellent resource for this type of work.

Quantitative online methodologies for testing advertising are similar to the experimental design methodologies used for interface testing that we discussed in Chapter 14. Experimental testing is a powerful tool for determining differences in the impact between creative executions of all types, and advertisements are no different.

The study begins with a brief set of questions to segment respondents into relevant consumer groups. Afterward, the sample is randomly split into equally distributed cells.[3] The number of cells is determined by the number of advertising creative executions to be tested. Typically, the number of cells is equal to the number of advertising executions. However, if the brand already has recognition in the marketplace or among the sampled population, it is advisable to add an additional control cell to measure baseline brand metrics.

It is critical to structure sample size to allow for statistically significant analysis. When conducting experimental designs, we utilize the chi-squared[4] test to evaluate whether observed findings

---

[3]Methods of splitting samples into random cells were covered in Chapter 12.
[4]See Chapter 13 or www.hyperstat.com for more information on chi-squared tests.

can be attributed to differences in the advertising creative message or simply to randomness. The test is sensitive to sample size; larger samples provide more confident and actionable results. Depending on the source of the sample, cost may be an issue. A large component of panel cost is sample size. This is notably absent in sitecentric approaches. As a general rule, each cell should contain a minimum of 100 respondents. This size allows evaluation of major differences in the creative execution among the overall sample. Greater sample sizes are required to drill down into the data and conduct analysis by segment or to detect more subtle differences between the impacts of different creative executions.

Each cell is administered one of the tested advertising executions. After reviewing the advertisement, respondents immediately answer a follow-up survey. There are two exceptions to this process:

1. *Control cell:* Study designs including a control cell have respondents in this cell answer the follow-up study without exposure to any advertising executions. This data provides a baseline measurement of preexisting brand perceptions among the sample.

2. *Recall:* Occasionally, advertising tests attempt to measure how memorable each advertisement is. Advertising and element[5] recall is a proven predictor[6] of less tangible metrics like positive brand perceptions and purchase probability. To collect this metric, some study designs wait a day or two before asking respondents to answer questions about the advertising execution. While this recontact method can establish which advertisement is most memorable, other metrics suffer. Overall ratings of the advertising and brand will be less differentiated between cells

---

[5]Specific bits and pieces of the overall creative execution.
[6]It is not surprising that recall is largely responsible for predicting any further brand attitude improvements. A consumer must first notice an ad and register its message before the ad can have any more substantial impact.

after a few days, when much of the advertising effect has worn off. For this reason, we recommend redisplaying creative executions to respondents after collecting recall metrics, but before asking any more specific advertising-related questions.

To evaluate the impact of the advertisement, the follow-up survey itself covers five areas:

1. *Ratings of the advertisement:* Typically, this is the primary metric used to evaluate advertisements. The simplest approach can focus on the overall appeal of the advertisement: "Overall, how would you rate the advertisement?" However, breaking down the ratings to measure specific attributes of the advertisement may prove more relevant.

2. *Brand affinity metrics:* More important than customers' opinions of the advertisement is how it actually shaped their opinions of the brand. Strategic advertising campaigns are conscious of the perceptions the advertising seeks to impact. A variety of attitudinal question types can help evaluate this impact. Agree or disagree statements are commonly used, but Semantic Differential Scales (see Chapter 7) can also be effective.

3. *Purchase or usage probability metrics:* The attitude many advertisements attempt to affect the most is whether those exposed will be more influenced to try your Web site.[7]

4. *Advertising recall:* Traditionally, advertising recall is a predictive measure of increased brand affinity and increased likelihood of trial: *"What brand do you recall seeing advertising for in the previous study?"* Ad recall data should be *unaided,* meaning that respondents type

[7]Experimental designs are especially useful in pretesting creative for online products, because most other product categories involve a cost component. Online, trying most things is free; as a result, respondents typically overstate their trial intent. With an experimental design, bias is neutralized, and any advantage one creative execution has over another becomes evident.

FIGURE 15.1: Rating attributes of the advertisement

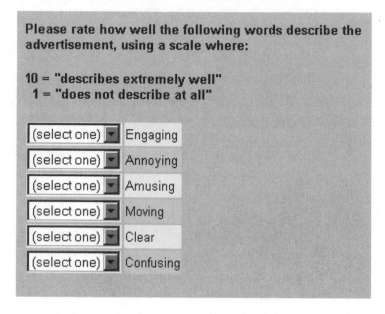

their answers into a text field rather than selecting from a list of possible responses.

5. *Element recall:* To augment general data on advertising recall, collect recall data for elements specific to the advertising creative. Element recall data helps determine which aspects of the advertisement, if any, are memorable. Theoretically, the elements most frequently recalled are those driving recall of the brand and therefore the effectiveness of the advertisement. This data can be either unaided or collected via lists containing both real and fake elements to select from (aided).

Analysis is done by noting differences in each metric between each tested creative and, when utilized, the control cell. Because cells were randomly generated and each group completed identical questionnaires, the only difference between cells is exposure to the advertising creative. Any significant differences in responses to the questionnaire must therefore be the result of differences in the creative. The process allows you to establish which advertisement

FIGURE 15.2: Brand affinity and purchase probability questions

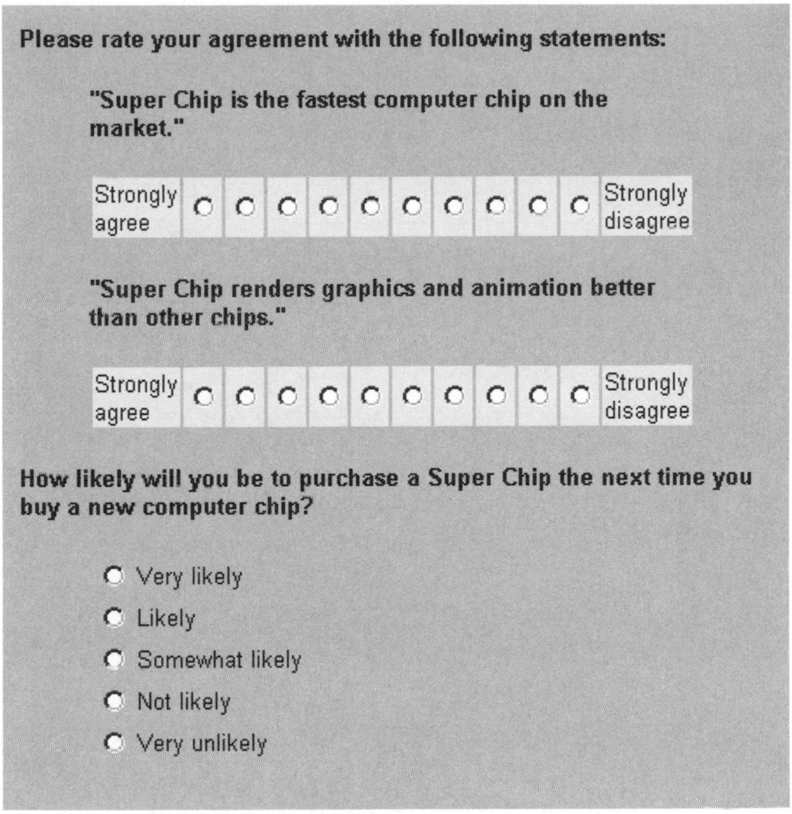

Please rate your agreement with the following statements:

"Super Chip is the fastest computer chip on the market."

Strongly agree ○ ○ ○ ○ ○ ○ ○ ○ ○ ○ Strongly disagree

"Super Chip renders graphics and animation better than other chips."

Strongly agree ○ ○ ○ ○ ○ ○ ○ ○ ○ ○ Strongly disagree

How likely will you be to purchase a Super Chip the next time you buy a new computer chip?

○ Very likely
○ Likely
○ Somewhat likely
○ Not likely
○ Very unlikely

has the most consumer appeal and is most effective at achieving the marketing objectives.

In analysis, you'll most likely see that the greatest differences will be observed in ratings of the advertisements themselves. These metrics pertain directly to the creative and are therefore most likely to show variation. Metrics specific to the product, such as brand perceptions and purchase probability, are less apt to be influenced by exposure to a single advertisement. These measures often require multiple advertising exposures before any effect can be measured (assuming the ad has the potential to impact perceptions in the first place). This is especially true for established brands for whom consumers have long-held preconceptions. New brands, on the other hand, will find brand perception and purchase probability

FIGURE 15.3: Unaided versus aided methods of collecting element recall data

(unaided example)

Please list any specific creative or messaging elements you recall from the advertisement?

Element 1 [   ]

Element 2 [   ]

Element 3 [   ]

Element 4 [   ]

Element 5 [   ]

(aided example)

Which of the following creative or messaging elements do you recall from the advertisement? (select all that apply)

☐ "Super Chip is Super Fast"   *Fake*

☐ A computer chip dressed in a superhero cape *Real*

☐ A computer chip lying on the beach   *Fake*

☐ "Super Chip, add punch to your PC"   *Real*

☐ Two boys playing video games   *Fake*

☐ Animation playing on a computer screen   *Real*

measures quite sensitive to change, since the advertisement represents the consumer's only experience with the brand.

EVALUATING THE RETURN ON INVESTMENT (ROI) OF ADVERTISING

As we mentioned earlier in this chapter, a great deal of the marketing research industry is focused on evaluating the effects of advertising.

After spending large sums to promote products to consumers, businesses want the ability to definitively state what affect this advertising had on driving trial of the product. Evaluating this is a complicated task, because a number of other factors beside advertising have significant influence on the adoption of online products. Search services, word of mouth, links from partner sites, press coverage, or any number of other factors could also be responsible for increased traffic patterns.

Even if the effects of advertising could be isolated, how would you measure the effectiveness of different media? What share percentage did radio, television, print, or Web advertising contribute to increased traffic?

To further complicate matters, there are a number of less-tangible aspects to advertising effectiveness you'll inevitably be interested in quantifying. Ultimately, advertising is primarily designed to drive sales and usage, but a potential customer goes though multiple stages of awareness before actually visiting your site. In the traditional model, consumers first see advertising for your product and become aware that it exists.[8] Then, over the course of multiple advertising exposures, perceptions of your product are shaped. Finally, positive perception of your brand is established and the customer makes the decision to visit your site. Much advertising effectiveness research concentrates on evaluating how advertising campaigns drive the process.

Aside from measuring bottom-line trial, which we discuss shortly, the basic questions asked to evaluate the effectiveness of an advertising campaign are:

1. *Did brand awareness increase during the campaign?*
   Aside from increased trial, this is the metric most advertising campaigns seek to affect. Brand awareness has been widely adopted as a fundamental benchmark of success, because it is easy quantify and track over time.

---

[8]The *direct response model,* often employed by e-merchants, seeks to present consumers with a specific product offering (often with an attractive price) that will motivate them to visit the site immediately to purchase the offered product.

Compared to softer measures like brand perception, awareness levels are concrete and clear to marketers.

2. *Do people recall seeing an advertisement for the tested brand?* Many studies have been conducted that show advertising recall is predictive of increased positive brand perceptions and purchase probability. These product-specific metrics are challenging to measure in a survey, since both are attitudinal and additive. Multiple advertising exposures are required to affect a customer's feelings for a product or the likelihood of selecting it over other brands. Many companies instead focus their research on easier metrics, like quantifying overall recall of the advertisement and the specific elements driving that recall.

3. *Did the advertisement change brand perceptions and purchase or trial probability?* Again, changes in brand perception and the likelihood that a customer will try your site are typically limited to newer brands lacking firmly established images. Extremely effective marketing campaigns, however, have the power to significantly impact these metrics for brands of any size. This is, after all, the reason companies advertise.

4. *What share of those reached were in the target market?* Earlier in this chapter we explained how to calculate the efficiency of a media purchase by dividing the cost of the advertisement by the number of qualified consumers you anticipate it will reach. Often, however, data available before an advertising campaign is insufficient for accurately calculating this figure. Post-advertising studies can provide a more accurate understanding and guide future media planning.

To accurately evaluate changes in awareness and brand perception attributable to mass media advertising campaigns, it is necessary to conduct research among a nationally representative population. Sitecentric methods are obviously insufficient, because customers are sampled upon accessing the site. Presumably these users are all aware of the brand to begin with. While brand perceptions can be measured among first-time users on a sitecentric level, repeat users are unsuitable candidates. For them, personal experience with the brand is far more responsible for their brand impressions than any advertisement could ever be.

Depending on the population you're attempting to understand, either a nationally representative Web panel or RDD phone sampling would be prescribed. Some mass-media campaigns have the stated objective of building awareness and brand identity among customers who have yet to venture online. Quantifying the effectiveness of these campaigns will require RDD phone research in order to include off-line users in the sampling frame. On the other hand, if you're comfortable limiting the evaluation of advertising effect to the online market, then nationally representative Web panels present a less expensive option that also allows the collection of more detailed information.

Advertising effectiveness research is quite costly and, ironically, the less you spend on advertising the more expensive this research will be. Attempting to create a measurable effect among a nationwide audience requires an extremely large amount of advertising. Based on approximately 275,000,000 residents in the United States, a 1% increase in brand awareness involves reaching and swaying 2.75 million individuals with advertising. Measuring a 10% increase requires a minimum reach of 27.5 million. Of course, most of those reached will not recall seeing the advertisement or the brand. If 25% of those exposed recall the tested brand, then the reach necessary to measure a 10% increase in brand awareness is over 100 million.

Due to the way these studies are conducted, a 10% increase is about the smallest measurable effect. Advertising effectiveness studies are executed via pre/post methodologies. A preliminary sample is interviewed before the campaign begins to establish a baseline measure of awareness, brand perceptions, and advertising recall. Toward the end of the advertising campaign, another sample is collected and asked identical survey questions to evaluate the change over time. Some research companies use an omnibus tracking strategy to obtain multiple measures over the course of the campaign. Unfortunately, the cost of conducting off-line research often necessitates smaller base sizes. Each sample may have a margin of error of plus or minus 5% or more. Thus, metrics may need to change by as much as 10% or more to be significant.

For these reasons, conducting advertising effectiveness research among a nationally representative off-line population is only recommended for large mass-media campaigns. Luckily, if you spend at this level, ad agencies will often contract with traditional marketing research companies that conduct omnibus studies to track the changes in advertising recall and brand awareness. One of the leaders in this field is Millward Brown (www.millward-brown.com).

Using a nationally representative Web panel is the other option for measuring increased awareness and brand perceptions. Panels are well-suited for those less concerned with quantifying the advertising effect on the off-line population, or those with advertising mixes that include large amounts of Web-based advertising.

ROI FROM A SITECENTRIC PERSPECTIVE

The baseline measure of advertising effectiveness is increased product trial. Measuring increased brand awareness, perception, or usage probability is little more than an attempt to predict how much additional product trial and regular usage will result from advertising. One reason these tangential metrics predominate is because directly measuring the effect of advertising on product trial is quite difficult off-line. Certainly, increased purchasing can be measured, but how can these increases be attributed to advertising? Increases may be due to business development, word of mouth, positive press, or any number of factors.[9] Even more difficult is establishing which media drove the most new trial. Was television, radio, print, or Web advertising most cost-efficient?

Sitecentric research is an excellent tool for obtaining an in-depth picture of marketing effectiveness and its relationship to trial. By surveying a representative sample of first-time users as they enter the site, you can accurately measure how visitors find out about your site. Identifying this *source of awareness* goes beyond simply evaluating the effectiveness of advertising. It expands your understanding to include your entire marketing mix. All sources driving usage of your site can be identified, quantified, and evaluated on a granular level.

Many sources beside outbound advertising are aggressively pursued by your marketing team to drive trial of your Web site. The public relations department pitches story ideas to journalists; business development teams craft content-sharing partnerships and link exchanges; booths at trade shows are bought and staffed; so-called viral marketing strategies, word of mouth campaigns, and direct mail are all used. Sitecentric ROI testing cheaply and easily enables the evaluation of all these marketing activities. Additionally, this approach isolates the effectiveness of individual outbound marketing campaigns such as television, print, radio, and the Web.

The effectiveness of each source can be determined by looking at a combination of:

1. the percentage of the marketing budget spent on that source, and

2. the percentage of new customers each source drove to the site.

---

[9]Print promotions with direct response objectives frequently use couponing or dedicated 1-800 numbers associated with the advertisement to measure the leads associated with a particular campaign or creative ad. Marketing that doesn't have a direct response component is far more difficult to quantify.

TABLE 15.1: Original source of awareness by first-time users

Web Advertising	15%
"Cool" or "Best" Site Page	5%
Search Engine	5%
Other Web Source	10%
Television Ad	15%
Magazine Article	5%
Friend, Family Member, or Colleague	10%
Magazine Ad	5%
Television Show	5%
Radio	10%
Trade Show	5%
Other	10%

Example:

For instance, assume that 10% of a $2 million marketing budget was spent on Web advertising. Looking at the source of awareness data in Table 15.1, we see that 15% of new site traffic is generated by Web advertising—the same percentage as television advertising. Now, assume that 60% of the marketing budget was spent on television advertising. Which source is more effective at driving traffic?

Web = 15% / 10% = 1.50 efficiency

TV = 15% / 60% = .25 efficiency

An effective marketing campaign attracts "qualified" users to the site. In addition to source of awareness information, sitecentric ROI studies may gather segmentation data to determine how qualified or potentially valuable each respondent is. An analysis of the segmentation characteristics of the users driven by each source of awareness establishes the marketing activities that deliver the most qualified leads. By factoring in marketing costs, sites can arrive at a cost-per-qualified visitor metric.

Example:

Assume that, of the 15% of new site traffic directed via Web advertising, 80% were members of the primary market segment.

Which source is more effective if only 40% of users directed to the site via television marketing are equally qualified?

Web = 15% * 80% / 10% = 1.20 efficiency

TV   = 15% * 40% / 60% = .10 efficiency

We strongly believe that sitecentric ROI studies are extremely useful for evaluating marketing effectiveness. Even more appealing is their ability to guide ongoing improvement of marketing strategy to maximize efficiency and minimize waste. Converting an ad hoc sitecentric survey into an ongoing tracking study requires minimal effort, tracking source of awareness and segmentation variables of first-time users provides a powerful marketing tool capable of enabling a data-driven approach to marketing your site. Changes to the outbound marketing mix can be made, evaluated, and then tweaked. If television advertising is not proving effective, for example, you might simply cancel the remaining commercials and shift the money to more cost-efficient sources. At the very least, research results will help you improve your strategy for the next campaign.

The value of sitecentric tracking research does not stop at guiding marketing strategy. In fact, that is just the tip of the iceberg. Many other aspects that affect the success of your online business can be monitored and used to evaluate site performance, customer retention, and changes in business strategy. Chapter 16 addresses this topic.

C H A P T E R

16

Tracking

U p to this point, our discussion has focused on the learning that can be obtained from ad hoc research. These one-time studies are directed at specific business objectives such as establishing market size, understanding customer characteristics, or determining the ideal feature set for a Web site. As we've demonstrated, ad hoc research is ideally suited to developing overall strategy. Despite the speed and efficiency with which online studies can be conducted, however, ad hoc research is still too slow to inform day-to-day business decisions.

The Web is a rapidly changing, fast-paced environment. Externally, any number of factors, from a shift in the composition of the Web population to a new trend sweeping the Internet industry, can impact usage of your site. Internal development teams scramble to create new content and implement new technology. Marketing staff chase down new opportunities and rearrange strategies to drive new qualified customers to the site. Business development and PR teams also do their part toward growing site traffic.

With all these activities happening simultaneously, a structured approach to evaluating changes to the site audience and usage is needed.

Meeting this need entails the design and/or implementation of a continual feedback system to track key metrics that reflect the success of your site. Such systems serve mainly to provide timely information on changes in site audience and usage. Having the ability to compare bottom-line site performance with any recent business activities (marketing, new features, redesign) allows decision makers to assess the impact of these activities and make continual adjustments as necessary.

Collecting a standardized set of regularly updated performance metrics not only takes the pulse of your online venture, but also arms your organization with a unified perspective. Far too often, different parts of the organization have access to vastly different information, and with it, an understandably disparate picture of exactly what's going on with the business. A continual feedback system puts everyone on the same page. It facilitates the development of a cohesive strategy, allowing superior data-driven decisions to increase your venture's likelihood of success. Without a unanimously accepted and readily available source of reliable data, evaluating (or arguing) the state of the business will eat up precious time and resources that could be put to far better use.

Most important, these systems provide immediate feedback on new business activities. The success of a new marketing campaign can be evaluated as soon as it is under way, allowing needed changes to be made or later portions scrubbed if the first portion proved unsuccessful at driving qualified site traffic. New content areas or implementations of new features can be monitored at launch to determine whether consumers visiting the site for the first time eventually become regulars. If the trial-to-usage conversion rate proves unsatisfactory, the problem can be identified early and changes to the content or marketing made before more customers have negative experiences. Even the trial generated by a recent press placement can be monitored, and the value of these new users quantified.

The ability to precisely evaluate the performance of day-to-day decisions will instill a valuable data-driven mentality in your organization. Rather than relying on conducting point-in-time ad hoc research projects to understand an issue, you can turn your entire site into a valuable learning tool. "Test, tweak, test again" will become the mantra of a staff devoted to a system that takes much of the guesswork and risk out of running a Web site.

TYPES OF TRACKING DATA

Two basic types of data are required to obtain the most detailed and actionable perspective on your site behavioral data and survey data.

Behavioral Data

The most common type of data used for ongoing tracking of Web sites, behavioral data is collected passively as users surf the site. Log files are updated with a variety of metrics each time a user requests a page from the Web server. The data from these server logs can be parsed, combined, and analyzed in a vast number of ways to provide extremely accurate information about the quantity of site usage, the areas and features used most, time of usage, depth of involvement, and a variety of other metrics we'll cover in detail shortly.

A significant shortcoming of Web server data is that it cannot uniquely identify a customer across multiple visits. As customers access a site, server logs can track their visits; but once they leave, the server cannot recognize them in subsequent visits. Obviously, tracking customer relationships longitudinally is a fundamental aspect of evaluating the success of business activities. Without it, a business cannot evaluate retention rates, measure the number of visits required before a customer purchases a product, or differentiate between the content that first-time and repeat customers utilize. To address these shortcomings, user tracking technologies combine cookie data with server log data. When customers first visit a Web site they are served cookies that uniquely identify them on that and subsequent visits. This allows repeat users to be identified as they enter the site and enables the association of previous usage data with subsequent site activities.

Survey Data

The combination of Web server logs and cookies is a powerful tool for tracking the behaviors of customers. Most companies, in fact, find this information sufficient to guide business practices and inform decisions. We believe that this is because most Web tracking technologies offer only this behavioral mix, and companies will make do with what's available. But in our opinion, simple tracking and reporting of behavioral data is shortsighted and fails to realize the true potential of a continuous feedback system. Only when they incorporate nonbehavioral metrics gained from primary research do these tracking system become truly comprehensive tools.

As we discussed in Chapter 15, constant tracking of users' initial source of awareness of your brand and the variables that allow users to be assigned to segments greatly increases your ability to evaluate the success of marketing campaigns and improve their efficiency going forward. Due to the referral metric in the server logs,[1] standard commercial Web tracking applications are limited to determining the effectiveness and ROI of online advertising campaigns and link-sharing partnerships only. The effect of any marketing that occurs offline is not captured. Bridging the gap to include traditional advertising and other off-line marketing activities requires survey data. Only by asking customers how they learned of the site can you establish what proportion of new users

---

[1]When a user clicks on a hyperlink or advertising banner to access your site, the location the user came from is captured in the server log as the *referrer*.

are driven via television, print, radio, press, word of mouth, or other awareness mechanisms. And, only by tracking the usage patterns of these users once they arrive can you evaluate the bottom-line ROI of each marketing vehicle.

This is only one instance of the power offered by the marriage of survey and behavioral data. Other survey metrics such as those used to drive segmentation or understand the audience can be associated with behavioral usage data to greatly enhance the type of everyday business decisions that can be informed with data. Content developers can closely monitor sections of the site utilized by the primary target segment(s). Advertising-supported sites can become the darlings of media planners everywhere by offering ad reporting that goes beyond simple counts of pageviews and clickthroughs, to include hard data on the detailed demographics of the customers their advertisements reached and (as the saying goes) much, much more.

The process of combining survey data with behavioral data does not require that every customer accessing the site be confronted with a survey solicitation. The same JavaScript random sampling process described elsewhere in this book can be leveraged to intercept a small fraction of users as they first access the site. Rather than a full-blown survey that might be employed in a major ad hoc research project, this sample will be asked to provide a few key pieces of data that developers and marketers wish to track. Answers from the survey are then encoded into cookies or simply stored in a database along with the unique ID used in the behavioral tracking cookie discussed earlier. To use an analogy, think of it as the radio tagging programs used to track the behavior of migrating species.

Tracking the usage habits of a subset of users is admittedly less accurate than gathering census data provided by the server, but the random subset of survey data combined with behavioral data provides more actionable information than server logs alone could ever hope to. Besides, pursuing one method does not preclude you from implementing the other. It is advisable to both monitor the subset of customers from whom you collect survey and behavioral data, and implement a commercial Web usage package to track the behavior of all users.

RECOMMENDED TRACKING METRICS

While vast amounts of data can be collected and reported on, the majority of value is derived from a few key metrics. Most of these metrics are already gathered through commercial Web-usage tracking applications like Web Trends (www.webtrends.com), Accrue (www.accrue.com), or Andromedia Aria (www.andromedia.com). Unfortunately, these packages are not set up to easily associate survey data with a subset of customers and report on these individuals separately—at least, not yet. Achieving this enhanced understanding of your customers requires linking these systems to external databases that you maintain yourself. Alternatively, you could choose to build a custom system to combine and report on these metrics. We caution anyone against custom-building an in-house tracking system, however, because the conversion of Web server logs into accurate user data is a tricky process that requires an in-depth knowledge of Web servers and Internet protocols. At this stage in the game, there is no need to reinvent the wheel. Your resources and time can be better spent tailoring an existing system to your specific needs.

Here we present the rationale behind some basic measures we've found most relevant to ongoing site measurement. These metrics will not apply to every scenario, and many sites will require additional metrics that are specific to their industry or site design to effectively measure day-to-day success. We indicate types of metrics that require the combination of survey and behavioral data with an asterisk. The remaining metrics are generally available in commercial Web-usage tracking products like those already mentioned.

People

Unique Users: The total number of individuals who visit your site each day. A fundamental measure of site activity, unique users provides a more accurate means of separating the number of users who have visited the site from the amount of interaction each user has had.

First-Time Unique Users: The number of people coming to your site for the first time. This metric provides the size of your trial population, and a basis for measuring the site's ability to convert trial to regular usage. This metric is key to a good understanding of both your marketing success (how much trial you are generating) and your attrition rates (how many users are failing to return over time).

Repeat Users: The act of returning for a second visit is an indicator that a user was intrigued by the initial experience and recognizes the value proposition of the site. This metric is a fundamental measure of success, because getting users to return to the site is a precursor to any deepening relationship. As the site develops, this metric will likely become very closely tied with revenue projections and goals.

New Users (in first week of usage following initial session[2]): Users who are new to your site make up an extremely important subset of the population to understand. These users are likely to experiment more, use different sections, and perhaps even view more pages on average than established users who have developed a specific routine. Most important, this is the user group that suffers the greatest level of attrition. Understanding the actions and composition of this group separate from established users and first-time users will be critical for improving trial-to-usage ratios.

[2]The relevant time frame for users to be considered "new" depends upon the usage cycle of your type of site. Some sites, like news providers, have a short cycle; users tend to revisit on a daily basis. E-commerce ventures, on the other hand, tend to see visitors again at the time of a purchase occasion, the cycle for which varies depending upon the types of products sold on the site.

Total Active Users: While total overall users will likely be reported for marketing purposes (as it represents the total installed base), it is important to consider that it does not normally exclude dormant users; as such, it does not indicate any user attrition issues that exist. For internal purposes, exclude users that have been dormant for a predetermined period of time (e.g., 1 month) to arrive at *Total Active Users.*

Conversion Rate: A calculated metric which measures the percentage of trial users who become repeat users. A goal of the site should be to drive the conversion rate of first-time users as high as possible through targeted marketing that brings qualified leads. While the number of first-time users is a signal of overall marketing success, the conversion rate indicates the overall efficiency of your marketing and the quality of the first-time user experience.

Activity

Page Views: The gross number of pages viewed, typically broken out by content section. Page views, due to their widespread acceptance as a performance metric, are a staple measurement of the relative popularity of certain areas.

Pages per Unique User: A basic measure of how many pages the average user looks at across your site. An increase or decrease in this metric may indicate a change in the involvement level of the audience.

Average Session Length: A measure of the average length of time a user spends at your site during any given engagement.

Self-Reported Data

Self-reported data is collected from a subset of customers via a short survey as they access the site. The variables collected are typically suggested by previous ad hoc research, and will vary from site to site. The data is combined with behavioral observations to provide a powerful context for interpreting ongoing business activities.

In addition to providing the development team with a solid understanding of audience composition, these metrics will prove exceedingly valuable in determining the effectiveness of the site's outbound marketing. By breaking these metrics down by each mechanism for driving awareness and trial (ad banner, partnership link, newspaper advertisement, etc.), you will be able to assess the quality of the traffic generated by each source. Tracking of referrals is discussed in the next subsection.

Self-reported metrics include:

Market Segment Membership*: The development of segmentation variables has been discussed throughout the book, and here is another place where it can pay handsome dividends. The ability to constantly track the behavior of various market segments will prove valuable in all aspects of site marketing and development efforts, allowing you to test the validity of your segmentation strategy. You might find, for example, that visitors initially considered to be the primary target market are not meeting expectations in terms of site usage or purchase volume. Such a situation would suggest that you revisit the segmentation scheme or else conduct additional research to understand why your product is not appealing to the group as anticipated.

Category-Specific Metrics*: Every site has some key metrics that enable you to quantify the value of a visitor. In commerce or advertising-supported sites, these are frequently behavioral metrics related to category consumption. Classification variables like gender, age, or occupation can also be vital for assessing the value of the user base. Beyond simple counts of users and pageviews, these self-reported metrics give you the ability to measure the success of marketing and site performance at reaching and retaining a valuable customer base.

These metrics tend to be unique to every site and scenario. An investment site might gather the following metrics:

- *portfolio size,*
- *frequency of trades,*
- *types of investments held, and*
- *investor experience level.*

An online retailer of cosmetics might seek these metrics:

- *age,*
- *gender,*
- *frequency of cosmetic purchase,*
- *types of cosmetics purchased.*

Referrals

Whenever a user accesses your site by clicking on a hyperlink or advertising banner, that fact is captured as referral data and saved in your server logs. Tracking this information provides feedback on the online marketing strategies that have directed the most traffic to the site. It also allows you to monitor daily changes that affect site traffic, such as an online news article or a high-profile link on another site. Referral information can be combined with other metrics to obtain a more granular understanding of the value of each marketing effort, allowing an ROI analysis like the one discussed in Chapter 15. Three types of referrals can be tracked:

Top Natural Referrals: A listing of Web links that send the most traffic to your site each day. These links could come from anywhere, not necessarily a source your marketing department has direct control over. For instance, a link in an online news article might direct 4,000 new users in a single day to your site; a mention in a "cool site of the day" feature could deliver you 1,000 new users.

Outbound Marketing: This is a list of traffic-generating links obtained through partnerships, ad banners, and other sources of outbound (typically purchased) online marketing. We track these separately because they are defined by the marketing department and should be individually tracked to measure the performance of various marketing activities.

Off-line Marketing (obtained from self-reported source of awareness data)*: This is the derived referral metric obtained via survey data. It is used to measure the efficiency and effectiveness of off-line marketing efforts. This data need not be restricted to include only paid sources of marketing exposure, and can run the full gamut of promotional mechanisms, including word of mouth and mentions in offline media. Interpreted with the aid of behavioral data, this information helps determine which sources are responsible for consumers' learning of, trying, and ultimately becoming valuable users of the site.

ANALYSIS

As the objective of the system is to provide actionable, current information to decision makers, the ability to interpret and respond to the metrics presented is critical. Overall, the applications of this data are vast, and data-driven teams will find limitless opportunities to expand upon and leverage the information to understand every facet of the site's performance. Lacking space to address all these treatments, we limit our discussion to the measurement of customers' deepening relationship with the site.

People Metrics

The revenue model of many sites is based on developing a growing audience of highly involved visitors who use the site repeatedly and heavily. Achieving this objective requires users to progress through the *value chain:*

Awareness → Trial → Usage → Preference

At each point along the value chain, sites inevitably lose some percentage of their potential customer base. Efficiently identifying and minimizing this attrition is the key to increased profitability. The metrics described throughout this chapter can provide the tools to track the site's ability to maximize the value of its audience.

Awareness → Trial

Though the level of awareness among the marketplace is impossible to measure without expensive representative RDD or panel-based sampling methodologies, the combination of awareness and a compelling reason to check out a new product results in trial. The level of trial the site has achieved in the marketplace is directly represented by the number of *first-time unique users* who visit the site each day.

Trial → Usage

Once trial has occurred, a user will decide whether or not the product has provided a compelling reason to return. The success of a site in driving users through to this next stage of the relationship is indicated by the percentage of new users who return. This is measured by the new users metric that tracks customers during their first week (or other relevant time frame) after first accessing the site.

Usage → Preference

Once users begin using the site, they discover whether the value proposition holds true. If it does, users graduate to a stage at which they prefer to use the product over competitive products. The alternative is attrition. Monitoring levels of attrition among the new user population is an excellent indicator of the shift from usage to preference. Attrition is evidenced by a failure of the average total active users metric to keep pace with the average number of new users.

In addition to observing and reporting on the sizes of populations achieving various levels of the value chain, it is also useful to
compare and contrast the audience profiles of meaningful subgroups of the user population. Understanding the usage patterns
and composition of these groups will help you develop effective
marketing and product development strategies that recognize the
needs of new users without alienating the core revenue-generating
audience. Subgroups might include:

- first-time users,
- repeat users,
- new users (first week of usage), and
- target segments (based on self-reported segmentation variables, if collected).

REPORTING

There are two approaches to reporting on site usage data: Web-
based interface and daily email updates.

Web-Based Interface

An interactive online application that displays, charts, and graphs
site usage data is the standard tool for analysis. These Web applications allow immediate and dynamic access to the data and are
extremely valuable for in-depth analysis. Specific findings of interest can be "drilled into" to evaluate possible causes. Time series
and legacy data are easily manipulated to compare past business
activities to current issues. Results are depicted in easily inter-
pretable tables, or as graphical charts that can be exported for use
in reports or forwarded to decision makers. Leading developers of
Web-usage tracking products like Web Trends, Accrue, and
Andromedia have invested heavily in the development of these
analysis tools, and feature interactive demos on their product Web
sites.

Daily Email Updates

While providing in-depth access to the data, Web-based interfaces require the end user to be proactive. It is not realistic to expect busy executives, producers, and marketers to make a habit of regularly culling though usage data. Instead, the most relevant metrics should be digested and distributed via daily email updates. This approach provides decision makers with the information needed to run a data-driven business without getting bogged down with details. If complex questions arise, they can be addressed via the Web-based application.

The email report, like the one presented here that was developed for an online investing site, should be designed to summarize the site's current performance on the metrics outlined in previous pages.

People

	Today	*7-day avg.*	*% Change*
Unique users			
First-time users			
% of traffic from first-time users			
New users visiting			
% of new user conversion			
Total repeat users visiting			
Total active user count			

Usage Data

T = today   7d = 7-day moving average   %C = percent change

	Total			Site Section 1			Site Section 2			Site Section 3		
	T	7d	%c	T	7d	%c	T	7d	%c	T	7d	%c
Sitewide												
Page views												
Unique users												
Pages per user												
Session length												
	T	7d	%c	T	7d	%c	T	7d	%c	T	7d	%c
Repeat Users												
Page views												
Unique users												
Pages per user												
Session length												
# of sessions												
	T	7d	%c	T	7d	%c	T	7d	%c	T	7d	%c
New Users												
Page views												
Unique users												
Pages per user												
Session length												
# of sessions												
	T	7d	%c	T	7d	%c	T	7d	%c	T	7d	%c
First-Time Users												
Page views												
Unique users												
Pages per user												
Length of session												

Profile Data

T = today   7d = 7-day moving average   %C = percent change

	Total			Site Section 1			Site Section 2			Site Section 3		
	T	7d	%c	T	7d	%c	T	7d	%c	T	7d	%c
Sitewide												
% in primary segment												
Avg. portfolio size												
Avg. trade frequency												
Investor experience												
	T	7d	%c	T	7d	%c	T	7d	%c	T	7d	%c
Members												
% in primary segment												
Avg. portfolio size												
Avg. trade frequency												
Investor experience												
	T	7d	%c	T	7d	%c	T	7d	%c	T	7d	%c
Early members												
% in primary segment												
Avg. portfolio size												
Avg. trade frequency												
Investor experience												
	T	7d	%c	T	7d	%c	T	7d	%c	T	7d	%c
New Members												
% in primary segment												
Avg. portfolio size												
Avg. trade frequency												
Investor experience												

Referral Data

Top Referrals	Rank	Total Referrals	% of Total Referrals
1			
2			
3			
4			
5			
6			
7			
8			
9			
10			

Tracked Outbound Referrals	Rank	Total Referrals	% of Total Referrals
1			
2			
3			
4			
5			
6			
7			
8			
9			
10			

Derived Referrals from Survey Data	Rank	Total Referrals	% of Total Referrals
1			
2			
3			
4			
5			
6			
7			
8			
9			
10			

Metrics by Referral (for each referral)

Referral #1	Today	7-day avg.	% Change
% who became new users			
% who became repeat users			
Segmentation (% primary)			
Median portfolio size			
Median frequency of trade			
Median investor experience			

Referral #2	Today	7-day avg.	% Change
% who became new users			
% who became repeat users			
Segmentation (% primary)			
Median portfolio size			
Median frequency of trade			
Median investor experience			

PRODUCTS

Traffic analysis packages cover a wide range of both functionality and price. At one end are shareware packages that can be down-loaded for free and used to interpret basic site usage activity. The opposite end contains packages costing upward of $15,000 that are customized to provide detailed enterprisewide reporting on specif-ic business issues that face e-commerce or ad-supported sites.

A number of good online resources exist for learning more about and comparing the cost and capabilities of these products. You may want to start with these:

- *Wired Digital's Webmonkey* (hotwired.lycos.com/ webmonkey/e-business/tracking/)

  This collection of articles educates the reader about both the metrics available for traffic analysis and the specific products available in the marketplace.

- *CNET's Builder.com* (www.builder.com/Servers/ Statistics/)

  Maintains a section devoted to understanding your Web site's traffic in a manner that is meaningful to your busi-ness. This section also contains reviews of traffic analysis software.

Glossary

A priori Segmentation strategy that uses a predetermined hypothesis to divide the market.

Active measurement Measurement technique that requires participants to actively record and report their behavior, typically through the use of a diary.

Ad hoc research Research conducted on an as-needed basis to explore a specific business issue.

Advertising effectiveness research Research discipline focused on quantifying the ability of advertising campaigns or creative to achieve key objectives.

ASP Active Server Pages, a Microsoft server-side scripting language.

Additudinal data Data focusing on what a consumer thinks, including opinions, preferences, or perceptions.

Attribute importance assessment Research to identify the specific product and brand performance attributes with the greatest impact on a consumer's purchase decision.

Awareness Having at least a cursory knowledge of the existence of a brand.

Backend script Server-side programming that allows the Web server to behave "intelligently."

Behavioral data Data focusing on what a consumer does, including purchase activity, leisure activities, and Web site usage.

Beta test Time period just before a site's official launch when the fully-operational product is used under normal operating conditions to identify any programming bugs or last-minute interface issues.

Bivariate analysis Analysis technique that investigates the relationship between two variables. Often synonymous with cross-tabular analysis.

Brand perceptions Attitudes that consumers have toward a brand.

Brand tracking Form of continuous measurement to detect small shifts in awareness or perceptions of brands. Typically employed to identify impacts of advertising on tested brands.

Category penetration The share of consumers currently purchasing or using a particular type of product or service.

Classification data Data defining characteristics of consumers, including personal attributes such as age, gender, or income.

Client-side scripts Programming algorithms downloaded as text, then compiled and executed on the user's Web browser.

Cluster analysis Analysis technique typically employed in segmentation research to group respondents, based on shared characteristics.

Concept statement Short description encapsulating a new product concept.

Concept testing Research approach designed to obtain early feedback on new product ideas before they are fully formed.

Confidence interval Range of values around the statistic where the "true" (population) statistic can be expected to be located (with a given level of certainty).

Confidence level The probability that the true population statistic will lie within a given range (confidence interval) of the indicated sample value.

Conjoint analysis Research technique in which respondents trade off different combinations of product or service attributes to arrive at the ideal feature set for a product or service.

Consumption level The volume (often dollar volume) of a product or service used by consumers.

Continuous tracking A study designed to take measurements on a continuous basis rather than at specific points in time (e.g., quarterly).

Convenience sample Sample obtained on a nonprobability basis.

Cookie Small text file stored on the user's computer that can be written to or read by the server and can be used as an unique identifier or to store supplementary information.

Copytesting Advertising effectiveness research technique used to pretest advertising creative.

Cost-of-entry The bare minimum required to participate in a market.

CPM Cost-per-thousand consumers reached.

Creative Advertising industry term employed as a general descriptor of advertising content.

Data collection Process of gathering data in a research study.

Data weighting Statistical manipulation of sample data to bring it in line with known population statistics.

Differentiated marketing approach Marketing strategy to develop specific marketing or products for each segment pursued.

Directory service Services like Yahoo! or Looksmart by which sites are grouped and searched in a logical hierarchy.

Discussion list Similar to USENET, discussion lists allow users to communicate in an open forum on very specific areas of interest. Discussion lists often use email as their communication mechanism, rather than USENET newsgroups.

Distribution channel Means by which a brand reaches its customer and provides goods and services.

Experimental research design Study designed to hold all factors but one constant, to isolate that factor's impact.

Field The portion of a study involving the sampling and interviewing of respondents.

Focus group Small in-person group sessions designed to elicit opinions about a particular research topic.

Focused marketing approach Marketing strategy choosing to focus on a subset of the total market.

Front page Term commonly used in Web publishing to refer to the main entry point of a Web site.

Incidence The proportion of a particular type of consumer or respondent in the population or sample.

Interface The collection of navigation tools, graphics, and text elements by which a user interacts with a Web product.

JavaScript Common Web-based scripting language executed on the Web browser (client-side).

Liquid capital Cash or other assets easily convertible to cash.

Longitudinal Analysis focused on understanding shifts in metrics over time.

Market Group of consumers to whom products and services are marketed.

Market size The total number of potential customers for a product or service.

Measurement bias The potential difference between the true state (behavior, perceptions, etc.) of the population and the measurement obtained through a measurement tool.

Measurement spheres Term coined to define the major areas of measurement for online products. The four major spheres are the market overall, the Internet, the online marketplace, and the existing customer base.

Media consumption Television watching, radio listening, magazine or newspaper reading, and Website viewing habits.

Media measurement Services like Nielsen, Arbitron, or MediaMetrix that measure consumers' viewing, reading, or listening habits of specific programs, radio stations, or Web sites.

Moderator Leader of a focus group who facilitates discussion and ensures the agenda is covered within the allotted time frame.

Multivariate analysis Analysis investigating the interrelationship of more than two variables simultaneously.

Nationally representative Samples or studies conducted and analyzed such that results accurately represent the national population.

Nonresponse bias Bias introduced into a sample when individuals selected for the study cannot be contacted or refuse to participate.

Observational data Data gathered by monitoring consumer activity.

Omnibus survey Survey made up of questions from multiple clients, each paying a small fee on a per-question basis.

One-off Study conducted once to address a particular issue and not likely to be repeated.

Panel Preselected group of consumers who agree to complete surveys, often profiled to allow easy contact of respondents with particular attributes.

Passive measurement Measurement techniques that monitor participants' behavior. Typically achieved via tracking software or hardware voluntarily installed on participants' computers or televisions.

Perceptual mapping Data analysis and summary technique to graphically plot brand perceptions for several brands, allowing comparisons to be made between perceived similarities and differences.

Perl Popular programming language for developing Web-based applications.

Population Group of consumers a research study attempts to understand.

Post hoc Segmentation strategy that allows data to drive the discovery of relevant consumer groups.

Primary research Original research conducted to address specific organizational objectives.

Projectability Ability of a sample to represent a given population.

Psychographics Catch-all term for metrics describing the personality, attitude, and belief makeup of an individual.

Purchase behavior tracking Point-of-purchase data leveraged to identify shifts in purchase levels of products. Typically employed in packaged goods industries via supermarket club cards or frequent shopper programs.

Purchase probability The likelihood that a consumer will purchase a given brand.

Qualitative research Major division in research approaches, primarily concerned with obtaining soft, subjective insight into the underlying issues surrounding a research problem.

Quantitative research Major division in research approaches, primarily concerned with obtaining concrete, objective measurement of factors central to the research objective.

Query string Means of passing variables from the Web browser to the Web server by way of including it in the URL.

Quota sampling Sampling technique to obtain predetermined quantities of respondents with specific characteristics.

Random Digit Dial (RDD) Random sampling technique widely utilized in telephone-based research.

Random rotation Frequently used to reduce bias in online research by randomly ordering questions or response choices.

Random sample Sample whose constituents were selected at random.

Reach The number of people an advertisement has the opportunity to reach.

Recall Measurement of an advertisement's ability to be remembered by consumers who view it.

Rental list List of consumers accessible for a fee.

Research objective Concise statement defining the goals of a research study or program.

Respondent Individual participant in a research study.

Respondent fatigue Burnout experienced by a survey respondent when confronted with long questionnaires or difficult questions.

Respondent incentives Cash or other consideration given to survey respondents in exchange for participation.

Response rate Percentage of users selected for participation in a study who actually complete a survey.

Response validation Process of checking respondent answers to be sure they make logical sense or fit the study's data requirements.

Sampling The process by which a subgroup of consumers is selected to participate in a study.

Sampling frame The subset of a population available and able to be contacted for sampling.

Screening Process used to identify respondents qualified to participate in a study.

Search engine Services such as Altavista or Hotbot that search the Web for pages matching detailed search criteria.

Secondary research Previously existing research.

Segmentation Process of dividing up a market into smaller subgroups that may benefit from specialized product or marketing approaches.

Server-side scripts Programming algorithms compiled and executed on the Web server.

Sitecentric Online research leveraging a sample of consumers who are intercepted as they access a particular Web site.

Snowball sampling Also known as referral sampling, snowball sampling asks each qualified respondent to provide additional respondents to contact. Typically employed to survey low-incidence populations.

Solicitation page Web page inviting sampled users to participate in a survey.

Subscriber information service Information retrieval service like Lexis-Nexis that searches through articles or other information on a subscription or pay-per-use pricing basis.

Switching behavior A consumer's propensity for or history of switching to new brands.

Syndicated research Research conducted and then resold to multiple client.

Top-2 box Term used to refer to the two uppermost choices in a ratings scale.

Tracking study Study conducted multiple times during its lifespan to provide up-to-date information or the topic being studied and to identify any changes occurring over time.

Trial Having firsthand experience with a brand.

Undifferentiated marketing approach Marketing strategy treating all market segments identically.

URL Universal Resource Locator. Commonly called a Web address.

Usage Regular purchase or usage of a brand.

USENET A distributed bulletin board system on the Internet comprised of users who post and read messages across thousands of available categories, known as *newsgroups.*

Wave An individual stage of a study involving multiple interview occasions.

Web-server logs Text files or databases that contain records of a Web site's activity.

INDEX